Thinking With the Church

FCCT | Free Church, Catholic Tradition

Barry Harvey and Bryan C. Hollon, editors

PUBLISHED VOLUMES:

Jeff W. Cary
Free Churches and the Body of Christ: Authority, Unity, and Truthfulness

Scott W. Bullard
Re-Membering the Body: The Lord's Supper and Ecclesial Unity in the Free Church Traditions

Thinking With the Church

Toward a Renewal of Baptist Theology

Derek C. Hatch

CASCADE *Books* • Eugene, Oregon

THINKING WITH THE CHURCH
Toward a Renewal of Baptist Theology

Free Church, Catholic Tradition 3

Copyright © 2018 Derek C. Hatch. All rights reserved. Except for brief quotations in critical publications or reviews, no part of this book may be reproduced in any manner without prior written permission from the publisher. Write: Permissions, Wipf and Stock Publishers, 199 W. 8th Ave., Suite 3, Eugene, OR 97401.

Cascade Books
An Imprint of Wipf and Stock Publishers
199 W. 8th Ave., Suite 3
Eugene, OR 97401

www.wipfandstock.com

PAPERBACK ISBN: 978-1-5326-1116-2
HARDCOVER ISBN: 978-1-5326-1118-6
EBOOK ISBN: 978-1-5326-1117-9

Cataloguing-in-Publication data:

Names: Hatch, Derek Christopher, 1981–, author.

Title: Thinking with the church : toward a renewal of baptist theology / Derek C. Hatch.

Description: Eugene, OR : Cascade Books, 2018 | Free Church, Catholic Tradition 3 | Includes bibliographical references and index.

Identifiers: ISBN 978-1-5326-1116-2 (paperback) | ISBN 978-1-5326-1118-6 (hardcover) | ISBN 978-1-5326-1117-9 (ebook)

Subjects: LCSH: Baptists—Doctrines. | Theology, Doctrinal.

Classification: BX6331.3 .H37 2018 (paperback) | BX6331.3 .H37 (ebook)

Manufactured in the U.S.A.   12/07/17

Unless otherwise noted, Scripture quotations are from New Revised Standard Version Bible, copyright © 1989 National Council of the Churches of Christ in the United States of America. Used by permission. All rights reserved worldwide.

To Sarah and our children

Contents

Series Preface ix

Acknowledgments xi

Introduction: Baptist Theology, Wandering in the Wilderness 1

Part One

1 Calvinism on Campus 15
2 *Ressourcement* and Ontology 37

Part Two

3 Bible and Tradition:
Listening for the Word of God 65

4 Individual and Community:
Beyond the Legacy of E. Y. Mullins 99

5 Truth and Freedom:
Making Theological Sense of Religious Liberty 131

Conclusion: The Liturgical Ground of *Ressourcement* 162

Bibliography 177

Index 193

Series Preface

Barry Harvey and Bryan C. Hollon, editors

WHY A BOOK SERIES entitled *Free Church, Catholic Tradition*? As he does on so many other occasions, Augustine eloquently articulates the benefits of engaging in the kinds of conversations that we hope it promotes. "Dear reader," he writes near the outset of *De Trinitate*, "whenever you are as certain about something as I am go forward with me; whenever you hesitate, seek with me; whenever you discover that you have gone wrong come back to me; or if I have gone wrong, call me back to you. In this way we will travel the street of love together as we make our way toward him of whom it is said, 'Seek his face always.'" Though Augustine's words here are addressed to individuals, the wisdom of what he says extends to the ecumenical spirit of our times. When set in this ecclesial context, his admonition provides both the content and the spirit that we hope will characterize this series.

The immediate context for this series is the growing number of scholars in Free Church communions who are interested in drawing upon the great tradition of the church catholic to deepen and enrich their own denominational heritage with its wisdom. We hope in particular that it will offer an effective means for getting the work of scholars from these church bodies into the wider theological conversation and that it will encourage others to join this conversation. The larger context is the modern ecumenical movement, which was given birth early in the twentieth century, developed in a variety of ways over the next several decades, and now in the twenty-first century has taken on new and diverse forms.

While ecumenism has many facets to it—ecclesiological, political, cultural—Jürgen Moltmann has helpfully identified its theological significance in his book, *The Church in the Power of the Spirit*. The ecumenical movement, writes Moltmann, has moved the churches away from the anathemas of the past, and ushered them down a path marked by dialogue and co-operation, culminating in toleration and the arguing out of differences within the one church. The ecumenical path, says Moltmann, leads theologically to living in council. He concedes that though the hope of an ecumenical all-Christian council, where Christianity would speak with one voice, is not at all likely in the foreseeable future, that hope nevertheless already sheds light on the present "wherever the divided churches are beginning to live in council with one another."

Living in council entails, on the one hand, consulting other churches and searching other traditions when asking questions affecting one's own communion. The days of returning always to the same dry wells to resolve internal problems and answer pressing questions are over. In particular, Free Churches that have entered into council with other churches are discovering new insights and fresh reservoirs of meaning. The *Free Church, Catholic Tradition* series has its first and most pressing *raison d'être* here, as more and more believers in these churches find ways of life and thought in the great tradition of the church that in their opinion are desperately needed in their own communions.

In addition, says Moltmann, living in council means intervening in the questions of other churches in an effort to cut through old provincial divisions. Though the idea of intervention may sound overly-intrusive (one thinks of reality television shows in which friends and family members perform "interventions" on loved ones who are addicted or otherwise caught up in ways of life that are not healthy), if it is in fact the case that the whole church is present in every individual church, what one body finds problematic or troublesome has important implications for the others: "it is then impossible to say that the controversy about papal infallibility is 'an internal problem for Catholics' or that the dispute about infant baptism is 'an internal problem for Protestants.'" Of course, if such interventions are not done prudently, carefully, humbly, and above all charitably, they will be of no avail.

The volumes in this series thus seek to cut across some of these well-established, though theologically problematic, divisions that have kept Free Church communions in particular from the riches of the Catholic intellectual, moral, and liturgical tradition, and to reconnect believers in these churches with the insights and wisdom of the church catholic. We also hope that Catholic theologians, together with Protestants from the magisterial traditions, would also find in the series a forum for shared inquiry with their "separated brethren," that together we might seek the face of God in the midst of our fragmented context.

Acknowledgments

IN THE CLASSROOM, I introduce my students to theology by saying that it is a conversation through time, bound up with friendship and community. Books in the field of theology are no different, drawing in those tied together within the mystical body of Christ. To be sure, innumerable people have shaped my work and vocation as a theologian—too many to thank in this short set of acknowledgments. However, several folks should be set apart from the crowd for special recognition.

First, this study began as a dissertation at the University of Dayton, so it is appropriate to express my gratitude to my student colleagues and professors there, without whom I certainly would not be the theologian I am today. More specifically, each member of my dissertation committee (Bill Portier, Dennis Doyle, Kelly Johnson, Bill Trollinger, and Barry Harvey) both encouraged and challenged me in my pursuit of this work. Additionally, Sandra Yocum, Brad Kallenberg, Michael Cox, Ethan Smith, Ben Peters, and Tim Gabrielli were invaluable in the development of my thinking. I was blessed to have them as interlocutors then, and I am privileged to call them friends now.

This book, though, is not my dissertation. While it certainly bears the marks of that earlier work, it also embodies continued thought on the subject matter as well as further experience with the theological questions facing baptist peoples. One laboratory for such thinking has been my work for the past five years as a professor at Howard Payne University. There, in conversations with engaged and intelligent students as well as with dedicated colleagues, I have cultivated deeper reflection on and more nuanced articulation of the nature of Baptist theology and its renewal. Among those within this community for whom I am especially grateful are Donnie Auvenshine, whose capable leadership as Dean of the School of Christian Studies and supportive encouragement as a friend have helped bring this project to completion, and Millard Kimery, whose friendship and conversation about life, literature, and philosophy have honed my thinking and my maturity as a scholar.

Theology at its best is for the sake of the church catholic. As a lay participant in the weekly liturgy of Baptist churches, I have had the pleasure of knowing and working with several pastors and ministers who were charitable dialogue partners as well as adept theologians in their own right. I am tremendously grateful for the leadership and ministry of Dorisanne Cooper, Rodney Wallace Kennedy, and Rodney McGlothlin. Furthermore, I am thankful for the work of Barry Harvey and Bryan Hollon in creating and managing the *Free Church, Catholic Tradition* series, which has provided a wonderful venue for this book. To Charlie Collier, Matthew Wimer, Brian Palmer, and others at Wipf & Stock, I am appreciative for their support of good theological scholarship.

Without doubt, my family deserves honor and acknowledgment for the completion of this work. My parents, Mitchell and Vanessa, have expressed support and encouragement throughout my academic work and have nurtured a love of learning from the early years of my education. Moreover, this work has grown up and matured alongside my four children: Philip, Simon, Joseph, and Rebekah. Walking through life with them has certainly cultivated deep love and joy as well as the always-important virtue of patience. I become a better theologian as I learn to be a better parent to them. Finally, my wife Sarah has been a faithful partner whose contributions in the field of social work and ministry have invaluably shaped my own theological vision. More importantly, she has endured with immense grace the burden of being married to an academic. For that alone, she deserves unending gratitude. The journey that led to this book's appearance is one that we have shared together, and it is a journey that will continue to shape us as we strive to be faithful spouses, parents, and followers of Jesus Christ, to whom ultimately all thanks and praise is due.

—Feast of Christ the King, 2016

Introduction

Baptist Theology, Wandering in the Wilderness

I TEACH THEOLOGY AT a small liberal arts Baptist university in the southern United States. As anyone in this setting can attest, this experience presents a dilemma that occasionally takes the form of an existential crisis: Baptists and theology do not always seem to mix well. In my academic formation, I occasionally encountered people who would warn me about theological education, as though I would "lose my faith" if I was not careful. Even among the properly educated, this prejudice against theology is evident. In the history of institutions such as my own, departments that housed theological studies were often known by the name "Bible Department," and, perhaps to reassure anxious Baptist congregants, the theology done was sometimes labeled "biblical theology" or "practical theology." Even though some of these titles have been changed, they have given way to others such as "Department of Religion" or "School of Christian Studies."[1] Moreover, among faculties and in the curricula at these institutions, one might find one or two theologians, yet numerous other faculty members in the areas of biblical and ministerial studies, and a relatively lighter course requirement in theology when compared to other competencies. This structure states a clear message: theological studies may be important and necessary, but it would be unwise to give it full reign within the department or the curriculum.[2]

---

1. Seminaries are occasionally an exception to this observation (e.g., Mercer University's McAfee School of Theology). However, even though one can find only a handful of Baptist institutions that do identify a Department or School of Theology (e.g., Houston Baptist University and Hardin-Simmons University's Logsdon School of Theology), the overall practice of avoiding this label is still prevalent, and it is notably in contrast to Catholic colleges and universities, which will more frequently use the term "theology" to label an entire department (which includes theological studies, biblical studies, and ministerial studies) in their school.

2. To be fair, though, my current institution is something of an exception as it

This antipathy concerning theology carries over into Baptist churches as well. One time when my family joined a congregation after moving to a new town, I was asked what I taught at the nearby university, to which I answered, "Theology." This must have sounded like gibberish to my new fellow church member, because he seemed very interested in my thoughts on rocks and soil. (That is, he thought my area was "*Geol-ogy*." I corrected the mistake by stating that I taught "Bible," and all was well from that point on.) Sunday school classes often do not know what to do with a theologian (or sometimes a scholar of Christianity in any area). Is this person a danger to the "heartfelt" shape of the Christian faith, or is she something of an encyclopedia of Christian facts that can be accessed when needed?

Needless to say, then, Baptists and theology have had a strained relationship, one that has had serious effects on their work in this area. Indeed, James William McClendon Jr. once observed that, despite their robust experience of the Christian faith, Baptists have produced little theological work of their own during their four hundred years of existence.[3] This statement and these observations serve as the backdrop for this volume, for if Baptists have been virtually mute when it comes to theology, what will become of our distinct practices and our participation within the church throughout the ages that stretches back to the apostles? In order to illustrate what is at stake in this concern, we should examine Baptist reflections on one of their signature practices: believers baptism.

Case Study: Baptists on Baptism

Relatively soon after their emergence on the ecclesial landscape in the seventeenth century, Baptists embraced the practice of believers baptism. This is a clear mark of Baptist existence, and even though Baptists are not the only Christians who baptize nor the only Christians who practice believers baptism, Baptists are continually reminded of the importance of this "church ordinance" every time they state the name of their "Baptist"

---

requires almost all majors in the School of Christian Studies to take courses in the history of Christianity, biblical interpretation, and Christian doctrine, providing a robust theological foundation for these students' intellectual formation. Further, while theological studies is part of a major labeled "Practical Theology" (including many ministerial studies courses), there are several courses within that category that warrant being called theology in a proper sense.

3. McClendon, *Ethics*, 20–26.

church.[4] It is prominently discussed in Baptist confessions of faith and is numbered among the notable "Baptist Distinctives."[5] For Baptists, then, when baptism occurs, it is often seen as a major event. That is, since they hold that only believers are to be baptized (i.e., what is called by some *credo*baptism), there is often surprise and delight at the baptism of a new convert (unexpected because it is not explicitly tied to any routine developmental stage of the person's life).[6]

Due to baptism's central place in Baptist life, one might expect Baptist laypeople to have a certain level of clarity about the fundamental theological contours of the practice itself. For instance, what occurs in the act of baptism? Who is operative and when? Is there a requisite form for the practice and, if so, what is it? These and other questions are central to understanding baptism. Without answering them, it is difficult to make clear what the nature of the act is and why it is performed. One would assume, therefore, that if anyone had a sufficiently thorough articulation

---

4. Baptists have generally refused to use the term *sacrament* to label baptism for many reasons, including (1) the aversion to any indication that baptism is salvific in itself, and (2) the fact that most Baptists understand baptism to be a representative act in some manner. Instead, the term "ordinance" is often used, indicating that the act is in obedience to Jesus's commands. See Brackney, *Doing Baptism Baptist Style*. There is also some preoccupation with avoiding any term (e.g., sacrament) that might have Catholic associations. W. T. Conner, a Baptist theologian from the first half of the twentieth century, remarked: "Christ has instituted two ceremonial ordinances and committed them to his people for perpetual observance—baptism and the Lord's Supper . . . Over against this view is the view of the Roman Catholic Church that these two ordinances, with five others, are 'sacraments' that convey grace to the participant" (*Christian Doctrine*, 273).

5. "The London Confession (1644)," art. xxxix in Lumpkin, *Baptist Confessions of Faith*, 167; "The Second London Confession (1677)," art. xxix in Lumpkin, *Baptist Confessions of Faith*, 291; "The Orthodox Creed (1678)," art. xxviii in Lumpkin, *Baptist Confessions of Faith*, 317. All versions of the Southern Baptist Convention's *Baptist Faith and Message* (1925, 1963, 2000) state that baptism is an act performed by immersion on the basis of a Christian believer's faith. The "Baptist Distinctives" effort began in the late twentieth century as a response to the conservative resurgence within the Southern Baptist Convention. For more on these developments, see Hankins, *Uneasy in Babylon*. The distinctives are intended to be thematic touchstones for historic Baptist identity and witness. Believers baptism by immersion is discussed as one distinctive, along with biblical authority, soul competency, salvation by grace through faith, the priesthood of believers, regenerate church membership, congregational church polity, local church autonomy, religious liberty, and voluntary cooperation among churches. For more information, see www.baptistdistinctives.org.

6. Lyles, "The Local Church," in Greer, *Baptists*, 50.

of the practice of baptism (and consistent answers to these questions), it would be the Baptists. However, this seems to be far from the case.

While one might discover silence on certain key theological points regarding baptism, what one finds primarily is a multitude of answers that move in divergent theological directions. To be sure, there is some sense of commonality among Baptists, but this agreement often concerns aspects of baptism that have minimal theological significance. Baptist historian Bill Leonard observes this pattern among Baptists, noting, "While Baptists generally agree that the immersion of Christian believers should be the normative mode [of baptism], they divide over the identity of proper candidates and the meaning of the act itself . . . The proper age for baptism is another matter that reflects Baptist diversity."[7]

Leonard rightly identifies this diversity, especially regarding the meaning of baptism itself. He indicates, though, that it is a positive aspect of Baptist life, allowing for a multitude of voices without any significant unity. However, what seems to be innocuous might better be described as confusion. With a brief glance, one can observe that some Baptists regard the practice to hold some spiritual or almost salvific quality. Others describe it as a representative or symbolic act. For these folks, baptism signals an inward change, from leading a life of sin to following Christ. Finally, occasionally baptism is viewed as primarily sociological in significance for Baptists, serving only as a rite of entry into the body of believers. Such disparate understandings of this central act of Baptist life and thought can contribute to serious theological chaos for Baptist people.

Further, while explanations of the meaning of baptism are often puzzling, it is also not evident that Baptists have a clear (or consistent) understanding of the details of the act itself, such as who is acting in the event, as well as when and how. For instance, it is not unusual to hear discussions of baptism that are explained in terms of an individual "deciding to follow Jesus."[8] This points to baptism as part of a wholly free and personal act on the part of the believer (i.e., one chooses God; baptism reflects that specific exercise of the will).[9] Along these lines, Baptist

7. Leonard, *Baptist Ways*, 1. It is often a refrain of Baptist discussions of baptism to mention that the original (and therefore proper) meaning of the Greek word *baptizō* is "to dip or immerse."

8. Cf. Reynolds, "I Have Decided to Follow Jesus," in Forbis, *The Baptist Hymnal*, #305.

9. "A voluntary spirit lies at the very heart of the Baptist self-understanding." Brackney, *Baptists*, 71.

historian Leon McBeth states, "[T]he nature of faith and baptism are such that they require a personal decision and commitment."[10] Baptism is also occasionally portrayed as an act of obedience to Christ's commands (Matt 28:18–20). Explanations of baptism as an aspect of a covenant—between God and the corporate person of the congregation— could be included here as well. Thus, this understanding of baptism affirms human ability to choose to follow God. Conversely (but with a similar result), Baptist theological leaders (i.e., pastors, church teachers, and professors) have highlighted that God is in control from the beginning of conversion to its culmination in baptism (i.e., the divine will is working at every stage of the process). On one hand, then, the emphasis is placed on the individual's initiative without any salvific ramifications (e.g., obedience to Christ, marking someone for church membership).[11] On the other hand, partly in order to avoid anything that sounds like "works righteousness," the practice of baptism is described as God's activity alone.

Sadly, this cognitively dissonant set of circumstances is not even recognized as such by Baptists, who often seem content to leave major aspects of their theological discourse uninterrogated and under-articulated. Even when the currents of contemporary theological discourse align with Baptist convictions, Baptists have failed to notice. For example, American Baptists Norman H. Maring and Winthrop S. Hudson, in discussing the need for a theology of baptism, pointed out that Karl Barth's 1943 lectures on baptism received little attention from Baptists in the United States, even though the prolific Swiss theologian agreed with their positions: "Barth came out strongly in those lectures in opposition to infant baptism, contending that New Testament baptism required persons to come to the rite only upon a personal profession of faith. He also supported immersion as the appropriate mode."[12] This, combined with a general apathy for theologically accounting for the act of baptism, stands as a "serious gap."[13]

Curtis Freeman also observes this confusion regarding baptism, centering it on two phenomena: rebaptisms and the increasing frequency of baptizing young children. Due to the stated importance of baptism,

10. McBeth, *Baptist Heritage*, 81.

11. All this while stating that not even baptism is necessary for entrance into the kingdom of God. See Pinson, et al., *Beliefs Important to Baptists*, 54–55.

12. Maring and Hudson, *Baptist Manual of Polity and Practice*, 151.

13. Ibid., 152.

Baptist groups and national bodies keep numerical baptismal records, often allowing these to serve as one major metric for a particular congregation's health.[14] What Freeman finds interesting is that approximately sixty percent of reported baptisms in the Southern Baptist Convention are rebaptisms, with most of those occurring with people who were baptized as infants. However, "more than a third are rebaptisms of believers who have been previously baptized in Southern Baptist churches."[15] This is troubling and strikes at the need for a theology that makes the practice of baptism intelligible: "The prevalence of such repeat believer's baptisms . . . is a startling indication that the doctrinal integrity of believer's baptism itself may be collapsing under the pressures of evangelical decisionism, atomistic individualism, and theological minimalism."[16]

Additionally, Freeman and other Baptists have become concerned that over time believers baptism has transitioned from being primarily received by adults, then by adolescents, and now by children. In 1993, Leonard commented on this trend:

> Statistical analysis of current SBC baptismal statistics would indicate that anywhere from 10 to 20 percent of that number, depending on the church and the region, is composed of persons six years or younger. Thus the SBC has opened the door to semi-infant baptism. A believers' church that baptizes preschoolers is committing heresy against its theology of conversion and its ecclesiology.[17]

For his part, Freeman describes this practice as amounting to "toddler baptism" and cites data from 2011, reporting that children under

---

14. In addition, Baptists also initiate campaigns focused on increasing the number of baptisms. For example, in 1954, the Southern Baptist Convention began a campaign called "A Million More in '54." More recently, a downward trend in baptisms among Southern Baptist churches generated the need to appoint a Pastors' Task Force in 2013 to study the decline. See Conway, "Pastor Task Force Addresses Declining Baptism Rates."

15. Freeman, *Contesting Catholicity*, 368.

16. Ibid. Freeman also states that the rebaptisms of the previously paedobaptized also presents theological challenges in the face of the common Baptist practice of open communion, where anyone who counts themselves as a baptized disciple of Jesus may participate. Requiring rebaptism for membership creates a higher wall for membership than for sharing in the bread and the cup. See ibid., 369–70.

17. Leonard, "When the Denominational Center Doesn't Hold," 909. For a more recent treatment of this development, see Camp, "Troubled Waters."

age eleven accounted for about 33 percent of recorded SBC baptisms.[18] Leonard notes that many factors indirectly contribute to this shift, including sensitivity to children who were raised within Baptist communities, alleviating the concerns of Christian parents, and possibly even the appearance of statistical growth for a particular congregation.[19] He also rightly links this shift in practice with a shift in theological convictions, but gives too much credit to Baptist theological reflection when he states, "[I]n the 20th century Southern Baptists modified their theology of the 'believers' church' to permit the baptism not simply of children but of preschoolers."[20] In other words, Leonard implies that Baptists decided to move in this direction, overtly changing their theology of baptism or the church, thus permitting a shift in practice. What seems more likely and is supported by the discussion above, is that some degree of theological imprecision, incoherence, or confusion regarding baptism and ecclesiology opened the door for novel ways (and people) for Baptists to baptize, despite their stated theological convictions.[21] Thus, if Baptists intend to take seriously the fact that there is "one Lord, one faith, one baptism, one God and Father of all" (Eph 4:5–6), then significant theological renewal will be necessary.

The Purpose of This Book: A Different Type of Reform

The requisite revitalization of Baptist theological reflection cannot simply restate Reformation ideas, since those have proven insufficient in offering life and shape to Baptist theology. That is, continual discussion of binaries such as divine sovereignty and human free will as well as the Reformation principles of grace alone (*sola gratia*), faith alone (*sola fide*), and scripture alone (*sola scriptura*) will only repeat the problems plaguing Baptist life and thought. More specifically, the necessary reform cannot reify existing denominational boundaries. In other words, for Baptists, attempts to focus solely on principles of Baptist identity (e.g., "distinctives"), while helpful in describing some aspects of Baptist history, occlude others and

---

18. Freeman. *Contesting Catholicity*, 369.
19. Leonard, "When the Denominational Center Doesn't Hold," 909.
20. Ibid.
21. This is not to say that one cannot detect an altered theology of baptism and ecclesiology from the ways in which Baptists perform baptism. Indeed, such theological convictions are embedded within the particular practices of Baptists, a point that will prove helpful in later chapters.

make it difficult for Baptists to conceive of their ecclesial existence within the broader sweep of the great Christian story.

Peter Leithart makes a similar observation concerning Protestantism's stance toward Catholicism. He notes that "Protestantism is a negative theology; a Protestant is a not-Catholic. Whatever Catholics say and do, the Protestant does and says as close to the opposite as he can."[22] The result of such posturing is that a vast wealth of resources and a broad chorus of voices are deemed unavailable to Protestants because they are considered "too Catholic." By contrast, Leithart proposes that the way forward lies with what he calls "Reformational Catholicism," which "is defined as much by the things it shares with Roman Catholicism as by its differences."[23] The result is that, even though some disagreements remain, "a Reformational Catholic gratefully receives the history of the entire Church as his history."[24] Likewise, Baptists should find ways to return to all of the sources of the Christian faith, especially those that have been previously neglected or avoided.

Moreover, reform cannot come from sources that produce something of an evangelical spiritualism. This is seen in two primary places. First is a movement that emphasizes being "spiritual but not religious" (SBNR), often criticizing the church and Christians for being hypocrites and placing stress on the interior dimensions of faith and spirituality. Occasionally this is motivated by a desire to emulate the social awareness and activism of persons like Dorothy Day, Mother Teresa, and Martin Luther King Jr.[25] Certainly religious institutions have need for improvement, but as one critic of SBNR pointed out, "Religion can provide a check against my tendency to think that I am the center of the universe . . . Spirituality without religion can become a self-centered complacency divorced from the wisdom of a community."[26] Another avenue for pursuing evangelicalism as an identity is to embrace what some would call a postmodern denominationalism. Here, something of a Christian cafeteria line is presented where one does not commit to a particular tradition, but meanders from one station to the next. At times, adherents of this

22. Leithart, "The End of Protestantism," para. 2.
23. Ibid., para. 5.
24. Ibid., para. 10.
25. Despite this admiration for this and other figures, SBNR proponents often overlook the fact that Day, Mother Teresa, and King all were incredibly immersed within the logic and liturgies of their respective religious communities.
26. Martin, *Jesuit Guide to (Almost) Everything*, 47, 50.

approach offer neologisms, such as Bapto-Presby-Methodo-Lutheran, in order to locate themselves. While these attempts are creative in deriving their names, with few exceptions, they ultimately reduce to generic evangelicalism, which has been persuasively argued to be inadequate as a stable identity.[27]

McClendon expounded on the reason for the dearth of Baptist theology: Baptists have failed to take their own story, and the depth of the broader Christian narrative, seriously.[28] Because of these challenges facing Baptists (and by extension, many free church Christians), a different type of theological method of reform is offered in this book: *ressourcement*, or a return to the sources of the Christian faith in order to discover (or recover) a more robust vision for theological renewal. While this does involve attending to the past, this sort of reform is not a simple recycling of the usual material and restating previous conclusions. Instead, as one theologian notes, "To get away from old things passing themselves off as tradition it is necessary to go back to the farthest past—which will reveal itself to be the nearest present."[29] Thus, central to *ressourcement* is a fundamental embrace of history, tradition, and catholicity. These concepts can be foreign to Baptists and are different from many efforts at reform that they have undertaken, and yet these terms address the precise concern named by McClendon and others regarding Baptists' underdeveloped theology. The focus in this book, then, even while remaining wholeheartedly Baptist, will be on the contributions and practices of the entire Christian church.

For Baptists and other free church Protestants, *ressourcement* will involve greater attention to the use of Scripture over time, and perhaps attention to patristic and medieval methods of biblical interpretation. It will also necessitate recovery of certain forgotten theological conversations, especially the relationship between nature and grace (or the natural and the supernatural). While Protestants have occasionally used these terms (though Baptists rarely have), they have a firm intellectual home within Catholic thought, where centuries of robust discussions about nature and grace have taken place. *Ressourcement* will also involve re-examination

---

27. Hart, *Deconstructing Evangelicalism*. One exception would be the moniker "Bapto-Catholic," which has been used to indicate not a blended or blurred denomination, but a reintegration of Baptist life and thought into the whole (i.e., catholic) Christian tradition. See Jorgenson, "Bapto-Catholicism."

28. McClendon, *Ethics*, 26.

29. De Lubac, *Paradoxes of Faith*, 20.

of foundational Baptist theological convictions, not in order to discard them, but to understand their importance against the backdrop of the vitality of the church across the centuries. This book's hope is that what will emerge is a more robust Baptist theology that is situated within the broader trajectory of the Christian tradition, adeptly addressing central questions of Baptist practice and providing fertile ground for engagement with the depth of wisdom within the Catholic church. In short, it is aimed at helping Baptists to think with the church.

The work of *ressourcement* is to return to the sources, but not in order to repristinate what is found there, such as some quests to find the "New Testament church" to the exclusion of other ecclesial formulations.[30] Instead, *ressourcement* means to revisit the sources of the Christian faith and return to one's own tradition renewed for the present. To do so involves embracing the entirety of the church and seeing a given tradition's gifts to that whole. Accordingly, Baptists have an important contribution to make to the church catholic (i.e., the whole church). However, the Baptist contribution is threatened when Baptists refuse to enter into deeper dialogue with the wider church in order to be strengthened by it. In what follows, then, we will find some areas where Baptists can learn from their fellow Christian pilgrims so that they are bolstered and made capable of offering their own significant gifts to the wider church.

Overview of Forthcoming Chapters

This volume is divided into two parts. In the first, I will discuss what has displaced robust reflection on the depth of the Christian tradition in Baptist theological conversations: questions about divine sovereignty and human free will. Chapter 1 will treat the prevalence of this fascination with the doctrines of grace (sometimes referred to as the five points of Calvinism) among Baptist and evangelical students and authors, as well as the ways in which these questions have captivated Baptists' imaginations. Chapter 2 will offer a different response to these questions in the form of the Catholic encounters with Reformed categories of thought in Molinism and Jansenism. While there are marked similarities between the content of these proposals and their positioning vis-à-vis one another,

---

30. This restorationist impulse is seen in the Stone-Campbell Movement as well as among some Baptists. One historical text concerning Baptists that utilizes this motif is Weaver, *In Search of the New Testament Church*.

the Catholic response, as detailed by French Catholic *ressourcement* theologian Henri de Lubac, is vastly different than seen in the Protestant world. Such an account will serve as a historical and theological lesson for responding to the present concern within Calvinism. Moreover, it will chart a methodological trajectory for the remainder of the book, revealing what *ressourcement* looks like and how it might inform the sort of theological renewal Baptists need.

In the second part, the *ressourcement* impulse will be directed toward several crucial theological challenges involving central convictions of Baptists: the Bible, the church, and religious liberty. In each case, anemic theological discussions have created numerous aporia that leave Baptist theological convictions vulnerable to co-optation by modernity, the nation-state, and the market. Thus, each chapter proceeds by identifying these deficiencies and looking to theological reflection from the rest of the church for necessary resources to move forward as the people of God shaped into the image of Christ. Moreover, each chapter is framed with a pair of terms that characterize the current conversations about that topic (Bible and Tradition, Individual and Community, Truth and Freedom). Oftentimes, because of the present state of Baptist theology, the best that can be hoped for is juxtaposition of the two ideas and various attempts to "balance" them. However, this approach is inadequate, since to elevate one side of the pair also involves reducing the emphasis on the other. By the conclusion of each chapter, a proposed resolution will emerge, one that sees both ideas as mutually participatory (and therefore not oppositionally situated). Such a relationship is fitting in light of the fact that the paradox of the incarnation as fully human and fully divine resides at the heart of the work of theology.

Chapter 3 addresses Baptists and the Bible. While much ink has been spilled on this topic, little of it has discussed the problems of the ways that Baptists have claimed the Reformation emphasis of *sola scriptura*, where the Bible stands over the church and tradition.[31] As will be shown, over time this has contributed to the inadequacy of the Bible for Christian faith and practice (even while the Bible retains its prime rhetorical place). Chapter 4 concerns the Baptist concept of the church. With a strong emphasis on soul competency, Baptists have progressively had difficulty articulating the place of the church within the Christian life. Further, they often identify the entire church with a local congregation.

---

31. For a good discussion of an alternate reading of *sola scriptura* as *suprema scriptura*, see Harmon, *Baptist Identity and the Ecumenical Future*, 33, 76, 78.

While discussing soul competency and its legacy, this chapter will ask what would be required for Baptists to take seriously the ties that bind us together as well as the notion of the church as catholic. Chapter 5 will address the signature Baptist idea of religious liberty. Upheld as a hallmark of Baptist history, religious liberty has become a doctrine often confused with liberal notions of freedom, where questions of truth are dismissed a priori. Through the lens of *ressourcement*, this chapter reframes the discussions of religious liberty by arguing for a theological account of religious freedom that does not marginalize the political aspects of theological discourse or particular truth claims.

By way of conclusion, the focus will shift from theological ideas to the embodiment and practice of those ideas in the liturgy of the church. In other words, returning to the sources requires embracing the church's ancient axiom, *lex orandi, lex credendi* ("the law of prayer/worship is the law of belief"), and reforming our liturgical life accordingly. In this manner, the embodied gestures of robust Christian worship become the fertile soil for renewing Baptist theology. With this in mind, the work of Benedictine liturgist Virgil Michel on the formative qualities of the liturgy will provide significant insights for not only thinking and speaking well as Baptists, but for reconstituting ourselves as fellow participants in the mystical body of Christ within the church catholic.

Part One

1

Calvinism on Campus

> We know what God could not possibly be: for example he could not be a god. Why? Because gods are bits of the world or anyway bits of the universe. They stand alongside heroes and human beings and teacups, none of which are gods. Gods are different; they are a superior kind of being ... [T]he gods are items in the universe. Top items maybe, but still items.
>
> —HERBERT MCCABE[1]

ON THE CAMPUSES OF many Baptist and free church colleges and universities, one can discern a common theological trend: students are captivated by the conversations surrounding divine sovereignty and human free will. To be sure, this is not the only influence on the theological scene, but it is a prominent one.[2] These discussions typically involve various forms of what has been described elsewhere as "the new Calvinism" or "neo-Calvinism," but here preference will be given to the moniker "resurgent Calvinism."[3] In dialogue with students and underneath a variety of

---

1. McCabe, "The Trinity and Prayer," 56.

2. Along with the fascination with the interaction between divine and human agency, one can find Lockean nominalist political anthropology, revivalistic pietism, Gnostic spirituality, and an emphasis on social justice also embedded (to varying degrees) within theological discussions among contemporary Baptists and free church Christians.

3. Van Biema, "10 Ideas Changing the World Right Now." I derive the term "resurgent Calvinism" from Collin Hansen's description of this movement's popular strength and the renewed interest in Reformed theological categories it has generated. Cf. Hansen, "Young, Restless, Reformed," 32–38. I will also point out that I am using the terms

religious discourse, one can detect concerns about God's justice against God's love, God's renown and passion for God's own glory, and the role that human beings play in the economy of salvation. This set of ideas certainly has intellectual and historical links to the sixteenth-century Protestant reformer, John Calvin, yet its deeper sources are actually much more recent. While people such as R. C. Sproul, D. A. Carson, and J. I. Packer figure prominently in students' exposure to this theological perspective and its tacit formation, the work of John Piper, former pastor of Bethlehem Baptist Church in Minneapolis, Minnesota, looms large in their imaginations. His focus on the works of Calvin and other Reformed thinkers such as Jonathan Edwards and Charles Haddon Spurgeon underscores the supremacy of God over all reality. While Piper's prominence throughout the Christian world and his emphasis on what he calls "Christian hedonism" has grown through his widespread preaching and his numerous books (such as *Desiring God*, *God's Passion for His Glory*, *The Pleasures of God*, and *Future Grace*),[4] his involvement in and influence on the youth-focused Passion movement has also significantly communicated this resurgent Calvinist perspective to the theological imaginations of college students.[5]

Others have made similar observations and discern the same trend among Baptist and free church college students.[6] H. Leon McBeth described a broader movement among Baptists to reclaim a Reformed

---

"Calvinist" and "Reformed" synonymously, even though there are subtle semantic, historical, and conceptual differences between them.

4. For Piper, "Christian hedonism" is a philosophy of life that seeks happiness by pursuing God's pleasure in God's own glory. In doing so, Piper declares that "God is most glorified in us when we are most satisfied in him" (*Desiring God*, 50), which serves as a paraphrase of the Westminster Shorter Catechism, "the chief end of man is to glorify God by enjoying him forever" (ibid., 23).

5. This set of conferences was started in 1997 by Louie Giglio and Jeff Lewis. However, the entire organization was influenced by Piper, as is indicated by the shared use of Isaiah 26:8, which became the motto for Passion and the theme for the initial conference sermon, which was preached by Piper. Not surprisingly, Piper has spoken numerous other times at Passion gatherings. In May 2000, thirty thousand college students attended an outdoor worship gathering called "One Day," at which Piper and other Passion figures spoke.

6. Knox, "Baptist College Professors Discuss Influence of Calvinism on Campuses"; Weaver and Finn, "Youth for Calvin." Weaver and Finn identify three sources for this resurgence: Calvinistic campus ministries (e.g., Reformed University Fellowship), Reformed-influenced contemporary Christian musical artists (e.g., Bebo Norman and Caedmon's Call), and popular authors and speakers (e.g., John Piper).

emphasis, seeing in this trend four factors that contribute to this resurgent Calvinism as providing "unchanging truths for changing times."[7] Arminian theologian Roger Olson describes an encounter where he was not considered a Christian because he was not Calvinist.[8] Peter Thuesen discusses the peculiar American fascination with the operations of divine providence, seeing it as "the proverbial elephant in the room of American denominationalism."[9] Indeed, for many Christians, it serves either as "the rock of Christian certainty" or "the most dangerous of doctrines."[10]

The impact of this school of thought is not recognized from a distance. Indeed, as a former student of a Baptist institution (and now a professor at another), these observations are derived from my own experience as well. When I was a student, numerous cafeteria and dorm room conversations centered on questions of divine sovereignty and human free will. For instance, could some lose their salvation by simply deciding to no longer believe in the truth of the gospel? Or, was it impossible to remove oneself from God's hands? I encountered classmates who were committed Calvinists (i.e., adherents of the doctrines of grace or the so-called five points of Calvinism) and others who were "on the fence." As a teacher as well, I have crossed paths with students who are captivated by the same queries and perceive the heart of the gospel to be at stake therein. Consequently, students can be found asking questions such as whether God's sovereignty extends to determining the actions of human beings and nature, whether salvation is a personal human decision or foreordained by God before the foundations of the world, whether God's grace is intended only for the elect, but not the damned, and whether God chooses that some people will not receive salvation.

Beyond personal conversations, though, one can observe other instances of resurgent Calvinism. For example, chapel worship bands tend to sing songs that emphasize Reformed themes of God's holiness over human depravity.[11] Moreover, the books that students read independent

---

7. McBeth, *Baptist Heritage*, 775. The four factors fueling the re-emergence of Calvinistic themes are: (1) a sense of return to original Baptist roots, (2) reaction against shallow evangelism practiced by Southern Baptists, (3) historical and theological links to fundamentalism, and (4) adoption of themes gleaned from contemporary society (e.g., inevitability beyond human control) (ibid., 774–76).

8. Olson, *Against Calvinism*, 15.

9. Thuesen, *Predestination*, 6.

10. Ibid., 3.

11. For example, the original author of "Amazing Grace," John Newton, presented

of class reflect this emphasis. One is likely to find interest in texts by Mark Driscoll, David Platt, Francis Chan, R. C. Sproul, J. I. Packer, Matt Chandler, and even Piper himself, among others. These authors diffuse the resurgent Calvinistic themes into multiple fields beyond just theology, including missions, biblical studies, gender roles, and personal relationships (including dating and marriage). Thus, regardless of what form it takes, students have significant contact with this resurgent Calvinist perspective.

What prompts such widespread interest in resurgent Calvinism? Sociologists Christian Smith and Melissa Lundquist Denton have described the religious sensibilities of American teenagers with the term "Moralistic Therapeutic Deism." According to them, the creed for its adherents states that a creator God who ordered the world into existence wants all people to be good, nice, and fair to each other; the goal of life is to be happy and feel good about oneself; God's only particular involvement in someone's life is to resolve a problem; and good people go to heaven when they die.[12] The divine being found in this "religion" is "something like a combination Divine Butler and Cosmic Therapist: he is always on call, takes care of any problems that arise, professionally helps his people to feel better about themselves, and does not become too personally involved in the process."[13] Consequently, many young people cannot articulate important religious topics, such as "repentance, love of neighbor, social justice, unmerited grace, self-discipline, humility, the costs of discipleship, dying to self, the sovereignty of God, personal holiness, the struggles of sanctification, glorifying God in suffering, hungering for righteousness . . ."[14] Smith and Denton offer this summary:

---

strong Calvinistic themes of redemption and salvation in the hymn's text, with God's grace restoring sight to the "wretch" who is singing. The contemporary attraction of these motifs is evident in a revised version of the song, written by Louie Giglio and Chris Tomlin, that mainly sets the hymn to new music, with the exception of adding a common refrain and using an alternate final stanza. Numerous contemporary worship songs appropriate portions of the Psalter for their lyrical content (e.g., Matt Redman's "Better is One Day"—Psalm 84, "Let Everything That Has Breath"—Psalm 150, "10,000 Reasons"—Psalm 103, and Chris Tomlin's "How Great is Our God"—Psalm 104). While this embrace of the Psalms as material for writing worship songs is not an exclusively Reformed emphasis, it dovetails with Calvin and the Reformed tradition's preference for singing the Psalms. See Webber, *Worship Old & New*, 113.

12. Smith and Denton, *Soul Searching*, 162–63.
13. Ibid., 165.
14. Ibid., 149.

> What very few U.S. teens seem to believe, to put it one way, is that religion is about orienting people to the authoritative will and purposes of God or about serious, life-changing participation in the practices of a community of people who inherit the religiocultural and ethical tradition. As far as we could discern, what most teens appear to believe instead is that religion is about God responding to the authoritative desires and feelings of people.[15]

With the emergence of this trend, one which concerns many religious scholars, some have seen the fruits of individualism and relativism.[16] Journalist Collin Hansen proposes that young people, once they leave their moralistic therapeutic congregations, are attracted to and transformed by "the transcendent God they behold through Reformed theology."[17] In other words, these youth are drawn to resurgent Calvinism because of their prior experience with the anemic religion of Moralistic Therapeutic Deism. Once they encounter it, then, these young Reformed adherents tightly latch onto the terms of the Calvinist argument and the way those terms shape theological discourse. The result on the ground is a multitude of students on college campuses who strongly describe themselves as Calvinist.

As can be observed, one notable characteristic of resurgent Calvinism (and one it shares with the work of its Reformed ancestor) is its theological rigor. It certainly does not lack for specificity or ease of access. The five-point Calvinist TULIP—Total depravity, Unconditional election, Limited atonement, Irresistible grace, and Perseverance of the saints—is simple, and is seen as the definitive statement of the relationship between human beings and God and the process of salvation as a whole. Although this paradigm has deep roots in the decisions of the Synod of Dort in the seventeenth century, it is usually taken for granted in lay theological conversations. Thus, even those who disagree with such positions (usually calling themselves Arminians) couch their rebuttals in terms similar to the Calvinists, perhaps arguing that a "five-point" approach robs mission work of its driving impulse or that God's love is violated if human beings cannot freely reciprocate. Occasionally, in an effort to present something of a middle-position that leans away from troublesome aspects of the TULIP (e.g., limited atonement or irresistible grace), a student will declare

15. Ibid.
16. See, e.g., Mohler, "Moralistic Therapeutic Deism—the New American Religion."
17. Hansen, *Young, Restless, Reformed*, 24.

that he or she is a "three-point" or a "four-point" Calvinist. Certainly, even if confused, statements such as these are attempts to nuance one's theological opinions in the face of perceived dangers. Nonetheless, the formative power of the resurgent Calvinist theological perspective is on full display. Even half-Calvinists or non-Calvinists find themselves using Calvinist terms to state such.[18] Consequently, the categories are concretized as the sum total and quintessential paradigm of Christian theology.

Because of this renewed interest in Calvinist theology, numerous books have appeared that engage these terms. Some are authored by pastors from either an Arminian (e.g., Rob Bell) or a Calvinist perspective (e.g., Chandler), even if this is not explicitly acknowledged in the text.[19] At times, some books have attempted to directly address the conundrum, often by offering an apology of the author's own position.[20] One recent set of these books has been written by Roger Olson (*Against Calvinism*) and Michael Horton (*For Calvinism*). While each defends their respective positions, they jointly thematize their key differences in terms of synergism and monergism. That is, Horton views the operation of God's grace, especially in salvation, as monergistic so that "everything that happens is not only foreknown but determined by God."[21] God alone is the one who saves, with no assistance from another agent. This, he writes, is "an affirmation of *sola gratia* in the history of the church of Jesus Christ."[22] Moralistic therapeutic deism, then, consists of the Pelagian chickens of American revivalism coming home to roost.[23] Olson, on the other hand, argues that God's grace is synergistic, that "salvation includes cooperation by the person being saved."[24] The salvific initiative resides with God,

---

18. In similar fashion, emergent church pastor Brian McLaren counters Calvinism by redefining the TULIP as Triune love, Unselfish election, Limitless reconciliation, Inspiring grace, and Passionate, persistent saints. McLaren, *Generous Orthodoxy*, 218–19.

19. Bell, *Love Wins*; Chandler, *The Explicit Gospel*.

20. See, e.g., Walls and Dongell, *Why I Am Not a Calvinist*; Peterson and Williams, *Why I Am Not an Arminian*; Hunt and White, *Debating Calvinism*.

21. Horton, *For Calvinism*, 59.

22. Ibid., 20–21.

23. Ibid., 51. Horton also notes that Arminianism "lists" in the direction of semi-Pelagianism (ibid., 33).

24. Olson, *Against Calvinism*, 50.

but God also makes room for human beings to play a role through the exercise of free will, akin to the reception of a gift that is not earned.[25]

One outcome of resurgent Calvinism's influence is a renewed interest in doctrine among students. In fact, numerous young Reformed thinkers speak of such a concern.[26] That is, having experienced a relative dearth of theological conversation within their churches of origin, they gravitate toward Calvinism and its respondents because it offers robust theological depth.[27] Nonetheless, while the quantity of critical attention directed at Calvinist ideas and their contemporary forms is justified, the ramifications of this focus need to be interrogated. For instance, it creates a dichotomy between two different viewpoints, understanding their rhetorical distance to be inclusive of all possible theological positions.[28] There are no other options except those that exist between synergism and monergism. Hence, students will occasionally ask friends and professors if they are Calvinist or Arminian, sometimes even anachronistically describing figures from earlier periods of Christian history in such terms (e.g., Augustine, Polycarp, Thomas Aquinas) and reading Scripture through their particular lens of the dichotomy (e.g., seeing the pervasiveness of sin in the existential angst of Romans 7).[29] In short, whether and to what extent one subscribes to Reformed thought becomes the sum total of Christian theology.

In many ways, this fascination with the doctrine of divine providence should not be a surprise. The story of Baptist history cannot be told

---

25. "God's grace is the effectual cause of salvation, but the human person's faith as response to prevenient grace is the instrumental cause of salvation" (ibid., 170).

26. Hansen, "Young, Restless, Reformed," 34.

27. McLaren describes his own journey in similar terms: "When I was growing up, there was anti-intellectualism rampant in Evangelical Christianity. At that time it was mostly in the Reformed churches (Presbyterian, Christian Reformed, etc.) that one found much intellectual vigor and life of the mind. Reformed writers and speakers like Francis Schaeffer, R. C. Sproul, Ravi Zacharias, Os Guinness, J. I. Packer, and others gave me a challenge and permission to think, and forever grateful, I made use of that permission" (*Generous Orthodoxy*, 210).

28. Some have offered the portmanteau "Calminian" to claim a middle or hybrid position, though this is somewhat suspect and perhaps impossible. See Olson, *Arminian Theology*, 67–69. Nonetheless, while acknowledging these semantic difficulties, James Leo Garrett uses this term to describe the thought of Baptist theologian David Dockery. Garrett, *Baptist Theology*, 704, 711, 725.

29. There is even a Reformed-inflected Bible translation, the English Standard Version. J. I. Packer was the general editor for the translation, and Calvinist scholars such as Wayne Grudem and Vern Poythress served on the translation committee.

without mentioning one of the earliest significant divisions—between the General Baptists and the Particular Baptists in England. Particular Baptists embraced Calvinistic ideas codified in the five-point TULIP (especially that redemption was reserved for the particular elect), while General Baptists rejected these principles and largely stood as anti-Calvinistic.[30] In the United States, early Baptist confessions of faith reflected a concern with Reformed theology. The Philadelphia Association, the first of its kind among Baptist churches in the American colonies, patterned their 1742 confession on the *Second London Confession of Faith* written by Particular Baptists in 1689.[31] Meanwhile, the *New Hampshire Confession of Faith* (1833) took a more moderate approach to the Calvinism/Arminianism debate. As Bill Leonard states, this was "an effort to 'have it both ways,' retaining election but extending it to all who chose to believe."[32] This confession became the basis of the initial version of the Southern Baptist Convention's *Baptist Faith and Message* in 1925.

Furthermore, in the twentieth century, the debate surrounding resurgent Calvinism extended to the contours of Baptist life. In the wake of the conservative/moderate crisis that resulted in the creation of the Cooperative Baptist Fellowship in 1991 and several rival state Baptist conventions, one of the points of theological difference within the remainder of the Southern Baptist Convention was the issue of divine sovereignty versus human free will. In 1982, Founders Ministries formed with the expressed aim to call Southern Baptists back to their foundation in the doctrines of grace. This push was aided by a historical examination of Baptists' roots in the Reformed tradition.[33] This divide within Southern Baptist life continues into the present. Since 1996, the Southern Baptist

30. For more on the General and Particular Baptists, see Bebbington, *Baptists Through the Centuries*, 43–63.

31. The *Philadelphia Confession* was nearly identical to the *Second London Confession of Faith*, except for two added articles. See "The Philadelphia Confession (1742)," in Lumpkin, *Baptist Confessions of Faith*, 348–53. Cf. "The Second London Confession (1677)," in Lumpkin, *Baptist Confessions of Faith*, 235–95.

32. Leonard, *Baptists in America*, 86. "[We believe] That Election is the gracious purpose of God, according to which he [graciously] regenerates, sanctifies, and save sinners;" and "[We believe] That the blessings of salvation are made free to all by the Gospel . . . and that nothing prevents the salvation of the greatest sinner on earth except his own [inherent depravity and] voluntary refusal to submit to the Lord Jesus Christ" ("The New Hampshire Confession of Faith," art. ix, vi, in Lumpkin, *Baptist Confessions of Faith*, 364, 363).

33. Nettles, *By His Grace and For His Glory*.

Theological Seminary has been headed by an avowed Calvinist, R. Albert Mohler Jr. One of his first steps taken was to re-emphasize Southern Seminary's Reformed-leaning confessional statement, the *Abstract of Principles*.[34] As a counterweight to Mohler's influence, Paige Patterson, president of Southwestern Baptist Theological Seminary since 2003 (and president of Southeastern Baptist Theological Seminary, another SBC institution, from 1992 to 2003), holds to the classical Arminian emphasis on human free will as a constituent part of salvation. Yet, even though it is easy to map this debate onto these SBC seminary presidents, it goes further than ideas to include personnel and day-to-day operations of the convention.[35] Moreover, even though only 10 percent of SBC pastors described themselves as Calvinist in a 2007 study, nearly 30 percent of new seminary graduates understood themselves as Reformed.[36] This developing trend is hailed by some, feared by others, but is recognized as a major controversy by many.[37]

Because this resurgent Calvinist movement is an ever-present topic of conversation, it warrants at least brief discussion. James McClendon observed that, when compared to the rest of the Christian tradition,

---

34. All professors who teach at Southern Seminary are required to affirm this statement. The *Abstract of Principles* was written in 1858 by Southern Seminary's first president, James Petigru Boyce, and is derived largely from the *Second London Confession of Faith*, a statement from seventeenth-century Baptists that borrowed heavily from the *Westminster Confession of Faith*. See "Abstract of Principles," in Leith, *Creeds of the Churches*, 339–43.

35. While the Arminian perspective has been the historically prevalent perspective within Southern Baptist life, the Calvinist perspective is now represented beyond Mohler's presence at Southern. Former Southern Seminary students, faculty, and administrators now occupy the presidencies of Midwestern Baptist Theological Seminary (Jason Allen), Southeastern Baptist Theological Seminary (Daniel Akin), the North American Mission Board (Kevin Ezell), the Ethics and Religious Liberty Commission (Russell Moore), and LifeWay Christian Resources (Thom Rainer). The current president of the International Mission Board (David Platt) also holds similar Calvinist beliefs.

36. Stetzer, "Calvinism, Evangelism, and SBC Leadership," in Clendenin and Waggoner, *Calvinism*, 13. These developments have prompted some interesting conversation partners. For instance, in 2015, moderate Baptist Roger Olson was invited by Paige Patterson to speak on the campus of conservative Southwestern Seminary about Calvinism and its alternatives (a rare point of agreement between these two men).

37. For more, see the essays in Clendenin and Waggoner, *Calvinism*, especially Yarnell, "Calvinism: Cause for Rejoicing, Cause for Concern," and Finn, "Southern Baptist Calvinism: Setting the Record Straight."

Baptists have "produced only a little formal theology."[38] To the extent that students and laypeople are more interested in theological conversations, this is admirable and good. However, questions remain about the adequacy of the resurgent Calvinist theological outlook, requiring attention to what it says, but also to what it neglects to say. That is, is it sufficient for sustaining the faith of the church across the centuries? Will it be acceptable for addressing the challenges of the contemporary world? To answer these questions, more needs to be said about the theological streams flowing out of the Reformation and into this contemporary movement.

Augustine and the Reformation Heritage

Of course, this largely Protestant debate concerning human free will and divine sovereignty (i.e., predestination) has deeper roots, emerging in part from the theological reflections of Augustine of Hippo (354–430 CE). As many scholars have observed, throughout his work Augustine wrestled with questions such as: What capabilities for good remain within a human being after the Fall but before the reception of redemptive grace? What is the theological significance of existence? What is the relationship between sin and existence? To say that Augustine wrestled with the same issues, however, is not to say that his reflections on those issues were consistent over time, In fact, this is certainly not the case. Augustine progressively became more negative about human capacities and continually more adamant that God's activity supersedes all other actors. Thus, any inheritors of Augustine's ideas (e.g., Reformed theologians) must acknowledge and assess the tremendous complexity within his thought. Part of that complexity are the categories of nature and grace (or the natural and the supernatural), even though they are generally overlooked by later generations. For Augustine, though, how these two terms and their relationship are conceived is important for understanding many other dynamics within Christian theology.

For example, in his *On Free Choice of the Will*, Augustine describes human free will as a good that comes from God. Consequently, no righteous act can be performed without free will.[39] Moreover, while he maintains that all good things come from God as a gift, he also notes that

---

38. McClendon, *Ethics*, 20.
39. Augustine, *On Free Choice of the Will* II.17–18.

God's foreknowledge does not impinge upon human free will.[40] What results from Augustine's thoughts on this topic is a tension between divine sovereignty and human free will in a manner that does not allow one to obliterate the other. Crucial to this understanding is his refusal to situate divine and human will as two externally related forces, which facilitates some measure of cooperation by analogy between these two powers as part of their intrinsic relationship. What grounds Augustine's understanding of agency is God as the source of being. Creaturely freedom acts in response to this gift of being. Thus, creation does not experience divine providence as an external power in competition with human agency. Instead, there is an intrinsic and noncompetitive relationship between the two. This is reflected in Augustine's statement within the *Confessions*: "You were more inward to me than my most inward part; and higher than my highest."[41] Here inwardness is clearly not a shift of one's gaze toward the private since the soul's most inward part is also linked to its highest part, where interiority opens out to God. As Denys Turner notes, "The *itinerarium intus* is also an *ascensio superius*. The two metaphors of inwardness and ascent themselves intersect at the point where God and the self intersect, so that that which is most interior to me is also that which is above and beyond me; so that the God who is within me is also the God I am in."[42] Thus, Augustine's understanding of divine and human will bring together the personal/intimate and the transcendent in metaphysical harmony.[43]

The relationship between the natural and the supernatural is displayed in Augustine's *magnum opus*, *The City of God*. There, Augustine reads the history of the Roman Empire against the drama of salvation history. However, instead of creating a dichotomy based on these different narratives, he views the natural realm as plagued by sin, but still containing admirable qualities and goals: "[I]t is wrong to deny that the aims of human civilization are good, for this is the highest end that

---

40. Ibid., III.1–2.

41. Augustine, *Confessions* III.6. Many have tried to construe statements such as this as evidence that Augustine simply redeploys Platonic thought in Christian guise. For a discussion of how Augustine's appropriation of Plato involved moving away from certain Platonic ideas, see Taylor, *Sources of the Self*, 127–39.

42. Turner, *Darkness of God*, 99.

43. This intersection is also evident in Augustine's discussion of the image of God within the human person, which takes the form of a triunity of memory, understanding, and will. Cf. Augustine, *On the Trinity, Books 8–15*, XIV.11.

mankind of itself can achieve. For, however lowly the goods of the earth, the aim, such as it is, is peace."[44] Further, in discussing the deeds of pagan heroes, he states, "[T]here was not to be the divine grace of everlasting life along with His holy angels in His heavenly City . . . On the other hand, if God did not grant them at least the temporal glory of a splendid Empire, there would have been no reward for the praiseworthy efforts or virtues by which they strove to attain that glory."[45] Augustine continues by noting that these pagan heroes "subordinated private property to the common welfare . . . resisted the temptation to avarice . . . [and] indulged in neither public crime nor private passion."[46] Consequently, he argues that these persons should be honored. That is, even though "[t]he reward of the saints is altogether different," this does not mean that the ideas and activities of the pagan are utterly irredeemable.[47] Natural virtue that coheres with the vision of the eternal city, incomplete though it may be, is to be recognized for what it is and praised.

Similarly, while one may be tempted to view Augustine's distinction between the earthly city and the heavenly city as a dualism so that one avoids the former and embraces the latter, Augustine states that there is a good deal of overlap between the two:

> [T]he earthly city which does live by faith seeks only an earthly peace, and limits the goal of its peace, of its harmony of authority and obedience among its citizens, to the voluntary and collective attainment of objectives necessary to mortal existence. The heavenly City, meanwhile—or, rather, that part that is on pilgrimage in mortal life and lives by faith—must use this earthly peace until such time as our mortality which needs such peace has passed away.[48]

Hence, there is a difference between the earthly and heavenly cities (and even one that makes the heavenly city better than its earthly counterpart), but this does not mean that everything related to the earthly city is worthy of condemnation; some of it is helpful for the heavenly city's pursuit of its appropriate end.

---

44. Augustine, *City of God* XV.4.
45. Ibid., V.15.
46. Ibid.
47. Ibid., V.16.
48. Ibid., XIX.17.

This understanding of the natural world coheres with Augustine's distinction of love involving the difference between using something (*uti*) and enjoying something (*frui*). In truth, three possibilities exist for everything: "Some things are to be enjoyed, others to be used, and there are others which are to be enjoyed and used."[49] These distinctions help to cultivate properly directed love, which means that both use and enjoyment can be good: "To enjoy something is to cling to it with love for its own sake. To use something, however, is to employ it in obtaining that which you love, provided that it is worthy of love."[50] That is, things merely used or utilized are worthwhile, yet they are significant for the contribution to a larger aim, a derivative good that is properly pursued in relation to the ultimate end, or that which is enjoyed.[51] In other words, even non-Christian material such as pagan philosophy can be loved for how it facilitates the enjoyment of the Triune God.

The magisterial Reformers (e.g., Martin Luther and John Calvin) inherited certain aspects of Augustine's theological outlook. However, since they received Augustine in different contexts, it is not certain that their appropriation of Augustine represents the fullness of his work. In short, while Luther and Calvin are significant luminaries within Protestantism, their contributions may be helpful, though perhaps only to the extent that they articulate a theological framework for cooperation of divine and human agency by analogy.[52] In other words, grace and nature cannot be externally related in a dualistic ontology. Rather, that which is natural must be integrally linked with the supernatural without being totally obscured (either by the operations of grace or the presence of sin). This is what other theologians have rightly called a "participatory ontology," where the created order participates (albeit imperfectly) in the life of God.[53]

Martin Luther (1483–1546) discussed the human will in a manner that at times left it little, if any, positive role in the Christian life. That is, to obey one's will was almost always to walk a path towards sin. For instance,

49. Augustine, *On Christian Doctrine* I.3.

50. Ibid., I.4.

51. "*Frui* is love in an absolute way; *uti* is love in a relative way." Fitzgerald, *Augustine Through the Centuries*, 513.

52. For more on Luther and Calvin concerning divine and human agency, see Placher, *Domestication of Transcendence*, 37–68.

53. See Boersma, *Nouvelle Théologie and Sacramental Ontology*, 16; Hollon, *Everything Is Sacred*, 7.

in his *Disputation against Scholastic Theology* (1517), he stated, "Man is by nature unable to want God to be God. Indeed, he himself wants to be God, and does not want God to be God."[54] Here Luther indicates that the order of the cosmos is challenged by the human will since human beings are not content to be servants of God. Moreover, this set of circumstances is described as being "by nature." Elsewhere in this treatise, he sharpens this point by stating, "No act is done according to nature that is not an act of concupiscence against God."[55] Once again, the inability of the human will to perform a good act is attributed to created nature. Statements such as these indicate that "nature" is something desperately in need of grace and entirely bankrupt on its own account. Thus, one could state that the pairing of nature and grace is more or less a pairing of sin and grace. That is, sin eliminates any possibility that the human will can (even in a minute way) pursue goodness. Only by the gracious aid of God in Jesus Christ does a human even approximate righteous activity. In the end, activities of human nature and activities of God's grace run counter to one another.

For Luther, then, to acknowledge that the human will has any capacity to desire God is to rob God's grace of its redemptive power. The result is that the human will is set against the will of God, unless, of course, the human will is united with the divine will to such an extent that there ceases to be a distinction between the two. This construal of the relationship between divine and human wills is solidified in the Lutheran *Augsburg Confession* (1530), prepared by Philip Melanchthon, which states in its second article, "[A]ll men [sic] are full of evil lust and inclinations from their mothers' wombs and are unable by nature to have true fear of God and true faith in God."[56]

John Calvin (1509–64) stands in continuity with Luther regarding the severe limitations of human free will.[57] He initially describes the corruption of the will as something that did not occur strictly by nature (i.e.,

---

54. Luther, *Disputation against Scholastic Theology*, 14.
55. Ibid.
56. "The Augsburg Confession," in Leith, *Creeds of the Churches*, 68.
57. This is not to equate the thought of Calvin to that of Luther, only to identify the nearly parallel trajectories of their ideas regarding the freedom of the will. They diverge at key places as well, e.g., the foundational Christic understandings of grace (Luther emphasizing the theology of the cross and Calvin focusing on the glorified Christ).

proceeding from human nature as created).[58] Calvin, however, takes issue with the use of the phrase "free will," stating,

> If anyone, then, can use this word without understanding it in a bad sense, I shall not trouble him on this account. But I hold that because it cannot be retained without great peril, it will, on the contrary, be a great boon for the church if it be abolished. I prefer not to use it myself, and I should like others, if they seek my advice, to avoid it.[59]

Thus, while it is possible to apply a valid sense to the term "free will" (i.e., the ability and freedom to choose between alternatives), Calvin is exceedingly concerned that people will understand free will in a Pelagian manner as "unrestricted power to choose either good or evil courses of action."[60] In other words, Calvin denies the fallen will any inclination for good, claiming that the philosophers' (e.g., Aristotle's) doctrine that "all things seek good through a natural instinct" has no purchase on the human will corrupted by sin.[61] In short, the fallen will, as part of the whole person, inclines entirely toward evil.[62] The implications of this understanding of the will are significant, as Dewey Hoitenga Jr. describes: "[I]f the will's prior instinct or inclination is morally evil without any qualification, there can be no motive left in the will for choosing a morally good alternative instead of an evil one; every choice is doomed from the start to be a choice of evil."[63]

Each in his own way, James K. A. Smith and J. Todd Billings dispute this reading of Calvin. Smith challenges the claim that Calvin is a nominalist (even though Calvin holds to some form of voluntarism).[64] Moreover, Smith highlights Calvin's affirmation of an "awareness of divinity" (*sensus divinitatis*) within human beings. In the *Institutes*, Calvin describes a "sense of divinity [that] is by nature engraven on human hearts."[65] Smith argues that this awareness, elsewhere described by Cal-

---

58. Cf. Calvin, *Institutes of the Christian Religion*, 2.1.11.
59. Ibid., 2.2.8.
60. Helm, *John Calvin's Ideas*, 160.
61. Calvin, *Institutes*, 2.2.26.
62. "But if the whole man [sic] lies under the power of sin, surely it is necessary that the will, which is its chief seat, be restrained by the stoutest bonds" (ibid., 2.2.27).
63. Hoitenga, *John Calvin and the Will*, 77.
64. Smith, *Introducing Radical Orthodoxy*, 95 n. 26.
65. Calvin, *Institutes*, 1.4.4.

vin as the "seed of religion," underscores humanity's "passional disposition to worship," even if that disposition is disordered.[66] Focused on desire rather than knowledge, this is similar to Augustine's restless heart from the *Confessions*, establishing human beings as primarily liturgical animals.[67] Thus, Calvin does not divorce humanity from God because humanity subtly, and perhaps unknowingly, has an inborn desire to see God.

Billings argues for "relative continuity with various patristic and medieval traditions."[68] While he states that Calvin is not a Thomist, a Scotist, or a Palamite, Billings views Calvin's theological work as characterized by a theology of participation that is centrally focused on love and believers' active work in the Christian life. Thus, one is not left with a unilateral gift from God to human beings, but a double grace. These gifts of grace, both of which arrive from outside of us, exist in a distinct, yet inseparable relationship, where the first gift, imputation of Christ's righteousness, is followed by a second gift, regeneration as a life of active gratitude and love, culminating in union with God, or "a kind of deification."[69] For Billings, then, "Calvin's strong account of divine agency enables, rather than undercuts, human agency in sanctification."[70] Central for his argument are key words such as participation, ingrafting, and adoption.[71]

In response to these objections about reading Calvin, two things should be noted. First, insofar as Smith and Billings are accurate in their

66. Smith, *Desiring the Kingdom*, 122–23. "There is a structural human propensity to worship a divinity, not to have *some* knowledge of the Creator God. This is precisely why it could never not be operative . . . If it is not directed toward the Triune Creator, it is misdirected toward an idol." Smith, *Introducing Radical Orthodoxy*, 180 n. 107.

67. Smith even invokes Augustine's famous phrase to make this point before commenting on Calvin's notion of *sensus divinitatis*. Cf. Smith, *Desiring the Kingdom*, 77.

68. Billings, *Calvin, Participation, and the Gift*, 190.

69. Ibid., 193.

70. Ibid., 17.

71. While it is beyond the scope of this book to delve further into this debate about the interpretation of Calvin, a few comments seem necessary. Billings's argument, while well-deployed and thought-provoking, leaves many unanswered questions, such as whether a truly participatory ontology can function when the verbs used to signal participation have passive connotation (e.g., adoption, ingrafting). Moreover, what of Calvin's denial of infused habits and the distinction between natural and supernatural virtues? Finally, since Billings's focus is on the activity of believers, one might ask about Calvin's stance toward the created order as a whole, rather than believers after justification. That is, does a genuinely analogical relationship (uniting, yet distinguishing, God and creation) exist in Calvin's work?

portrayals of Calvin, they only augment the need for attending to the whole Christian tradition. Smith depicts a Calvin who is more faithful to Augustine. That is, if correct, Calvin's use of *sensus divinitatis* resonates with Augustine's restless heart, marking humans as more than simply sinners devoid of any inclination toward God after the Fall. Moreover, if Billings is correct, then his rebuttal of Calvin's critics brings the Reformer closer to a patristic and medieval conception of participation through his thorough engagement with sources such as Cyril, Irenaeus, and Augustine. Second, both Smith and Billings focus their attention on Calvin himself, leaving open the question of how Calvin was received and appropriated by his later Reformed interpreters.

These interpreters also served as the architects of Calvinism, extending his ideas as they systematized his thought as well. As Diarmaid MacCulloch notes, "Calvin's successors became ever more dogmatic in their assertions, ruthlessly spelling out questions about salvation that Calvin had generally left understated."[72] Chief among these theologians was Theodore Beza, who followed Calvin in Geneva after his death in 1564, making him a prominent spokesperson for Reformed theology. Beza was instrumental in pushing Calvinist theology toward explicit double predestination, limiting Christ's atoning sacrifice to only the elect, as well as positing that the number and names of the elect and reprobate were foreordained by God before the Fall.[73]

While this system of Calvinist thought developed, internal critiques emerged. Jakob Arminius, a student of Beza, questioned his interpretation of Calvin, and eventually denied the irresistibility of God's grace, understanding that "alongside those whom God has eternally decreed to be elect to salvation there are those who choose to reject the offer of God's grace, and fall away into damnation."[74] Therefore, God does not foreordain these persons to damnation, but foresees it nonetheless, thereby (to Arminius's mind) preserving the Reformed emphasis on God's sovereignty over all of creation. Though Arminius died in 1609, his position persisted by being championed by the Dutch Remonstrants (precursors to contemporary Arminians), who were wrongly labeled as Pelagians and eventually condemned at the Synod of Dort (1618–1619). In response to this crisis, Reformed theologians constructed a rubric for orthodoxy that

72. MacCulloch, *Reformation*, 374.
73. Ibid., 375.
74. Ibid., 376.

set human free will over divine sovereignty. In English, this rubric is the popular TULIP that inspires so many young Calvinists today.[75]

Later-generation Calvinists (and for some, even Calvin himself) held a similar position to Luther: that which is not grace is sin. In other words, grace and nature are not seen as in any way compatible after the Fall (and, for Beza, even before the Fall). Indeed, Hoitenga notes that Calvin is rightly criticized on this point: "[Calvin] disparages nature to magnify grace. If both nature and grace are from God, there is no need to fear giving nature its full due in its fallen state."[76] Read in light of his later interpreters, Calvin goes so far as to deny that humans have a proper desire for the good, even if only a desire that is malformed and misdirected. Rather, the impotence of human beings in pursuing the good pervades the whole human person, leaving deficient desire and deficient actions, dividing the realm of God's grace from the realm of fallen humanity, where nothing but sin remains of the good creation of God. Moreover, with the actions of Reformed theologians at Dort, the possibility for any positive actions by humans was further denied by emphasizing the total depravity of human beings and the inability of human free will to resist God's grace, leaving grace and nature in an external (and oppositional) relationship.

The Folly of Resurgent Calvinism

As was observed earlier, resurgent Calvinism, even when grounded in its Reformation ancestors, fails to offer a genuine theological vision for Baptists. That is, Baptists and other free church Protestants do not need to pick a side regarding divine sovereignty and human free will since this will only exacerbate their theological confusion. Instead, what is needed is a way forward that embraces both without setting them in opposition to or in tension with one another. In fact, James McClendon indicates that presenting theological conversations in these terms (e.g., human will vs. divine sovereignty, Calvinism vs. Arminianism) has contributed to the relative dearth of significant Baptist theological scholarship mentioned

---

75. Ibid., 378. Horton describes this synod as "the closest thing to an ecumenical council in early Protestantism," and notes that even Cyril Lucaris, the sitting ecumenical Patriarch of Constantinople, "embraced the canons of the Synod of Dort and incorporated them into his 1629 Confession" (*For Calvinism*, 20).

76. Hoitenga, *John Calvin and the Will*, 85.

earlier.[77] Even when both human and divine agency are manifest, they are often located at the same level, situating them within a zero-sum game. What emerges from these observations is that any possibility for multiple causation by human and divine agency is diminished. In short, humanity and God do not work together or cooperate in any way, form, or fashion. Another way to describe these circumstances is in terms of univocity.[78] Emerging from the thought of medieval scholastic John Duns Scotus (1266–1308), univocal language proposes that God and creatures are positioned side-by-side under the same genus. This means that, despite differences in finitude, God and creatures fundamentally share in the category of existence, making attributive claims different only in degree and not in kind. That is, literally meaning, "single voice," univocal language is applicable in the same way for all objects. Thus, adjectives modify nouns in the same manner with no qualitative difference. For example, if both God and a person (e.g., Jim) are described as good, then they must be good *in the same manner.* God may possess more goodness than Jim, but the essence of that goodness is unchanged. Scotus's work, in short, flattened the ontological landscape so that God was bigger and grander than creatures, but God, like creatures, was also a being. This thinking was developed further by fellow Franciscan William of Occam. Here, the univocal ground of language individualizes beings who no longer participate in Being itself, God. With Occam's nominalism, the other locus for any connection between God and creatures is through the will. Yet, this is also problematic: "God and finite things have to be rivals, since their individualities are contrastive and mutually exclusive."[79]

The univocal language beneath resurgent Calvinism deepens Baptists' difficulties, because it reduces God's activity and human activity to the same level, so that God can act in a larger way than any single person, but the nature of that activity remains the same between God and humanity. In other words, God and humanity are set in an extrinsic ontological relationship. This makes simple juxtaposition of divine and human agency insufficient since it merely reiterates the competition between God and humans.

77. McClendon, *Ethics*, 24–26.

78. While univocal language is not the focus of this book (and therefore will not be thoroughly examined), it does require attention insofar as it is a contributing factor to Baptists' troubles.

79. Barron, *Priority of Christ*, 14. For more on the significance of the univocity of being, see Burrell, *Faith and Freedom*, 176–89.

Instead, what Baptists need is an ontology and an understanding of language (and, by extension, of their practices) that allows for human and divine activity to operate on multiple levels. In this conception, humans (and all of creation) participate in God, who is not a being in the universe bigger than other creatures but is Being itself, the ground of all creation. Like Herbert McCabe's declaration at the outset of this chapter, God is not a god, or an item in the universe. God transcends even existence itself, serving as its source and wellspring. Hence, "otherness" need not imply competition. Consequently, language applied to God and humans would function in an analogical rather than a univocal manner, recognizing the similarities between attributive terms and their simultaneous dissimilarity. Thus, Jim and God are both described as good but not in the same manner, because God is not merely the perfection or fullness of goodness, but God is the source of goodness as well, making all good human activity derivative of and intelligible in light of God's goodness in the first place. This perspective highlights what is needed—not cooperation on a single plane of activity (which produces the same zero-sum game), but cooperation by analogy, or participation in the noncompetitively transcendent and coinherent God.[80]

In his book *Predestination*, Peter Thuesen treats the evolution of predestination, or the doctrine of divine providence, from its European birthplace to its contemporary American home, discussing how various Christian groups have received this doctrine and adapted it to their experience on the American religious landscape. However, while Thuesen does discuss the common positioning of Calvinism against Arminianism, he notes that "the most interesting antithesis is not between predestination and free will but between predestinarianism and sacramentalism."[81] That is, what is really at stake in the debates about divine sovereignty and human free will relates to the mystical beauty and holiness of the sacramental ritual and questions concerning the presence of the divine in the world.[82] The result was that "in the predestinarian progression from the Reformation to the megachurch, the sacramental substance of Christianity attenuated to almost nothing."[83] In fact, this shift from a more sacramental outlook toward one that focused on singular agency has impinged

80. Cf. Barron, *Priority of Christ*, 205–7.

81. Thuesen, *Predestination*, 6.

82. Not surprisingly, then, Hans Boersma describes the needed participatory ontology as a "resacramentalized Christian ontology" (*Heavenly Participation*, 20).

83. Thuesen, *Predestination*, 217.

on theological depth as well, leaving contemporary theology (such as that performed by many Baptists) anemic and sterile.[84]

Thus, sacramental practices such as baptism might have been largely unintelligible in light of the debates about resurgent Calvinism. For Calvinistic thinkers, baptism cannot be an act pervaded by both divine and human agency. Because the human will is unable to pursue good, baptism's work is initiated and brought to completion by God alone, unpolluted by human influence. For Arminians, a better alternative is not available because their theological outlook also reproduces the quandary facing Baptists. Indeed, the Baptist landscape is littered with positions related to the intra-Reformed debate surrounding Arminius.[85] In short, the quest to define what agent is active and at which moment has left a maze of confusion in its wake. Neither Calvinism, nor Arminianism, nor anything in between offer significant resources for moving forward. Further, while the traditions that emerge from the magisterial Reformers do have Augustine as a theological forerunner, they also distanced themselves from the bishop of Hippo in significant ways, including his aversion to situating the divine and human wills externally.

—

The crisis concerning Calvinism grips the imaginations of contemporary evangelical college students and other laypersons. Once again, the questions that arise, even if misdirected, emerge from a budding love and appreciation for theological reflection. This is a good starting point for Baptists and free church Christians. However, more work needs to be done. This includes reshaping the operative questions that confront students. As hinted above, university students interested in theology might avoid the question, "Are you a Calvinist or an Arminian?" Rather, they might ask about a participatory ontology, or an understanding of the God-world relationship that makes sense of both divine and human agency. As highlighted throughout this chapter, though, this quest will be frustrating and endless unless different theological resources are brought to bear on this question. Indeed, even asking about a participatory ontology is not

84. Ibid. Thuesen concludes by gesturing toward artists such as Flannery O'Connor as the true inheritors of this sacramental sensibility, seen, e.g., in the life of O. E. Parker in "Parker's Back."

85. For more on Baptists' wide-ranging views regarding Calvinism (and their impact on the dynamics of Baptist life), see Thuesen, *Predestination*, 193–208.

a wholly new question as it has its roots in the very beginning of the Christian tradition. Thus, Baptists should view this quandary as a first step toward joining with the great tradition by consulting the ancient writers of the Christian faith as well as Scripture. This will aid Baptists in finding a truly participatory ontology as they broaden the conversation beyond the Reformation heritage and find new dialogue partners as they explore the relationship between God and the world. As a move toward answering this question and cultivating the necessary theological vision, both of these tasks will be pursued in the next chapter through attention to a similar debate, one that ends very differently than the impasse found in Reformed history and at the heart of resurgent Calvinism. Moreover, through this historical examination, we will find a method for theological renewal that will open up new doors for Baptist theology within the heart of the church.

2

Ressourcement and Ontology

> All theologians have recognized that God is something greater than can be conceived; and hence they affirmed that He is super-substantial, and above every name, and the like. In the case of God they have not expressed to us one thing by "super," another by "without," another by "in," another by "non," and [another] by "before"; for it is the same thing for God to be supersubstantial Substance, Substance without substance, insubstantial Substance, non-substantial Substance, and Substance before substance.
>
> —NICHOLAS OF CUSA[1]

IN THE PREVIOUS CHAPTER, the crisis created by imaginations captivated by resurgent Calvinism presented a problem for the shape of Baptist theology. As was discussed, what is needed is not a clear determination regarding whether one is an Arminian or a Calvinist. Instead, a participatory ontology will open up space for new questions that will revitalize Baptist and free church theological reflection. However, as was also seen, we will have little success avoiding a univocal perspective when confined to the conventional Protestant interlocutors. So much of the theological story has already been told when one starts here that the result is virtually the same. Instead, a different kind of reform will be necessary, one that will renew not only theological convictions but theological vision as well. Surprisingly, though, to properly appreciate this new kind of reform, we

---

1. Nicholas of Cusa, *God as Not-Other*, 1113.

must observe a theological dispute very similar to the resurgent Calvinist one we just left behind.

In this chapter, then, we will evaluate a Catholic analogue to the Calvinist/Arminian controversy among Protestants. After doing so, the differences between the Protestant and Catholic versions will become clear through the work of twentieth-century French Jesuit Henri de Lubac, whose efforts for *ressourcement* called Catholic theology back to its wellspring. Finally, de Lubac and others' emphasis on the theology of nature and grace will offer resources for a more participatory ontology and exhibit how the methodology of *ressourcement* can renew Baptist faith and practice going forward.

Divine Sovereignty and Human Free Will in a Catholic Key

Earlier, we surveyed the insufficiency of the Protestant magisterial Reformers in providing resources for Baptists and free church Protestants confronted by resurgent Calvinism. However, these debates concerning the sovereignty of God and human free will did not occur only among Protestant Reformers. Indeed, Catholics were forced to address them as well, beginning with the Council of Trent. When addressing justification, the council rejected the Protestants' accent on "grace alone" (*sola gratia*) by decreeing, "[W]hile God touches the heart of man through the illumination of the Holy Ghost, man himself neither does absolutely nothing while receiving the inspiration, since he can also reject it, nor yet is he able by his own will and without the grace of God to move himself to justice in [God's] sight."[2] Moreover, the "faith alone" (*sola fide*) of the Reformers was rebuffed as expressing the conviction that "sins are forgiven or have been forgiven to anyone who boasts of his confidence and certainty of the remission of his sins, resting on that alone."[3] Expanding on this, the council affirmed the need for both grace and good works.[4]

2. Council of Trent, "Decree concerning Justification," ch. V, in Leith, *Creeds of the Churches*, 410.

3. Council of Trent, "Decree concerning Justification," ch. IX, in ibid., 413. "Moreover, it must not be maintained, that they who are truly justified must needs, without any doubt whatever, convince themselves that they are justified, and that no one is absolved from sins and justified except he that believes with certainty that he is absolved and justified" (ibid.).

4. "If anyone says that the sinner is justified by faith alone, meaning that nothing

Thus, the first canon of the council reaffirms the church's opposition to Pelagianism,[5] while canon four anathematizes a monergistic outlook on salvation.[6] In short, while the impetus for the response found at Trent was located in the Protestant Reformation, the council sought to avoid the two problematic positions that were hazards to Protestant thinking at that time and even today.

Despite the efforts of the Decree on Justification at Trent, Catholics continued to confront similar theological questions about the relationship between grace and free will. In response to Luther's argument that human will is incapable of doing anything good without God, Catholic humanist Desiderius Erasmus (1466–1536) defended free will, stating, "By free choice . . . we mean a power of the human free will by which a man can apply himself to the things which lead to eternal salvation, or turn away from them."[7] This argument was picked up by many Jesuits, most notably Luis de Molina (1535–1600), a Spaniard who authored a controversial work on the operations of divine grace in 1588. Affirming the centrality of divine grace in bringing about a good act, Molinism (as Molina's ideas were labeled) safeguarded human freedom by arguing that human free will does not conflict with God's "middle knowledge" of "futuribles" (e.g., future human consent to divine grace).[8] Thus, grace's

---

else is required to co-operate in order to obtain the grace of justification, and that it is not in any way necessary that he be prepared and disposed by the action of his own will, let him be anathema" (Council of Trent, "Decree concerning Justification," canon IX, in ibid., 421).

5. "If anyone says that man can be justified before God by his own works, whether done by his natural powers or through the teaching of the law, without divine grace through Jesus Christ, let him be anathema" (Council of Trent, "Decree concerning Justification," canon I, in ibid., 420).

6. "If anyone says that man's free will moved and aroused by God, by assenting to God's call and action, in no way co-operates toward disposing and preparing itself to obtain the grace of justification, that it cannot refuse its assent if it wishes, but that, as something inanimate, it does nothing whatever and is merely passive, let him be anathema" (Council of Trent, "Decree concerning Justification," canon IV, in ibid., 420).

7. Erasmus, *On the Freedom of the Will*, 47.

8. This middle knowledge (*scientia media*) was distinct from God's natural knowledge (concerning all individuals as well as all possible actions and circumstances related to all individuals) and God's free knowledge (concerning which contingencies will undoubtedly be actualized). As one commentator describes Molina's position, "Whereas by God's natural knowledge God knows what an individual *could* do if placed in a particular set of circumstances, by middle knowledge God knows what an individual *would* do when placed in the same particular set of circumstances." Bryant,

efficacy is founded upon its union with human agency. Opposing Molinism was Domingo Báñez (1528–1604), a Spanish Dominican who argued that divine grace was efficacious by bringing about the will's consent, rather than depending upon the variations in the will's activity and divine foreknowledge of its merits.[9] For Báñez, who followed the thought of Augustine and Aquinas, grace must be gratuitous or it is not grace at all.[10]

The dispute between Jesuits and Dominicans was not limited to Spain, however. In Leuven, Michael Baius (1513–89), a Belgian Catholic theologian, taught that humanity's original state of innocence was natural and that the benefits of such innocence (e.g., final destination in heaven) were owed to humanity and not based on a gratuitous gift of grace by God. After the fall, human beings were utterly incapable of any good apart from the empowerment of divine grace. Despite his appeals to Augustine's anti-Pelagian writings, the mention of pre-lapsarian perfection and its obligated "gift" opened Baius to charges of Pelagianism. Baius's ideas were countered by the Italian Robert Bellarmine (1542–1621), the first Jesuit to teach theology at the Dominican school in Leuven. Bellarmine's defense of Catholic thought against the Protestant Reformers heightened his suspicions of Baius's evaluation of human free will after original sin.

Eventually, these hardened lines between the Jesuits who defended human free will without disturbing God's governance and the Dominicans who argued for the absolute priority of God's sovereignty led to a crisis addressed by a Roman Catholic commission known as the *Congregatio de Auxiliis* (1594–1607). Taking its name from the debate about the nature of the "aid" (*auxilium*) of God's grace, Pope Clement VIII formed this commission in 1597 to ascertain whether the "infallible efficacy of grace is due to the very nature of grace itself or to God's eternal knowledge of the use each man would make of all possible graces."[11] While the commission's deliberations were tense and spanned three papacies, the eventual decision of Pope Paul V on the feast of St. Augustine in 1607 produced no wholesale condemnation of one side or the other. In other

---

"Molina, Arminius, Plaifere, Goad, and Wesley," 95.

9. Hill, "Báñez and Bañezianism," 49.

10. Interestingly, Molina's position has experienced a renaissance of sorts recently, with Protestant evangelical scholars embracing it as an alternative to Calvinism. See Craig, "The Middle Knowledge View," in Beilby and Eddy, *Divine Foreknowledge*, and Keathley, *Salvation and Sovereignty*.

11. Cited in Ryan, "Congregatio de Auxiliis," 169.

words, the Dominicans were not declared Calvinists and the Jesuits were not labeled as Pelagians. Both were allowed to defend their respective positions without condemning the other. Each were also required to limit their writings on the subject for a season. What is important for the purpose of this study is the treatment of each position given by the Catholic hierarchy. While the Protestant version of this debate forced people to decide whether they were Calvinist or Arminian, at two different historical points in the Catholic version, one side of the debate could have been elevated at the expense of the other as the fullness of the truth, and yet, this did not occur. In other words, the Council of Trent, by condemning the extreme positions of Pelagianism and monergism, left ample space for a variety of theological reflection. The *de Auxiliis* controversy ends in a similar manner, allowing Molinism and Baianism to defend their positions without claiming superiority.

These debates continued, however, in the work of Cornelius Jansenius (1585–1638), a Dutch bishop and theologian who spent most of his teaching career in Leuven. Following Baius, Jansenius argued that the original state of humanity was based entirely on God's grace, but also that God could not have possibly created humanity in any other manner. He saw a significant pessimism within the works of Augustine that prompted him to oppose the casuistry and theological flexibility deployed by Jesuits, especially in the mission field.[12] In his posthumously published *Augustinus* (which was supposedly developed by reading all of Augustine's works ten times and the works on grace thirty times),[13] Jansenius described "[h]umanity . . . as radically corrupt and the human will to good therefore nonexistent."[14] Any mention of human nature necessarily involved discussion of sinfulness. As historian Robert Bireley describes, Jansenius's work offered "profound theological pessimism with its emphasis on the effects of original sin on human nature and its assertion of a divine determinism that seemed to exclude man's free will in the work of salvation."[15] The result of the publication of *Augustinus* was the condemnation of five propositions found therein, including the irresistibility of divine grace and the assertion that Christ's redemptive death was not meant for all people.

---

12. MacCullough, *Reformation*, 481–82.
13. Bireley, *Refashioning of Catholicism*, 188.
14. MacCullough, *Reformation*, 482.
15. Bireley, *Refashioning of Catholicism*, 188.

From this description, it is clear that, despite a lack of an organic or genealogical relationship between Reformation thought and Jansenius, Jansenism (and even Baianism) has theological themes that strongly resonate with Calvinism. In fact, contemporaries of Jansenius and his descendants (especially Jesuits) noted significant similarities between Calvinism and Jansenism. Both offer a deep pessimism about human nature as affected by original sin. Both view divine activity as fundamental in determining all of reality. Moreover, both claim Augustine as a theological foundation and as a lens for reading Scripture. This parallel makes for an important corollary in evaluating both positions and their perceived Augustinian heritage.

Ressourcement: An Excursus on Theological Method

What has been performed in this brief historical examination of Molinism, Baianism, and Jansenism is part of what twentieth-century theologians called *ressourcement*. This theological method, which involves "returning to the sources" of the faith, was represented prominently by twentieth-century French Jesuit Henri de Lubac (1896–1991), who saw thorough historical work as a path to theological renewal. In twentieth-century Catholicism, ancient and medieval texts were understood primarily through their interpreters. These voices grew into what Romanus Cessario has called "the commentatorial tradition," taking on a life of its own.[16] De Lubac, while genuinely interested in reading these texts faithfully, also observed how the particular interpretations of the commentatorial tradition—whether an accurate reading of the original text or not—affected contemporary Christian thought. Thus, in discussing *ressourcement*, he writes,

> How should we rediscover Christianity if not by going back to its sources, trying to recapture it in its periods of explosive vitality? How should we rediscover the meaning of so many doctrines and institutions which always tend toward dead abstraction and formalism in us, if not by trying to touch anew the creative thought that achieved them? . . . The task is not for everyone, obviously, but it is indispensable that it be done and forever done again.[17]

---

16. Cessario, *Short History of Thomism*, 12.
17. De Lubac, *Paradoxes of Faith*, 58.

Thus, de Lubac plumbed the depths of the Catholic tradition, aiming to re-read important patristic and scholastic texts rather than accept the prevalent manualist reading.[18] In the case of Aquinas, this involved recovering the Augustinian impulses (sometimes mediated through figures such as Pseudo-Dionysius) that animated the work of the Angelic Doctor. The result was not simply a new reading of an old name within the history of Christianity. Rather, the new (or perhaps renewed) reading brought fresh theological life to Thomas's works and his impact on contemporary theological discourse.

De Lubac's work was part of a movement within twentieth-century Catholic theology that stemmed from the conviction that "the renewal of Christian vitality is at least partially linked to a renewed exploration of the periods and of the works where the Christian tradition is expressed with a particular intensity."[19] Other contributors to this movement included French Dominicans Yves Congar, Marie-Dominque Chenu, as well as Swiss theologian Hans Urs von Balthasar, and German theologian Joseph Ratzinger (now Pope Emeritus Benedict XVI). Each in their own way embodied the *ressourcement* impulse, engaging the depth of the sources of the Christian faith. For de Lubac, his writings mainly brought about the renewal of a more integrated nature/grace schema, one that challenged the dominant form of Thomism in the early twentieth century and served as the foundation for numerous theological developments thereafter. Not surprisingly, his work (as well as much of the work of other *ressourcement* theologians) consisted of historical theological arguments. That is, dogma was not disconnected from historical development, though it was not reducible to history either.

In some cases, genuine *ressourcement* involved not only renewed readings of accepted texts, but also recovery of voices that had been marginalized and even forgotten, those whom Balthasar described as "the great among the vanquished who have fallen because of the machinations of smaller minds or of a narrow Catholicism that is politically rather than spiritually minded."[20] Some of these "vanquished" persons included early Christian theologian (and later, a condemned heretic) Origen of

---

18. "So ingrained has the habit become, that it calls for much time, and sometimes the most painstaking effort of analysis, for us to learn again how to read these texts, even when in themselves they are perfectly clear." De Lubac, *Mystery of the Supernatural*, 6.

19. De Lubac, *At the Service of the Church*, 95.

20. Balthasar, *Theology of Henri de Lubac*, 30–31.

Alexandria (c. 185–254 CE), Italian Platonist philosopher Giovanni Pico della Mirandola (1463–94), non-Marxian socialist Pierre-Joseph Proudhon (1809–65), and Jesuit mystic, paleontologist, and priest Pierre Teilhard de Chardin (1881–1955).

As de Lubac makes clear, *ressourcement* requires more than simply a willingness to examine older internal sources since this can often repeat the mistakes that produced present circumstances, as was seen with resurgent Calvinism in chapter one. Instead, it will require a full-blown embrace of the Christian tradition, especially as embodied by other Christian groups, including Catholics. This serves as something of an obstacle, since, as Dr. Tom More in Walker Percy's *Love in the Ruins* states, Baptists "don't like Catholics no matter what."[21] In other words, for Baptists and other free church Protestants, who have developed an aversion to tradition, a thoroughgoing anti-Catholicism sometimes prejudices any findings from that portion of the Christian tradition. Tradition has even been a bad word for Baptists and other free church Christians. Offering vociferous pleas that they have never been a creedal people or need "no creed but the Bible," an embrace of tradition has been perceived as a return to the old or a hierarchical top-down approach to church and theology. For many Baptists, this appears to violate the evangelical need to be "relevant" and "up to date" or cuts against the grain of Baptists' self-identity as dissenters. Nonetheless, there have been significant calls within Baptist life to reconsider this revulsion to tradition (and its attendant anti-Catholic sentiments) in favor of the depth and life offered by fellow Christian pilgrims.

In a review essay of Terrence Tilley's *Inventing Catholic Tradition* (2000), Baptist theologian Mark Medley discusses Baptists' use (or misuse) of tradition.[22] Stating that Baptists usually operate with a relatively static view of tradition (i.e., tradition is an object that is passed down), Medley refers to Tilley's use of a more differentiated definition of tradition that encompasses "the act of transmission (*traditio*), not just the content handed down (*tradita*)."[23] Medley sees in Tilley's work the possibilities for a theological conception of tradition, potentially rooted in ecclesiological practices: "Thinking about tradition not as 'things handed over,' but as 'socially embodied, interwoven, enduring practices' suggests

21. Percy, *Love in the Ruins*, 22.

22. Medley, "Catholics, Baptists, and the Normativity of Tradition." For more discussion of this topic, see Harmon, *Towards Baptist Catholicity*, 7–8.

23. Medley, "Catholics, Baptists, and the Normativity of Tradition," 121.

that knowing a tradition is a learned, acquired rule-ordered skill."[24] With this in focus, the life of the community of faith becomes crucial to the convictions that sustain it, meaning that "theological reflection on tradition emerges from and within the ordinary, concrete practices of communities of faith."[25]

Philip Thompson echoes these sentiments, treating the intersection of memory, history, and tradition. Thompson employs the work of Rowan Williams in delineating the difference between good and bad history. For Williams,

> Good historical writing . . . is writing that constructs a sense of who we are by a real engagement with the strangeness of the past, that establishes my or our identity now as bound up with a whole range of things that are not easy for me or us, not obvious or native to the world we think we inhabit, yet which have to be recognized in their solid reality as both different and part of us . . . [B]ad history is any kind of narrative that refuses this difficulty and enlargement—whether by giving us a version of the past that is just the present in fancy dress or by dismissing the past as a wholly foreign country whose language we shall never learn and which can only be seen as incomprehensible and almost comic in its savagery and ignorance.[26]

Thompson contends that Baptist historiography suffers from bad history precisely at the points where Baptist historians offer "as the truth of Baptist history a quite universalized ideal that any may appropriate" (e.g., "what Baptists have always believed").[27] Counter to this myopia is good history, which Thompson sees as crucial for the maintenance of memory and truthfulness regarding tradition.[28] That is, good history attends to everything that is found, even the material that seems foreign and strange, which can offer a critical perspective on the state of the present.[29]

---

24. Ibid., 122. Cf. Tilley, *Inventing Catholic Tradition*, 44.
25. Medley, "Catholics, Baptists, and the Normativity of Tradition," 123.
26. Williams, *Why Study the Past?*, 23–24.
27. Thompson, "Dimensions of Memory," 62. Thompson addresses the moderate Baptist perspective of continuity of convictions among Baptists in another essay; see "'As It Was in the Beginning'(?)."
28. He makes it clear that one cannot escape the influence of tradition, only one's conscious apprehension of its role. Thus, Thompson notes, "Baptists have made a tradition of rejecting tradition." Thompson, "Dimensions of Memory," 56.
29. Ibid., 63.

Cameron Jorgenson, using Alasdair MacIntyre's groundbreaking work on tradition, highlights that the embrace of tradition is not a choice one exercises. In other words, individuals do not stand alone but in traditioned communities that operate with a particular form of rationality. The result is that Baptists' impulses to dissent from the consensus of the whole are not automatically ruled out. Rather, since MacIntyre's notion of tradition makes room for argument and disagreement, these impulses are vital to the life of the tradition itself, provided they are continually situated within the tradition.[30]

This aversion to tradition has deeper consequences as it has fueled a long-standing oppositional stance toward Catholicism. Since the Reformation, Protestants have had a suspicious stance toward Catholics. As evangelical historian Mark Noll has observed, this has especially been the case within the United States, when growing numbers of Catholic immigrants to cities in the eastern United States in the nineteenth century threatened job prospects for Protestants.[31] This brought about hostile developments such as the founding of political organizations like the Order of the Star-Spangled Banner in 1849, which was reorganized in 1852 and renamed the American Party.[32] Their efforts to oppose any foreign entry into American public life, combined with sometimes violent actions against Catholics often made nineteenth-century America an inhospitable place for Catholics.

Overall Protestant suspicion of Catholics slowly waned, though, throughout the twentieth century (especially the latter half). Gradually, Catholics were seen as having a significant place within the American intellectual landscape, illustrated by their prominence in sociologist Will

---

30. Jorgenson, "Bapto-Catholicism," 188–89. While considerably indebted to MacIntyre, Medley is sympathetic with Tilley's use of James McClendon's conception of tradition rather than MacIntyre's, which "understands participation in a tradition as knowing how to argue," is "too limited to apply to . . . liturgical traditions and religious traditions where argument is not the central mode of discourse," and generally assumes that "the contents of the arguments, the *tradita*, are more important than the process of arguing, the *traditio*." Medley, "Catholics, Baptists, and the Normativity of Tradition," 122 n. 8.

31. Noll, *History of Christianity*, 208.

32. Ibid., 209. About the American Party, Noll continues: "[I]ts members were popularly called 'Know Nothings' because when they were questioned about the group's principles or activities, they would always respond 'I don't know'" (ibid., 209–10).

Herberg's 1955 study, *Protestant, Catholic, Jew*.[33] Further, in the latter half of the twentieth century, American Protestants perceived less danger from Catholics and more from what was called secular humanism. In other words, a new enemy entered the scene, bringing with it potential— both for fear and for timely alliances. Consequently, Protestant evangelicals began to warm to the idea that they could work with conservative Catholics, especially regarding social issues (e.g., abortion, marriage), leading to their inclusion in Rev. Jerry Falwell's Moral Majority as well as other efforts.[34]

While other Protestants softened their stance toward Catholics in the United States, Baptists have often displayed a more thoroughgoing antipathy toward Catholics. R. Albert Mohler Jr, current president of the Southern Baptist Theological Seminary, stated on national television in 2000 that the Catholic Church was a "false church" that teaches a "false gospel."[35] E. Y. Mullins (1860–1928) and George W. Truett (1867–1944) both viewed Catholics as an "other." As Lee Canipe explains, this stance toward Catholicism was prevalent among many of Truett's coreligionists: "For Baptists, the Roman Catholic Church represented the epitome of false religion and stood for everything that Baptists despised—autocracy, creedalism, hierarchy, 'proxy religion,' and so forth."[36] Mullins saw Catholicism as contrary to biblical Christianity as it embraced intermediaries that he perceived to be "human interference" and "religion by proxy" (e.g., infant baptism, episcopacy).[37] Thus, for Mullins, Catholicism was overly authoritative, quashing the freedom for the individual believer, especially in the area of biblical interpretation.[38] Truett stood as a champion of democracy and religious liberty, both of which he observed to

---

33. Herberg, *Protestant, Catholic, Jew*.

34. Cf. Marsden, *Fundamentalism and American Culture*, 242–43. A broader example of this is the 1994 "Evangelicals and Catholics Together" document (co-signed by Charles Colson and Richard John Neuhaus) that aimed to identify commonalities in order to witness to the modern world in the twenty-first century.

35. King, Larry, interview with R. Albert Mohler Jr. Cf. "Mohler calls Catholicism 'false church.'"

36. Canipe, "Echoes of Baptist Democracy," 418.

37. Mullins, *Axioms of Religion*, 54.

38. "[T]he doctrine of papal infallibility combined with that of an authoritative tradition forbids all private or divergent interpretations of Scripture. To discover and proclaim an interpretation of the word of God which contravenes in any essential particular that which bears the stamp of traditional or papal approval, is for the Catholic to invoke upon his head the anathema of the church" (ibid., 62).

be lacking within the Catholic Church.[39] With these statements in view, it is apparent why, in the final evaluation of Catholicism for Mullins and Truett, it stood as the "exact antithesis" of Baptist life and thought.[40]

Mullins and Truett were not the only Baptists who were suspicious of Catholic actions within the United States. In 1946, Joseph Martin (J. M.) Dawson (1879–1973), a Baptist pastor, became the first full-time director of the Baptist Joint Committee on Public Affairs (BJCPA; an organization that lobbies government officials in support of religious liberty),[41] holding this position until 1953.[42] A collective venture on the part of several Baptist denominations, the committee sought to inform Baptists of the significance of certain matters pertaining to church and state as well as serve as an advocate for Baptists in Washington, DC. Dawson was also instrumental in the 1947 founding of Protestants and Other Americans United for the Separation of Church and State (POAU), serving as its first secretary and acting director.[43] This group stood at the center of a wave of anti-Catholicism in the 1940s and 1950s. Such sentiments were fueled largely by the works of lawyer and author Paul Blanshard, who put forth arguments that Catholics in the United States should not be trusted and that their designs were for global supremacy.[44]

Baptists participated in this widespread wariness of Catholic activities within the United States. As Canipe writes, "At the heart of this Baptist antipathy lay an uneasy suspicion that Catholics in America owed their true allegiance not to the United States, but to the Pope and his

---

39. "Baptists joyfully cherish all these believers in Christ [who hold that Christ is their personal savior and love Jesus in sincerity and truth], as their brothers in the common salvation, whether they be found in a Protestant communion, or in a Catholic communion, or in any other communion, or in no communion." Truett, "Baptist Message and Mission," 117–18.

40. Ibid., 129. Mullins and his impact on Baptist life and thought will be the subject of chapter 4, while Truett will feature prominently in chapter 5.

41. Actually, this became the organization's name in 1950. Before that, it was known as the Joint Conference Committee on Public Relations. Leonard, *Baptists in America*, 167. In 2005, the organization changed its name to Baptist Joint Committee on Religious Liberty.

42. For more details on Dawson's work with the BJCPA, see Goen, "Baptists and Church-State Issues in the Twentieth Century."

43. This group has since abandoned part of its name. Now it exists as Americans United for Separation of Church and State.

44. See Blanshard, *American Freedom and Catholic Power*. His second book on this subject set Communism and the Catholic Church as parallel threats to American democracy. See Blanshard, *Communism, Democracy, and Catholic Power*.

designs for world domination. Behind every Catholic move, Baptists saw the potential for sabotage."[45] For instance, in 1919, a brief article appeared in *The Baptist Standard* (a state Baptist newspaper) describing a message delivered from the Pope by the papal undersecretary of state to President Woodrow Wilson where Pope Benedict XV had voiced admiration for the United States and its democratic principles. In response to these events, the article's author noted that the pope was "the autocrat of autocrats," called the sincerity of his praise into question, and quoted a *New York Herald* article that spoke of the possibility that the pope's ulterior motive was recognition of papal temporal power by the United States.[46] Reacting to this and other perceived seditious actions by Catholics in the United States, Baptists emphasized a fervent love of democratic government, which, as they saw it, ran against the grain of the Catholic Church.[47]

Following the Second Vatican Council, Baptist attitudes toward Catholics shifted to some degree. With the promulgation of the Declaration on Religious Freedom (*Dignitatis Humanae*) and the use of the vernacular for Mass, among other things, Baptists began to find limited affinity with Catholics. In his book, *Soul Liberty* (1975), Glenn Hinson, a Baptist historian, noted that prior to the council a reactionary mindset reigned, evidenced by the *Syllabus of Errors* (1864) and the quashing of Modernism (1907). However, with Pope John XXIII, Hinson viewed a new era for Catholics and their relations with Protestants. By using the phrase "separated brethren" to describe Protestants, Hinson perceived new avenues for ecumenical dialogue. More importantly, though, *Dignitatis Humanae* took steps to affirm religious freedom that resonated with what Hinson saw as a historic Baptist conviction. In other words, according to Hinson, Catholics, like Baptists, now understood that "God created persons free to seek truth according to their conscience," thereby precluding the use of external coercion to produce religious faith.[48]

While initially this may seem to be a softening of the anti-Catholicism previously seen by Baptists, in actuality, such sentiments appear to remain, even if not actively so. That is, Hinson's praise is based on the fact that Catholics have, in his view, come into greater agreement with Baptists. Moreover, despite his assessment, he retained Baptist opposition to

45. Canipe, "Echoes of Baptist Democracy," 418.
46. "An Autocrat's Democracy," 10–11.
47. See, e.g., Gambrell, "Rome in World Politics," 1.
48. Hinson, *Soul Liberty*, 119. The Declaration on Religious Freedom, and Baptists' possible reception of it, will be discussed in more detail in chapter 5.

other Catholic convictions, noting his displeasure that *Dignitatis Humanae* did not renounce Catholic support for parochial schools and was not clearly in support of separation of church and state. In summary, therefore, it remains probable that Baptist admiration of Catholics' decisions following the Second Vatican Council was less about Catholics' practices and more about those of Baptists.

Both of these concerns—aversion to tradition and anti-Catholicism—are obstacles to genuine *ressourcement* because they obstruct theological vision and limit the breadth of the tradition to offer fresh theological resources. Furthermore, the inability to return to all of the tradition's sources undercuts Baptists' vision of basic theological voices that are already in use (e.g., Scripture) and not in use (e.g., church fathers and mothers) as well as unique theological convictions that have become hallmarks of Baptist faith and practice (e.g., religious liberty and believers baptism).[49] What is also clear from this discussion and the comparison between resurgent Calvinism and the Molinist/Jansenist controversies is that history is a significant theological resource and invaluable for *ressourcement*. In other words, the sources to which we return are not to be repristinated. Instead, they dynamically offer life from the past to the present.

De Lubac, Ontology, and Nature/Grace

Moving away from these obstacles facilitates an engagement with and evaluation of the theological episode discussed earlier in this chapter concerning grace and free will in a Catholic key. Following de Lubac, the aim of such an examination is not simply to provide a historical account that stands (at least for our project) as an alternative to the sharp oppositional stances surrounding contemporary resurgent Calvinism (though it certainly does this). Instead, such historical work is part of a broader theological concern that might guide Baptists toward a more participatory (or sacramental) ontology. Setting aside any interest in stating whether Jansenism or Molinism is correct over the other (in fact, he saw both as theologically problematic), de Lubac interrogates the nature of the debate itself. On the one hand, a concern for humanistic freedom motivated Molinism. On the other hand, the strong emphasis on absolute

---

49. For more on a Baptist *ressourcement* of Scripture and religious liberty, see chapters 3 and 5, respectively.

divine freedom in Jansenism arose from a sense that humanity sorely lacked in this area. De Lubac states that Jansenius's "supralapsarian 'optimism' has determined his practical pessimism."[50] In short, the opposing positions of Molinism and Jansenism both presuppose that human activity is separated from divine activity.

Moreover, Balthasar discusses a shift in the understanding of "nature." While Augustine used the term to describe the *de facto* unity of "creaturely essence and free gift of grace," Protestant Reformers along with Baius and Jansenius located nature in original creation, which left it utterly ruined by sin.[51] According to de Lubac, this marked a departure from Augustine: "To [Augustine], man and God were not two powers in confrontation, nor two individuals who are strangers to each other . . . [T]here was no question for him of opposition between nature and grace, but of inclusion; there was no contest, but union. It was not a matter for man of annihilation but of closest unification and transformation."[52] In short, while Jansenism (and here we might add Calvinism) claims a thoroughgoing Augustinian heritage, de Lubac states that this is perhaps pushed to extremes: "If necessary [Jansenius] will be more faithful to Augustine than Augustine is to himself."[53] So what was the catalyst for this separation between Jansenius's Augustine and the real Augustine? How could he and Baius, while reading the Doctor of Grace, depart so sharply from him?

As a clue concerning what distinguishes these later Augustinianisms from their source, Louis Dupré points to the rise of nominalism in the post-Reformation Renaissance period. With an emphasis on things as named, nominalism unhinges reality from the words used to describe it. The result is that "words and forms became independent symbols of expression."[54] Because of this shift, what ties together various objects (e.g., two people) is not that they each share in the reality of personhood or humanity. Instead, what links them together is the similar appellation (i.e., "people"). Two results have emerged from this philosophical outlook. First, the natural order, which had been granted relative autonomy when discussed in the medieval period, became divorced from the su-

---

50. De Lubac, *Augustinianism and Modern Theology*, 68.
51. Balthasar, *Theology of Karl Barth*, 271–72.
52. De Lubac, *Augustinianism and Modern Theology*, 68.
53. Ibid., 40.
54. Dupré, *Passage to Modernity*, 41.

pernatural order. Creation became nature detached from the beauty of God's good order. Moreover, politics and the sciences were separated from theology as independent discourses. Second, the rise of nominalism implied an emphasis on voluntarism, placing the will at the center of existence. Freedom, then, eventually became the ability to choose, or to exercise volition, and God's transcendence was protected by safeguarding God's absolute freedom over the volition of other beings in the cosmos.[55]

While he was as concerned about nominalism as Dupré, de Lubac approached it through a different pathway, focusing his attention on how Molinism, Baianism, and Jansenism construed the relationship between the natural and the supernatural, or nature and grace. This was, in fact, not an altogether different concern since Dupré notes that nominalist developments fueled the emergence of a dualism between the natural and the supernatural.[56] Treatment of the historical discussion above became a significant portion of de Lubac's *Surnaturel*, a book that would later be described as a "turning point in the history of contemporary Thomism."[57] Countering what he saw as the prevalent extrinsicism between nature and grace, de Lubac argued that contemporary Thomists had misread Aquinas, especially concerning humanity's natural desire to see God.

For de Lubac, much of his focus centered on the historical development of an extrinsic relationship between the natural and the supernatural. Over time, the readers and interpreters of Thomas Aquinas (who was then designated as the philosophical foundation for Catholic theology) took the place of Thomas himself. For de Lubac, this meant that he needed to complexify the Thomistic picture and challenge the dominant reading. Central to this task was opposition to what de Lubac called the "pure nature" hypothesis. Intended to maintain the gratuity of God's grace (i.e., in no way obliging God to grant grace to humanity), this "hypothesis," which developed over the course of the fifteenth and sixteenth centuries, claimed that nature could be created without any intrinsic connection with the supernatural, leaving the natural and the supernatural with

---

55. Dupré notes that the seeds for voluntarism are planted before the rise of nominalism, but the strong emphasis on the will would not have come to pass without the cultural conditions provided by nominalism (ibid., 128).

56. Ibid., 178.

57. Bonino, "Foreword," viii. He continues: "In short, if in the year 2000 no one is any longer a Thomist in quite the same way he would have been in 1900 or even in 1945, it is partly because of Fr. de Lubac" (ibid.). The historical section of *Surnaturel* was later recast as the core of de Lubac's 1965 *Augustinianism and Modern Theology*.

separate final ends, each pursued independently by their own respective means. De Lubac recognized that the strategy of the pure nature hypothesis resulted in an excessive division of the natural and the supernatural with devastating consequences: "If we begin by dissociating the two orders completely, in order to establish the existence of a natural order that could be fully and finally self-sufficient, we are all too likely to end up by seeing not so much a distinction as a complete divorce."[58]

In the case of the historical discussion above, the radical Augustinianism of the Baian and Jansenian positions was refuted by means of the pure nature hypothesis, with Bellarmine identified as one of the most prominent initiators in his defense against Baius. Even though de Lubac acknowledged a role for hypothetical pure nature for the prelapsarian human condition (though not in humanity's actual state), he saw the responses to Baius and Jansenius as an overreaction that had serious consequences as later Thomistic commentators, such as Francisco Suárez, embraced pure nature. As Hans Boersma notes, this "served to highlight the autonomous character of the natural realm, and thus further separated that realm from the supernatural."[59] Thus, like the magisterial Reformation positions treated in the previous chapter, the pure nature hypothesis left the natural with nothing to do with the supernatural so that when discussing human nature, one is saying nothing about God.

While de Lubac observed that the Jansenists misread Augustine, those who supported the doctrine of pure nature tended to emphasize the Aristotelian influences on Aquinas's thought. In other words, the philosophical underpinnings of Thomistic thought were understood to stand on their own, not dependent upon revelation, granting created nature a greater sense of autonomy as a result. The hypothesis itself was characterized by the Aristotelian notion that if a being has a particular end, then it must be endowed with the ability to reach that end. Aristotle's example of the movement of stars was central to this interpretation of Thomas: "If nature had given the heavens an inclination toward progressive motion, it would have also given the means for that motion."[60] That is, if humanity has a natural desire for God, then humanity must possess the ability to achieve that end. De Lubac notes that fifteenth-century theologian Denys the Carthusian relied upon Aristotle to state that "Natural desire does

---

58. De Lubac, *Mystery of the Supernatural*, 35.
59. Boersma, *Heavenly Participation*, 65.
60. Quoted in de Lubac, *Mystery of the Supernatural*, 169.

not extend beyond its natural capacity. For nature in accordance with the natural order of things cannot be in vain, since God and nature create nothing in vain."[61] Along similar lines, sixteenth-century Dominican (and opponent to Martin Luther) Thomas Cajetan declared, "It does not appear to be true, that the created intellect naturally desires to see God; for nature does not bestow an inclination to something to which the whole power of nature cannot lead; a proof is that nature placed the organs for any potency deep within the soul."[62] Suárez, whose system has been described as "Christianized Aristotelianism,"[63] utilized Aristotle to write, "Nature, in giving them the inclination to a certain motion, gives them the organs for it."[64]

De Lubac observed that this reading of Thomas had permeated late nineteenth-century and early twentieth-century Catholic theology, exemplified in the work of his teacher Fr. Pedro Descoqs and the eminent Réginald Garrigou-Lagrange, OP, renowned Thomist of the manualist tradition and professor at the Angelicum in Rome. In response, he embraced a more Augustinian position, in fact claiming that a more Augustinian reading of Aquinas was more faithful to the Angelic Doctor. At several places he favorably quotes Augustine's famous line: "You have made us for yourself, O God, and our hearts are restless until they rest in you."[65] That is, humanity is created for communion with God, possessing a natural desire to see God and attain supernatural beatitude, yet this can only be fulfilled by God's gratuitous grace. Thus, when Aquinas states that "grace perfects nature" (*gratia perficit naturam*), it should be understood as a completion of nature by grace, fulfilling its natural desire: "[T]he supernatural does not merely *elevate* nature . . . ; it does not penetrate nature merely to help it prolong its momentum . . . and bring it to a successful conclusion. It *transforms* it."[66] Consequently, de Lubac charged that in

---

61. Denys the Carthusian, *De lumine Christianae theoriae*; quoted in de Lubac, *Augustinianism and Modern Theology*, 164.

62. Cajetan, *In Primam*; quoted in de Lubac, *Mystery of the Supernatural*, 138 n. 90.

63. McCool, *Neo-Thomists*, 19. De Lubac writes that no one did more to contribute to the use of Aristotle's remarks about the motion of stars than Suárez. Cf. de Lubac, *Augustinianism and Modern Theology*, 168.

64. Suárez, *De ultimo fine*; quoted in de Lubac, *Mystery of the Supernatural*, 148.

65. Augustine, *Confessions* I.1. Cf. De Lubac, *Mystery of the Supernatural*, xxxvii, 53.

66. De Lubac, *Brief Catechesis on Nature and Grace*, 81. See also Aquinas, *Summa Theologiae* Ia, q. 1, art. 8, ad 2. "[G]race is proportionate to nature as perfection is to the perfectible" (Aquinas, *De Veritate*; quoted in de Lubac, *Mystery of the Supernatural*,

de-emphasizing the fullness of this aspect in Aquinas's thought, Cajetan had not simply commented on Thomas's works. He had produced innovations that divided him from Thomas and distorted interpretations of the Angelic Doctor and his reception of Augustine: "Cajetan was in no sense 'clarifying' or 'developing' Thomist teaching on the matter; far from 'pushing it to its ultimate conclusion,' or bringing it to its goal . . . he was profoundly altering its whole meaning."[67] By laying out these arguments about Aquinas, de Lubac separated Descoqs, Garrigou-Lagrange, and other neo-Thomists from their avowed theological master, noting that perhaps Thomas himself would not be able to be a member of the neo-Thomist school.[68] Thus, de Lubac found that the relationship between Thomas and twentieth-century neo-Thomism was much different than advertised, concluding that "the mass of neo-Thomists . . . rediscovered not so much St. Thomas himself as the later forms of Thomism."[69]

Neo-Thomist understandings of the relationship between nature and grace were originally intended to protect the realm of the supernatural from being overtaken by the natural. With the growth of modern scientific methods (e.g., naturalism) and Cartesian philosophy, Catholic theologians feared the loss of any voice for the Church within the modern world. The solution was to divide the realm of nature from that of grace in order to maintain some distinct and separate sphere for work regarding the supernatural. De Lubac did not quarrel with the intended purpose of this more extrinsic construal of nature and grace, but he did argue that the results have not been as hoped:

> The supernatural, deprived of its organic links with nature, tended to be understood by some as a mere "supernature," a "double" of nature . . . Such a dualism, just when it imagined that it was most successfully opposing the negations of naturalism, was most strongly influenced by it, and the transcendence in which it hoped to preserve the supernatural with such jealous

---

23).

67. De Lubac, *Mystery of the Supernatural*, 9.

68. Ibid., 152. This statement is based on a quotation from Anatole France that it is rare "for any master to belong to the school he has founded as firmly as his disciples do." Indeed, de Lubac quotes Garrigou-Lagrange, saying, "God, the author of our nature, could not give us the innate natural desire for an end to which he could not lead us *ut auctor naturae* ['as the author of nature']. The order of agents would no longer correspond to the order of ends" (ibid., 149).

69. Ibid., 188.

care was, in fact, a banishment. The most confirmed secularists found in it, in spite of itself, an ally.[70]

In other words, by creating a situation where the supernatural was viewed as a separate superaddition to nature, the realm of grace was understood to be superfluous to the natural world, which operated according to its own methods and protocols (i.e., naturalistic scientific procedures).[71] In the end, the neo-Thomist schema prompted further neglect of the supernatural, leaving it to occupy the margins of knowledge and contributing to the construction of the secular.

This is similar to Dietrich Bonhoeffer's critique of liberal Protestant theology, which understood God to be what he termed a "stopgap":

> If in fact the frontiers of knowledge are being pushed further and further back (and that is bound to be the case), then God is being pushed back with them, and is therefore continually in retreat. We are to find God in what we know, not in what we don't know; God wants us to realize his presence, not in unsolved problems but in those that are solved.[72]

Likewise, once the orders of nature and grace had been severed by neo-Thomism, the natural realm, aided by the emergence of a nominalist ontology was free to pursue knowledge and explain occurrences in the world according to naturalistic science, thereby relegating God (and a more theological view of the world) to the "gaps" of human knowledge and contributing to the growth and influence of secularism.[73]

More troubling, though, are the political possibilities presented by the extrinsic relationship between nature and grace. In general, extrinsic relationships begin to develop with other paired concepts (e.g., faith

---

70. De Lubac, *Catholicism*, 313–14.

71. "[B]y this oversimple method of preserving the gratuitousness of the supernatural order, they were, to put it mildly, lessening its meaning." De Lubac, *Mystery of the Supernatural*, 178.

72. Bonhoeffer, *Letters and Papers from Prison*, 311. The letter is dated May 29, 1944.

73. De Lubac alludes to these gaps as well: "Today that secularism, following its course, is beginning to enter the minds even of Christians . . . [E]verything that comes from Christ, everything that should lead to him, is pushed so far into the background as to look like disappearing for good. The last word in Christian progress and the entry into adulthood would then appear to consist in a total secularization which would expel God not merely from the life of society, but from culture and even from personal relationships" (*Mystery of the Supernatural*, xxxv).

and reason, church and world). Anthropologically speaking, the human person is separated from Christology, foreclosing the possibility of what Nicholas Healy describes as "the mystery of Christ reveal[ing] the original purpose and meaning of creation itself—reveal[ing], we might say, the nature of nature."[74] This christological understanding of humanness is further reflected in the words of the Second Vatican Council: "Christ, the final Adam, by the revelation of the mystery of the Father and His love, fully reveals man to man himself and makes his supreme calling clear."[75] Without a Christ-formed anthropology, what constitutes humanity (and even progress for the human race) is separated from any christologically informed understanding of the human person. In other words, once nature is divorced from grace, human life is disconnected from the abiding presence of the Triune God, and theological positions no longer maintain any relationship to political commitments, enabling anyone (including a theologian) to have parallel (and competing) allegiances to church and state.

For de Lubac, the ramifications of the extrinsicism of his contemporary neo-Thomists was particularly problematic, as evidenced by his concern about the French conservative organization *Action française* led by atheist Charles Maurras. Within this right-wing movement, Maurras agitated against the anticlericalism of the French Third Republic, calling upon Catholics to support his organization in restoring the Roman Catholic Church and the French monarchy to prominence.[76] The group was condemned by Pope Pius XI in 1926. Nonetheless, it continued to shape French Catholic sentiments until the end of the Second World War, including promotion of the pro-Nazi Vichy government from 1940 to 1944. Among the Catholic supporters of the organization were Descoqs and Garrigou-Lagrange. As Fergus Kerr details, Garrigou-Lagrange "did not conceal his support for the Vichy regime nor his longstanding sympathies with *Action française*."[77] Moreover, Kerr points out that the Vichy government corresponded to the contours of Garrigou-Lagrange's neo-Thomistic outlook: "The Vichy state, in its traditionally Catholic isola-

74. Healy, "Henri de Lubac on Nature and Grace," 545.
75. Second Vatican Council, *Gaudium et Spes* §22.
76. Cf. La Soujeole, "Supernatural and Contemporary Ecclesiology," 321 n. 17.
77. Kerr, "French Theology," 112. He continues: "[Garrigou-Lagrange] was a close associate of the Vichy ambassador to the Vatican, who assured his government in a notorious dispatch that the Holy See had no objections to the Vichy anti-Jewish legislation, even providing supporting citations from Aquinas . . . " (ibid.).

tion, must have seemed as effective a way of making time stand still as the time-transcending system of the neo-Thomists."[78] De Lubac, observing these associations, argued that concern for the theology of nature and grace had important implications for the church's relationship with the world.

De Lubac and *Ressourcement*

Returning to the concern about univocity expressed in the previous chapter, de Lubac's construal of the relationship between the natural and the supernatural pushes back the extrinsicism of resurgent Calvinism and its respondents. There, God was an immense being (sometimes even articulated as a gigantic will) that was ontologically separate from creation. While the contours and audiences of each argument are different, this creates similar conditions to the "pure nature hypothesis." De Lubac, though not entering our present conversation directly, illustrates the dangers of such a view. To overly divide the divine from the created order facilitates a nature/grace dualism by removing the active presence of the divine from the created order. A naturalized world emerges that is separate from any supernatural end. In other words, it makes secularism possible by understanding the *telos* of nature to be found within nature itself. By contrast, as Bryan Hollon states, "A participatory ontology such as the one envisioned by de Lubac means that there can be no partition between the natural and the supernatural. In the end, nature and history are transformed and completed by God's supernatural grace."[79] The operative diagram would not involve a created being dwarfed by an immense being (God), but a dynamic relationship between a created being and being itself (or, that which makes existence itself possible) so that (as Augustine was observed in chapter 1), God is both higher than each being, yet intimately interior to each being.[80] Hans Boersma notes that

---

78. Ibid.
79. Hollon, *Everything Is Sacred*, 105.
80. A voice crucial to such insights is Pseudo-Dionysius the Areopagite (who is cited by Aquinas more than seventeen hundred times), a sixth-century theologian who argued that terms such as "wisdom" and "goodness" were not attributes of God, but names of God, so that to name any creature as wise or good would require ontological participation in the God who is wisdom or goodness. With regard to existence, Dionysius states that everything that exists participates in the God who is being: "Since God is a 'being' in a way beyond being, he bestows existence upon everything and

this ontological relationship between creator and creation maintains a distinction between the two without pushing that distinction to separation or division, properly orienting the natural toward its appointed end in the supernatural.[81] This yields a Creator/creature relationship where cooperation need not produce a zero-sum game since each being noncompetitively participates in the being of a transcendent and coinherent God.[82]

Recalling that Peter Thuesen named sacramentalism as the antithesis to predestinarianism, a better conception of the relationship between the natural and the supernatural might be found there. In the sacraments, material elements (e.g., water, bread, wine) are not separate from the reality to which they point. In other words, they are not *mere* symbols. This would imply a nominalistic and extrinsic relationship between the sign and the signified. Instead, the sacrament participates in the reality to which it points, underscoring a coinherent and intrinsic relationship between the two. When considering all of the created order through this lens, a participatory account of existence emerges: "[B]ecause creation is a sharing in the being of God, our connection with God is a *participatory*, or real, connection—not just an *external*, or nominal, connection."[83] Thus, instead of a dualism, there is a "participatory anchoring of the created order in the eternal Logos."[84]

Such an articulation of this participatory ontology will serve a significant role in a Baptist *ressourcement* by bringing the full resources of the tradition to bear on a crucial theological question of weighty ecclesial import. The physically created world is not divorced from the divine; instead, by virtue of being created, it holds a vital (or sacramental) link to the divine. At the heart of this nuanced intrinsic relationship between nature and grace is the human being created in God's image, an anthropological claim located within the broader theological orbit of Christology, where the enfleshed God-man reveals genuine humanity to itself and situates that humanity within God's gracious gifts to and for

---

brings the whole world into being." Pseudo-Dionysius, "The Divine Names," 66.

81. Boersma, *Heavenly Participation*, 31.
82. Cf. Barron, *Priority of Christ*, 205–7.
83. Boersma, *Heavenly Participation*, 24.
84. Ibid., 52.

the world.[85] This Christocentric focus will serve as the centerpiece for additional trajectories of *ressourcement* in later chapters.

The ramifications for returning to these sources of the Christian faith (especially for Baptists) are several. First, as de Lubac's work displays, theology cannot be construed as an isolated discipline, divorced from more basic philosophical questions or even cultural issues and events. Rather, theology is placed at the center of these disciplines and questions, carrying an important voice in (and occasionally, in opposition to) historical, cultural, and political movements. Second, regarding the focus and nature of a theologian's work—that is, the Christian faith itself—de Lubac states, "Christianity is not an object that we can hold in our hand: it is a mystery before which we are always ignorant and uninitiated."[86] That is, theology cannot be neat and tidy: "[T]heology is not, or ought not to be, a buildup of concepts by which the believer tries to make the divine mystery less mysterious, and in some cases to eliminate it altogether."[87] Instead, as one commentator notes, the mystery of the Christian faith (i.e., the "object" of theological study) unavoidably makes theology into a self-involving discipline: "The mystery . . . that the theologian encounters and reflects upon is at the same time an example, a model and a norm by which to live. The Christ event renews everything, draws the theologian who approaches it thoughtfully and studiously into a process of renewal as well."[88]

—

While the past two chapters have focused on the differences between Protestant and Catholic versions of the debates about divine sovereignty and human free will, the aim of this book is not to simply highlight the ways in which Catholics might be in a better theological place than Protestants. In other words, *ressourcement* is not about abandoning one's own tradition when a better opportunity arises. Instead, it is concerned

85. Cf. Second Vatican Council, *Gaudium et Spes* §22. David L. Schindler, crediting Paul McPartlan, points out that this text from *Gaudium et Spes* appears "in virtually the same form" in de Lubac's *Catholicism*. David L. Schindler, "Introduction to the 1998 Edition," in de Lubac, *Mystery of the Supernatural*, xi; cf. de Lubac, *Catholicism*, 342.

86. De Lubac, *Paradoxes of Faith*, 43.

87. De Lubac, *Mystery of the Supernatural*, 178.

88. Voderholzer, *Meet Henri de Lubac*, 111.

with situating one's own tradition within the broader sweep of the entire Christian faith, thereby gaining wisdom from ancient voices, a deeper theological vocabulary, and a wider set of pilgrim friends. All of these can contribute to greater theological reflection on the part of Baptists and other free church Christians. The univocal dilemma presented by the resurgent Calvinist crisis strikes at the heart of the Christian faith, including the questions about baptism discussed in the introduction. De Lubac and his *ressourcement* methodology offer a theological path forward for addressing univocity and embracing a more participatory ontology through an intrinsic relationship between nature and grace.

De Lubac's methodology also provides guidance for proceeding in this book. That is, in order to pursue the multifaceted theological renewal that Baptists need, a thoroughgoing *ressourcement* is necessary. This will involve examining foundational theological convictions and their historical reception by Baptists as well as resonances with the rest of the tradition. Like de Lubac's own historical work, this is about more than mere historical accuracy or getting the story straight. Instead, this historical focus will underscore the importance of history for theological discourse: "To engage with the Church's past is to see something of the Church's future."[89] In other words, *ressourcement* is neither splitting theological hairs nor dwelling on minute historical details, but it reveals the broader historical and cultural importance of theology, even in the present.

The next section of the book will treat three focal Baptist theological convictions, offering a thick historical account of their development and reception, including their potential obstacles. Afterward, these convictions will be placed in conversation with various voices within the Christian tradition with the hope of avoiding the pitfalls in their present form without sacrificing their center. That is, the aim is a more robust account of each conviction so that Baptist theology is renewed and strengthened as a part of the whole church's thinking. At the heart of each chapter will be a christological emphasis that takes seriously that Jesus is "the way, the truth, and the life" (John 14:6). In the next chapter, the theological conviction in focus will be Baptists' emphasis on the Bible as the primary (and sometimes sole) source for faith and practice.

---

89. Williams, *Why Study the Past?*, 94.

Part Two

3

Bible and Tradition

Listening for the Word of God

> Now, friends, . . . I want to tell you . . . why you can absolutely trust this church—it's based on the Bible. Yes sir! It's based on your own interpitation of the Bible, friends. You can sit at home and interpit your own Bible however you feel in your heart it ought to be interpited. That's right, . . . just the way Jesus would have done it.
>
> —ONNIE JAY IN *WISE BLOOD*[1]

IT SEEMS APPROPRIATE THAT any Baptist return to the sources should involve a fresh look at the Scriptures. Baptists have oftentimes described themselves as "people of the book" in order to highlight the role of the Bible (from the Greek *biblos* for "book") in their theological formation and way of life. Events such as Bible drill and Bible study and activities such as Scripture memorization, while not exclusive to Baptists, have held and continue to hold a prominent place in Baptist churches. This, however, does not tell the whole story. In fact, questions remain about what influence over Baptist faith and practice the Bible actually has. That is, over time, it is possible (and even likely) that Baptists have taken certain aspects of the biblical witness for granted, leaving them uninterrogated. To understand, then, the relationship between the Bible and the Baptists, more investigation is needed.

---

1. O'Connor, *Three by Flannery O'Connor*, 78.

This chapter aims to return to Scripture, not only to read its content anew, but also to re-examine how Scripture has been read (i.e., the particular hermeneutical approaches that have been embedded within Baptists' use of Scripture). After a discussion of common interpretive approaches to the Bible (both explicit and implicit) and their effects on the text of Scripture as a whole, the impact of the Protestant watchphrase "scripture alone" (*sola scriptura*) will be treated and evaluated in light of the ecclesial context of the Scriptures. In the end, this volume's goal of a Baptist *ressourcement* will involve viewing the Bible as a dynamic entity rather than an inert object, embedded within the life of the church with a greater appreciation for the role of tradition in the overall reading of the Bible.

Baptist Hermeneutical Strategies

Many Baptists and free church Christians have sought to safeguard the content of Scripture in order to protect its authority. This is done by several avenues, one of which is to set the Bible over any other sources for theological reflection. For example, occasionally the divine inspiration of the Bible is opposed to the human influence of tradition or experience. Here, the *sola scriptura* of the Reformation becomes *nuda scriptura*, or bare/naked Scripture. The Bible can also be protected by explicitly articulating what it means that "all Scripture is God-breathed" (2 Tim 3:16 NIV). Baptists, along with other evangelicals, have sometimes appealed to theories of inspiration that avoid the pollution of human beings. Thus, in order to move toward *ressourcement*, a brief survey of prominent Baptist and free church hermeneutical strategies will give a lay of the land.

Alexander Campbell, though not a Baptist, offers some interesting insights as to the trajectory of "Bible only" sentiments.[2] Campbell aimed to avoid what he observed were historical accretions to the scriptural text. These additions, like barnacles on the side of a ship, dirtied the Bible and prevented a plain reading of the Word of God. One had to remove these in order to clear one's vision. So much was this Campbell's goal that he intended to make every reading of Scripture a fresh one: "Beware of having any commentator or system before your eyes or your mind.

---

2. Campbell's thought is impacted by his encounters with Baptists, and many of the first Campbellites came from the ranks of the Baptists. I am indebted to D. Michael Cox for his invaluable insight into Campbell's life and thought.

Open the New Testament as if mortal man had never seen it before."[3] For Campbell, the Bible was "a book of facts, not of opinions, theories, abstract generalities, nor of verbal definitions."[4]

This thoroughgoing biblicism was informed by the prevalent philosophy of the day, Scottish Common Sense Realism. This emphasis on what plainly appeared in the text was joined to an inductive method of study popularized by Francis Bacon. In it, one only needed to assemble the relevant facts related to a subject and draw conclusions based on those facts. As George Marsden observes, this philosophical outlook saw that "the common sense of mankind, whether of the man behind the plow or the man behind the desk, was the surest guide to truth."[5] The result of this methodology was the discovery of objective facts that stood outside the fluctuations of history. When used with regard to the Bible, this gave rise to an aversion to complex theories of textual composition or discussions of interpretations of particular texts that were deeply sedimented within the tradition.[6] Instead, what seemed plain to the individual reader was the timeless biblical fact in view, not a time-bound interpretation or opinion. That is, as scientists had natural facts that occupied their attention, biblical "scientists" focused on their own set of facts—those found in the Bible. Thus, Campbell desired to read the Bible without Luther, Calvin, or Wesley "on [one's] nose."[7]

Related to Campbell's biblicism is a penchant for using only biblical terminology: "We choose to speak of Bible things by Bible words, because we are suspicious that if a word is not in the Bible, the idea which it represents is not there."[8] While this may initially seem like a good idea, one is immediately confronted with theological problems arising from the fact that words and phrases like "Trinity" and "eternally begotten" are not found in the biblical text. Does this mean that historically orthodox Christian convictions like Trinitarianism or the consubstantiality of the Father and the Son are numbered among the accretions to the

---

3. Campbell, "Address to the Readers of the Christian Baptist—No. I," 33.
4. Campbell, *Christian System*, 18.
5. Marsden, *Fundamentalism and American Culture*, 15.
6. As Eugene Boring states, "The Bible was like an object which could be studied empirically in the laboratory of open discussion; when people of goodwill agree on a viable method, they could not do otherwise but agree on the meaning of the Bible." Boring, *Disciples and the Bible*, 87.
7. Quoted in Harrison, "Alexander Campbell on Luther," 143.
8. Campbell, *Christian System*, 130.

Bible against which Campbell warned? Perhaps not, but the pathways to maintaining such convictions have certainly been limited.[9] For Campbell, there was "no creed but Christ, and no book but the Bible."[10]

Baptists were not immune to this approach to reading and interpreting Scripture. In fact, they embraced it, adopting it for their own use. In part as a response to the rise of scientific naturalism, several Baptist scholars sought to establish the truth of the biblical text by appealing to its factual character. A key player in this for Baptists was James Petigru Boyce (1827–1888). Trained under Charles Hodge at Princeton Theological Seminary, Boyce imbibed the Common Sense Realism that permeated Hodge's work.[11] Emphasizing facts as the centerpiece of knowledge, Boyce argued in his *Abstract of Systematic Theology* that reason and revelation were two modes of acquiring knowledge: "When we refer to reason as a source of knowledge distinct from revelation, we mean the information attained, by the use of this faculty, in connection only with the natural, as distinguished from the supernatural . . . By revelation, we mean the knowledge which God conveys by direct supernatural instruction, pre-eminently that given in the book known as the Bible."[12] Both avenues of knowledge are concerned with the gathering of facts. Theology, then, involved organizing these "facts about God [that] were

---

9. Curtis Freeman discusses a similar trend among eighteenth-century English Christians. Confronted by a neo-Arian heresy against which all were opposed, those who held to an extra-biblical Trinitarian declaration of faith were known as subscribers, while those who, like Campbell, sought to use only biblical terms were known as nonsubscribers. Even though these groups converged around Trinitarian orthodoxy at one point, over time (and as the Johannine Comma of 1 John 5:7 fell out of favor), "few who sided with the nonsubscriber position in succeeding generations remained trinitarian." Freeman, *Contesting Catholicity*, 161. As a result, when the Johannine Comma was dropped from the biblical text, "Baptists lost a vital link with patristic reflections and creedal formulations" (ibid., 181).

10. Boring, *Disciples and the Bible*, 16–19.

11. In his *Systematic Theology*, Hodge wrote that "the Bible is to the theologian what nature is to the man. It is his store-house of facts" (quoted in Marsden, *Fundamentalism and American Culture*, 113). Hodge's successor at Princeton, B. B. Warfield, continued this emphasis, stating that the task of theology consisted in "collecting the whole body of relevant facts" (quoted in Smith, *Bible Made Impossible*, 57). Christian Smith admits that Hodge and Warfield display greater sophistication in other places, yet these statements are representative of what was passed on to their students like Boyce (ibid.).

12. Boyce, *Abstract of Systematic Theology*, 47. This text by Boyce displayed the influence of Hodge as it was shaped after the latter's three-volume *Systematic Theology*. George, "James Petigru Boyce," 75.

propositionally set forth in the Scriptures and immediately available to the individual mind by means of commonsense reason."[13]

While the straightforward language of "Bible facts" has fallen out of favor within contemporary biblical interpretation, an emphasis on the words of the text remains. Many have attempted to safeguard these words through theories of inerrancy. For example, in 1978, the Chicago Statement on Biblical Inerrancy affirmed that "Scripture in its entirety is inerrant, being free from all falsehood, fraud, or deceit" with the denial that this only extended to "spiritual, religious, or redemptive themes, exclusive of assertions in the fields of history and science."[14] This is qualified by the caveat that claims of inerrancy apply "only to the autographic text of Scripture" (which is no longer extant).[15] Another, yet similar, attempt to hold on to the Bible alone is through verbal plenary theory of inspiration. In contrast to theories that focus on illumination (where human writers are enlightened as they work) and dynamic views of inspiration (where human authors cooperate with divine authorship in some manner), verbal plenary theories understand inspiration to extend to the very words themselves, so that "every word of the Bible is inspired."[16] Even though adherents deny that this is a dictation theory, the result is a biblical text where each statement "can be read as a true proposition to be affirmed."[17] Here the resonance with the biblicism of Hodge, Boyce, and Warfield is most prominent and is also present in contemporary conservative Baptists such as Paige Patterson and Al Mohler.[18]

In something of a contrast to this pure biblicism, Francis Wayland (1796–1865), former president of Brown University and pastor of First Baptist Church in Providence, Rhode Island, grounded the entirety of the Christian life in the text of the Bible. That is, the Bible stood at the heart of the experience of the Christian life:

> [T]he Bible is the word of the living God; the only manifestation that has been made to us of the will of our Creator and Judge, the only record of what he has done for our salvation; the only

13. Freeman, *Contesting Catholicity*, 78.

14. International Council on Biblical Inerrancy, "The Chicago Statement on Biblical Inerrancy," art. xii.

15. Ibid., art. x.

16. Lemke, "Inspiration and Truthfulness of Scripture," 152.

17. Ibid.

18. Colter, "Patterson Delivers Sermon on Inerrancy of Scripture"; see also Mohler, "When the Bible Speaks, God Speaks."

volume on whose pages are inscribed the conditions on which we may escape eternal wrath, and enter into the rest which remaineth for the people of God.[19]

Wayland, for his part, understood Scripture to stand not only as the primary source for theological reflection. Instead, it was "our only rule of faith and practice . . . We judge the Fathers, as they are called, by the New Testament. We judge tradition and the rites and usages of men by the same law."[20] The result of this theology of Scripture is that Baptists did not embrace any creed or confession and are rightly "delivered from the yoke of antiquity, tradition, and ecclesiastical usurpation."[21]

This focus on Scripture was situated within what Wayland described as "the absolute right of private judgment in all matters of religion."[22] In other words, the message of the Bible does not proceed from God to representatives of the church (e.g., priests). Rather, it is "a communication from God to every individual of the human race."[23] Any imposition of association, or confession, or creed, was viewed as an obstacle to the "perfect sufficiency of the Scriptures."[24] Thus, while Wayland grounded everything in the Bible (or as he stated, "the *New Testament*, the *whole* New Testament, and *nothing but* the New Testament"), determining the nature of the communication between God and the individual rests with that individual, unavoidably bringing experience to bear on reading the Scriptures and living the full Christian life.[25]

Like Wayland a generation earlier, E. Y. Mullins took a different approach to reading Scripture than the Boyce trajectory. Rather than

19. Wayland, *Principles and Practices of Baptist Churches*, 297.

20. Ibid., 133.

21. Ibid. "[T]he world will never be reformed, until Christians prune off all the beliefs and usages which have been ingrafted on the church, as it was left by the apostles, and in simplicity and truth adopt for their only and sufficient rule, the New Testament, as it was committed to them by our Lord and Saviour" (ibid., 134).

22. Ibid., 132.

23. Ibid.

24. Ibid., 133.

25. Ibid., 86; emphasis original. Wayland continues: "No matter by what reverence for antiquity, by what tradition, by what councils, by what consent of any branches of the church, or of the whole church, at any particular period, an opinion or practice may be sustained, if it be not sustained by the command or the example of Christ, or of his apostles, we value it accordingly . . . Hence, to a Baptist, all appeals to the fathers, or to antiquity, or general practice in the early centuries, or in later times, are irrelevant and frivolous" (ibid.).

emphasizing "Bible facts" that set the Bible on a similar (and antagonistic) plane as scientific knowledge, he stated that "the Bible is not a book of science nor of philosophy. It is a book of religion."[26] By religion, Mullins meant "all the relations between God and man."[27] Similar to Wayland, the focus on relationship brought experience and contextualization to the forefront of theological reflection. As Mullins wrote in *The Axioms of Religion*, "The progress of events and the conditions of Christian work are the best interpreters of Scripture . . . Every interpretation of Scripture assumes, or should assume, the divinely adapted fitness of Scripture to human need."[28] This should not be understood, however, to indicate that experience is the primary authority, but only that personal experience is the primary medium through which God's Spirit moves: "[W]hen we speak of making experience explicit in expounding the doctrines of Christianity, we are by no means adopting that as the sole criterion of truth . . . Jesus Christ is its sole founder and supreme authority as the revealer of God. The Scriptures are our only source of authoritative information about Christ and his earthly career."[29]

Thus, the biblical witness retains its importance because it is a sourcebook for understanding Jesus since it is "the greatest of all books of religious experience."[30] Despite this declaration, Mullins was concerned about attempts to wield the Bible as an external authority over personal experience (in a manner similar to the common Baptist view of creeds and ecclesiastical authority).[31] Because of this, Mullins, through discussion of several other axioms of the Christian faith, entrusted to the individual interpreter the ability to read the Bible for him or herself. This established within Christianity an absolute monarchy (between God and

---

26. Mullins, *Christian Religion in Its Doctrinal Expression*, 150. Mullins disliked any false tests forced on the Bible, whether a test from hostile atheists or one from well-meaning Christians that sought to get answers from Scripture that it was never intended to answer.

27. Ibid., 2.

28. Mullins, *Axioms of Religion*, 13.

29. Ibid., 3. While not present in the 1925 version, the 1963 *Baptist Faith and Message* echoed Mullins's language here. See Southern Baptist Convention, *The Baptist Faith and Message* (1963), art. i.

30. Ibid.

31. "Truth must be assimilated and understood, not imposed by authority of any kind, whether pope or church or Bible." Mullins, *Christian Religion in Its Doctrinal Expression*, 11.

the Christian) and a pure democracy (or access of interpretation) among the community of believers.[32]

Interestingly, while Wayland and Mullins did not embrace the biblicism of their fellow Baptists and other free church Christians, their approaches to Scripture begin with *sola scriptura* and bear close resemblance to that biblicism. For instance, both men not only set the Bible over other sources for theology, but they see Scripture as ruling the other sources entirely. The perfectly sufficient Scriptures need no help from church, tradition, or reason. In the words of the late-nineteenth-century hymn, because one's "faith has found a resting place, not in device or creed, . . . I need no other argument, I need no other plea."[33] Thus, even though personal experience is brought to the forefront, it is centered on one's personal experience with the Bible. Consequently, arguments that attempt to distance Mullins and Wayland from biblicism ultimately fail.[34]

With the rise of historical-critical approaches to Scripture, a dramatic shift occurred. In fact, as Michael Legaspi has pointed out, while this change centered on acquiring a deeper knowledge of the text of the Bible, the movement also transformed the Bible from living Scripture into a dead object—a text.[35] Various critical methods provided tools to get behind the text to see details of the lives of the original historical people and communities. The goal in this endeavor was to discover *what the text meant* when it was initially written. This became the heart of determining the "plain meaning" of the text. Commentaries devoted the vast majority of their pages to explicating the literal (past) meaning of a given text, establishing it as the arbiter of a good and bad interpretation. Once that was accomplished, the final remaining task was an interpre-

32. Mullins, *Axioms of Religion*, 131–32.

33. Edmunds, "My Faith Has Found a Resting Place," in Forbis, *The Baptist Hymnal*, #412.

34. Mohler argues that Mullins's embrace of experience places him alongside German liberal theologian Friedrich Schleiermacher, yet this overlooks the fact that Schleiermacher also claimed to hold a Bible-only approach. Mohler, introduction to *Axioms of Religion*, 8–9, 14. See Smith, *Bible Made Impossible*, 86.

35. Legaspi, *Death of Scripture*, x. Legaspi's study centers on the new academic programs developed by Johann David Michaelis at the University of Göttingen for studying the biblical text. The preface offers a distinction between the Bible as found within the Eastern Orthodox liturgy, where it is live and active and never read silently, but always read with and to the congregation within the context of prayer and song, and the Bible as found within a university biblical studies seminar, where it is read in isolation by individuals and understood to be static and set within the past (ibid., vii–viii).

tive move from what the text meant to what it means for contemporary readers (sometimes referred to as application). When this shift was fully complete, though, it transformed the meaning of the Bible into a narration of past events to be studied from a so-called objective perspective in abstraction from the liturgical and ecclesial ground of Scripture.

With concerns about "Catholic Allegorism," Baptists joined other Protestants in shunning anything but the literal/historical reading of the biblical text.[36] This made the historical-critical method of biblical interpretation appealing, though it did not escape the "Bible as storehouse of facts" sensibility. Excavating the historical, social, and cultural artifacts within the text and examining them located the text in the past. Any contemporary voice arose in the creative application of the text's past to our present. While this is immensely helpful in observing some of the depth of the biblical text, it is inadequate as a resting place.[37] One is constantly distanced from the Bible since it is a foreign object that speaks primarily about the past (and, only through some effort, might add wisdom for the present). The Bible is a wellspring of information, but not necessarily of mystery.

This survey of Baptist hermeneutical strategies, albeit very brief, brings a central theme to the forefront: the Bible stands alone. Insofar as it is possible, Baptists and other free church readers of Scripture have endeavored to discover the plain meaning of the text, whether that is identified with the critically discerned past meaning or the extrahistorical plenary sense of the text. Moreover, to say the Bible stands alone is also to highlight the ways in which individual readers can approach it without any serious concern for reading awry. Like Onnie Jay, readers can embrace the Bible in light of their own "interpitation . . . just the

---

36. Even as he acknowledges the proper motive of patristic allegory, Bernard Ramm states that the "curse of the allegorical method is that it obscures the true meaning of the Word of God." Ramm, *Protestant Biblical Interpretation*, 30. In fact, he strengthens his claim by identifying allegory as the primary error of the heretical Gnostics (ibid.).

37. In my own experience and my own teaching, historical-critical approaches to Scripture are helpful in opening students' eyes to new questions to ask the text, questions that have never occurred to them. In other words, this broadens students' horizons regarding what Karl Barth called "the strange world of the Bible." The result of this pedagogical approach, though, is not to make historical-critical methodology their preferred method of reading, but to move students from a first naiveté to a second naiveté, where the deeper mystery of the Scriptures can be pursued.

way Jesus would have done it."[38] There is no need for a community of readers or an understanding of the Bible based on consensus over time. With these broad contours established, it is worthwhile to examine whether this emphasis on the Bible as the sole source for Christian faith and practice facilitates successful discussion and resolution of challenges presented to the church by contemporary concerns.

Tearing the Bible Apart

One effect of the individualized approach to reading Scripture is that it leaves the Bible in a tenuous position. For both conservative and moderate Baptists, each individual's interpretation is viewed as valid on the basis of the plain sense of the text or the skill of the reader. At its best, this methodology fragments Baptists into groups of like-minded interpreters. Thus, conservatives gather with other conservatives where they sense that the Bible is viewed as the "inerrant Word of God." Likewise, moderates and liberals find their hermeneutical kin centered around the competency of the interpreter's soul. At best, these two approaches coincidentally arrive at the same interpretive conclusions. At worst, this reading strategy produces incommensurable readings that threaten to divide Baptists more sharply and tear the Bible apart.

Religious historian Mark Noll sees the American Civil War and its preceding tensions as a site for a similar disparity in interpretative approaches. Abolitionists in the North, fueled by spiritual energy from the Second Great Awakening, opposed the institution of slavery vehemently. In the South, slavery was defended with equal passion. Not only were moral and economic arguments offered on both sides, but religious arguments were prominently proclaimed. The result was a plethora of denominations (Presbyterians, Methodists) that split along sectional lines. In short, according to Noll, the Civil War, while certainly a national predicament, also stands as a religious war and a theological crisis.[39]

The Bible was also a participant in this struggle. Noll notes that Scripture "provided a vocabulary for traditional deference but also innovative egalitarianism."[40] For instance, in antebellum America, slaves

---

38. O'Connor, *Three by Flannery O'Connor*, 78.

39. Noll, *History of Christianity*, 314–17. See also Noll, *The Civil War as a Theological Crisis*.

40. Noll, *History of Christianity*, 404.

took great hope in the depiction of God as liberator found in stories such as Moses and the Hebrews' escape from Egypt (Exod 14–15), Shadrach, Meshach, and Abednego in the fiery furnace (Dan 3:19–30), and the declaration of Jesus's ministry of setting the captives free (Luke 4:14–30). However, these same slaves had to make "a sharp distinction between the Bible that their owners preached . . . and the Bible they discovered for themselves."[41] The slaveowners emphasized scriptural passages that taught the need not to steal (Exod 20:15), to remain in one's life station (1 Cor 7:20; Col 3:18—4:1), and to obey authorities (Rom 13:1–4). Baptists were not immune from the confusion of these debates. In fact, their participation reveals the root of the problem. In the North, Baptists voiced extreme opposition to the practice of slavery.[42] In the South, while there was some concern that slaveholding should have limits,[43] there was no indication that the institution (one that was viewed as having biblical warrants) should vanish altogether. Clearly the Bible was a contested site at this time.

In 1822, Richard Furman, a prominent South Carolina preacher and significant slaveowner himself,[44] communicated with the governor of the state on behalf of the Baptist Convention of South Carolina. In his address, Furman argued that "the right of holding slaves is clearly established in the Holy Scriptures."[45] He referred to Old Testament examples of slaveholding, mentioned the existence of slavery throughout the Roman Empire, and noted that the equal spiritual relationship between converted masters and slaves did not necessitate an equal relationship in physical or legal terms. Furman's certainty on the matter is further displayed:

> Had the holding of slaves been a moral evil, it cannot be supposed, that the inspired Apostles, who feared not the faces of men, and were ready to lay down their lives in the cause of their

---

41. Ibid., 405.

42. The Maine Baptist Association described the institution as "'the most abominable' of all systems of iniquity that had cursed the world" (quoted in Bebbington, *Baptists Through the Centuries*, 94).

43. David Bebbington notes that in 1808 the Mississippi Baptist Association "resolved that its member churches should take disciplinary action against members 'whose treatment of their slaves is unscriptural'" (ibid., 141).

44. For more about Richard Furman's entanglement in the institution of slavery, including evidence of the treatment of his slaves, see Rogers, *Richard Furman*, 221–30.

45. Furman, "Exposition of the Views of the Baptists," 253.

> God, would have tolerated it ... But, instead of [ordering Christian masters to liberate Christian slaves], they let the relationship remain untouched, as being lawful and right, and insist on the relative duties.[46]

Furman's defense of the institution of slavery offered moral justification because slaveowners had a responsibility to provide for the well-being of the slaves, often (according to Furman) resulting in better living conditions than prior to enslavement.[47] Moreover, Christian slaveowners brought slaves into an encounter with the gospel, which might not have occurred had slavery not existed. He cautioned any opponents of slavery that ending the institution would have disastrous consequences for the spiritual health of slaves and for general order of the South.[48] Perhaps more troublesome than the conclusions Furman reached was that he justified them on the basis of the Bible, which "produce[s] one of the best securities to the public, for the internal and domestic peace of the state."[49]

Debates about slavery among Baptists continued and heightened tensions. Through several controversies surrounding whether the Home Missionary Society of the Triennial Convention would appoint a slaveowner as a missionary,[50] the Acting Board of the Convention decided in 1845 to bar from appointment any candidate who was a slaveowner: "If ... any one should offer himself as a missionary, having slaves, and

---

46. Ibid. It is clear from this quote that Furman read the text of Paul's letter to Philemon as one that maintains the physical boundaries of master and slave, even as Onesimus's relationship to Philemon is "no longer as a slave but as more than a slave, a beloved brother ... both in the flesh and in the Lord" (Phlm 16).

47. Furman stated that "Divine law never sanctions immoral actions" ("Exposition of the Views of the Baptists," 253).

48. Ibid., 254. This address occurred after a slave rebellion in South Carolina led by Denmark Vesey, a former slave living in Charleston, which provided Furman with an unfair depiction of what the South would look like if slaves had their freedom and access to the same privileges (including firearms) as the rest of the citizenry.

49. Ibid.

50. In 1844, Georgia Baptists nominated James Reeve as a missionary, explicitly stating that he was a test case as a slaveowner. The Home Missionary Society neither accepted nor denied his application, stating that "it is not expedient to introduce the subjects of slavery or anti-slavery into our deliberations." American Baptist Home Mission Society, "Minutes." After this non-response, Alabama Baptists asked a series a hypothetical questions intended to determine whether the Triennial Convention would in fact appoint a slaveholder as a missionary (especially since southern states also sent funds to the Convention to support their missionary candidates). These questions elicited a more definitive rejection.

should insist on retaining them as his property, we could not appoint him. One thing is certain, we can never be a party to any arrangement which would imply approbation of slavery."[51] The response from Baptists in the slaveholding South was swift and certain, indicating their view that the decisions of the Triennial Convention amounted to "war within our gates."[52] As a result, the southern state Baptist conventions met in Augusta, Georgia, on May 8–12, 1845, and formed a new entity, the Southern Baptist Convention (SBC). It was clear that the central issue of this development was the opposition or promotion of slavery. William Bullein Johnson, a South Carolinian who became the first president of the new regional body, stated that the abolitionist Baptists in the North had "acted upon a sentiment they have failed to prove—That slavery is, in all circumstances, sinful."[53]

Though slavery was the catalyst for such a divide among Baptists, the crucial player in this drama was the Bible. While many Baptists argued that this issue was settled in Scripture, it was not so simple to adjudicate since appeals to the Bible appeared from both abolitionists and pro-slavery advocates, with each side claiming not only particular texts, but particular interpretations of the same texts. Interestingly, Johnson declared his loyalty to *sola scriptura* in his first address as SBC president, noting, "We have constructed for our basis no new creed; acting in this matter upon a Baptist aversion for all creeds but the Bible."[54] In the end, however, the Bible was torn apart in this controversy and ultimately excluded as an arbiter in moral and theological disputes of this sort. While everyone appealed to the Bible, their convictions were shaped by stronger (though more subtle) philosophical and cultural influences (e.g., sectional solidarity or the cultural and economic impetus for slavery). As a result, the only recourse for Baptists was separation (in 1845) and outright war (in 1860).[55]

51. Acting Board of the General Missionary Convention, "Reply of the Foreign Mission Board to the Alabama Convention," 259.

52. Johnson, "Address to the Public," 119. Johnson had also served as president of the Triennial Convention from 1841–44.

53. Ibid., 120. In 1995, the Southern Baptist Convention passed a resolution condemning "historic acts of evil such as slavery" and apologizing for its role in "condoning and/or perpetuating individual and systemic racism in our lifetime."

54. Ibid.

55. Walter Shurden notes that when the SBC met in 1861 in Savannah, Georgia, only one month after the Battle of Fort Sumter and three months after the formation of the Confederate States of America, "the delegates . . . defended the right of

The theological crisis presented by the Civil War was not lost on the era's actors. Even President Abraham Lincoln, in his Second Inaugural Address in 1865, pointed out that "Both [Northern and Southern Christians] read the same Bible and pray to the same God, and each invokes His aid against the other."[56] The hermeneutical scandal revealed by the Civil War raises numerous questions about the stance of Baptists and other free church Christians toward the Bible. Can "Bible alone" genuinely work as the basis for faith and practice? Does reading the Scriptures require at least a minimum ability of inquiry and study? Finally, and more importantly, does a singular reader need the rest of the church in order to properly understand the Bible and live faithfully?

Problems with *Sola Scriptura*

At the heart of the tension surrounding the Bible is not the Bible itself, but that Baptists and other free church Christians set the Bible in isolation from other aspects of Christianity. That is, while the magisterial Reformers (e.g., Luther, Calvin) did not aim to flatten the biblical witness to only the literal or plain meaning of the text, centuries of heavy emphasis on *sola scriptura* have robbed Scripture of its meaning and authority so that many contemporary readers see biblical interpretation as "an enterprise best done without the church or even in spite of the church."[57] This principle has been increasingly used to protect the Bible from the perceived accretions of tradition and history, resulting (in theory) in a "pure scripture" (*scriptura pura*) that would be plain to readers. After encountering the text in its literal sense, one would simply need to acclaim, "The Bible says it; that settles it." Over time, the biblicism that developed had several specific characteristics that closed off more dynamic alternatives.[58] As the Bible was increasingly viewed as a manual (e.g., BIBLE =

---

secession, pledged themselves to the Confederacy, and substituted 'Southern States of North America' for 'United States' in the SBC constitution." Shurden, *Not an Easy Journey*, 139.

56. Lincoln, "Second Inaugural Address."

57. Williams, *Evangelicals and Tradition*, 96.

58. Christian Smith identifies ten such characteristics: divine writing, total representation, complete coverage, democratic perspicuity, commonsense hermeneutics, solo scriptura, internal harmony, universal application, inductive method, and handbook model. For Smith, evangelicalism's approach to the Bible is summed up in these qualities, even if not all characteristics are present everywhere (*Bible Made Impossible*, 4–5).

"Basic Instructions Before Leaving Earth"), the emphasis rested primarily on discovering the "biblical" approach to a particular topic (e.g., gender roles, economics), a rhetorical stance that stated more about the alternative (i.e., it is non-biblical or unbiblical) than about the perspective in view.[59]

However, the outcome of these developments was not a text that had one plain meaning, but a text that had several (and sometimes divergent) meanings, with no method of discerning the hermeneutical way forward. As Christian Smith states, "on important matters the Bible apparently is not clear, consistent, and univocal enough to enable the best-intentioned, most-highly skilled, believing readers to come to agreement as to what it teaches."[60] Gerald Schlabach writes that the emphasis on Scripture alone soon caused more problems than it solved:

> [D]octrinal disputes quickly dashed early Reformation hope in the principle of *sola scriptura*—that if only the Bible were available for all believers, accretions of tradition and human teaching would lose their force and the renewal of authentic Christianity could proceed unfettered. The Bible did not turn out to be quite so self-interpreting; even learned Reformers with the best interpretive skills of the day soon found themselves disagreeing with one another over doctrine.[61]

With this in view, doubling down on the Princetonian plan of viewing the Bible as a book of facts or importing personal experience as the primary interpretive lens have not proven to be successful strategies for taking the Bible seriously, let alone taking it seriously as the church's book. In fact, persistent arguments against genuine alternatives have only furthered the problem.[62] Even affirmations of biblical inerrancy are insufficient since affirming the inspiration of the original autographs of Scripture has no

---

59. The two most prominent organizations on either side of the issue of gender roles reflect this tendency, with advocates of traditional roles represented by the Council for Biblical Manhood and Womanhood, and advocates of progressive understandings of gender represented by Christians for Biblical Equality.

60. Smith, *Bible Made Impossible*, 25.

61. Schlabach, *Unlearning Protestantism*, 34.

62. See, e.g., William Underwood's critique of the call for communal discernment within biblical interpretation found in the "Baptist Manifesto" (Re-envisioning Baptist Identity: A Manifesto for Baptist Communities in North America). Underwood wrongly links the Manifesto and its authors to fundamentalism, arguing that private interpretation of the Bible is the safest and most Baptist way forward. Underwood, "The Future of Baptist Higher Education at Mercer University."

necessary purchase on the present text which was produced after multiple layers of copying and transmission. Even if such claims are accurate, they are ultimately useless, as Smith rightly indicates: "People standing on a sinking ship in the middle of the ocean are not helped one bit by the in-fact-totally-correct observation that if they were on another ship they would not be sinking."[63]

Thus, even though Baptists have stated unequivocally that the Bible is "the true center of Christian union," anything but union has occurred.[64] In fact, as Baptist deliberations ahead of the Civil War demonstrate, the divisions wrought from these disputes about the Bible have resulted in significant violence, including Christians killing other Christians. Consequently, to retain the Bible as a crucial source for Christian life and thought, a naked Bible will be insufficient (and perhaps even dangerous) as it will only recreate these problems in new contexts.[65] Along these lines, twentieth-century Dominican Yves Congar, citing numerous theologians, notes that *sola scriptura* fails as a principle because it is one that is not owned by Scripture and is in fact contradicted by Scripture.[66] Congar links Jesus to church and tradition in order to strengthen this claim: "Neither Jesus, who wrote nothing, nor St. Paul ever said: 'You will believe only what is written in the Gospels or in my letters', but we do find: 'You will believe what has been transmitted and taught to you.'"[67]

Echoing Congar, James McClendon argues that, unlike methodologies that distance the reader from the life of the church, there is no split between what the biblical text meant and what it means. Instead, biblical

---

63. Smith, *Bible Made Impossible*, 40.

64. Southern Baptist Convention, *The Baptist Faith and Message* (1925, 1963, 2000), art. i. I am also aware that this is not a problem isolated to Baptists. Jaroslav Pelikan notes that "Bible only" will also fail to unite divided groups within the sweep of Christian history (e.g., Eastern Orthodox, Roman Catholic, and Lutherans): "The history of Jewish-Christian relations, and then the history of the divisions within Christendom, is at one level the history of biblical interpretation." Pelikan, *Whose Bible Is It?*, 4.

65. One could see an analogue between the antebellum discussion among Baptists and the late-twentieth-century culture wars. In these discussions (especially concerning gender roles and women's participation in ministry), Baptists on both sides have appealed to Scripture for wisdom. Once again, though, the naked Bible has failed to provide a way forward beyond ideological opposition (i.e., appeals to Scripture often reproduce the convictions already accepted from broader cultural and philosophical trends).

66. Congar, *Meaning of Tradition*, 34.

67. Ibid.

reading is a traditioned reading, situated within the readings and worship of the apostles, the church fathers and mothers, and ministers, theologians, and lay people across the centuries. McClendon writes that this "baptist vision" is not the same as a flat biblicism: "[S]ay that Scripture in this vision can be expressed as a hermeneutical principle: *shared awareness of the present Christian community as the primitive community and the eschatological community*. In a motto, *the church now is the primitive church and the church on judgment day*."[68] The Bible is not, then, a book that any individual can approach in solitude. It is the church's book. Thus, while historical-critical methods emphasize the importance of context (e.g., situating the prophetic ministry of Amos within the prosperity and security of the eighth-century BCE kings, Jeroboam II of Israel and Azariah of Judah), the follow-up question concerns which context. As McClendon points out, the historical, social, and cultural context of the biblical text, while very important, is not the primary context. Rather, it is the ecclesial and liturgical context that is in view.[69] Thus, to recover this context and a deeper sense of Scripture's authority and meaning, Baptists will need to undertake a *ressourcement* of the Bible's relationship with the wider church and its history.

Ressourcement

Congar's emphasis on "what has been transmitted and taught" brings a more robust sense of tradition to the fore. He discusses the nexus of the biblical witness and the Christian tradition by offering a distinction between the two: "The holy Scriptures have an absolute value that tradition has not, which is why . . . they are the supreme guide to which any others there may be are subjected."[70] This distinction is significant because it norms the judgments of the magisterium so that they cannot work against the grain of the Bible. Yet, Congar is also clear that he is

---

68. McClendon, *Ethics*, 30; emphasis original. For an appreciative critique of McClendon's understanding of Scripture within the "baptist vision," see Cary, *Free Churches*, 158–65.

69. Joel Green makes this point by reminding readers of the liturgical response to each week's lections: "This is the Word of the Lord / Thanks be to God." As Green states, "The question, then, is how to hear in the words of Scripture the word of God speaking in the present tense. This *is* (and not simply *was* and/or might somehow *become*) the Word of the Lord" (*Practicing Theological Interpretation*, 5).

70. Congar, *Meaning of Tradition*, 100.

not reinforcing the Scriptures as "the absolute rule of every other norm, like the Protestant scriptural principle." In other words, the Bible is not "the *sole* principle regulating the belief and life of the Church."[71] In fact, tradition "envelops and transcends Scripture."[72] In short, in response to the evangelical emphasis on Scripture as the complete revelation of God with no admixture from humans, Congar writes, "It would be misleading to say that Scripture was wholly divine and tradition purely human: Scripture too is human and historical."[73] Congar continues by stating that the work of the Holy Spirit permeates both Scripture and tradition such that "a certain continuity [runs] though [them]."[74] Thus, the Church needs both Scripture and tradition in order to be faithful to her vocation: "[T]he Church verifies and proves her teaching by Scripture. But she interprets Scripture in her tradition and decides controversies by means of her Magisterium, with reference to Scripture and tradition."[75]

For the purposes of the present discussion, Congar offers a different sense of Scripture as well as tradition than the prevalent Baptist view. For Baptists and free church Christians, the Bible is often viewed as the sole source for theological reflection and development of the Christian life, a source that is plain to all readers. This fragments readers of the Bible from one another, making each individual reading equally valid. Congar, though, moves biblical interpretation away from individual Christians isolated from one another. Instead, the vitality of the church permeates Scripture, bringing a communal dimension to hermeneutics.[76] Individual readers of Scripture are not left behind, but their readings are set in orbit around the church's reading. Thus, as a recent international dialogue between Catholics and Baptists stated, the Bible is "never read 'alone,' that is, without the context of a community which translates it, proclaims it

---

71. Ibid.
72. Ibid., 101.
73. Ibid., 99.
74. Ibid.

75. Ibid., 101. Elsewhere, Congar declares, "[T]here is not a single point of belief that the Church holds by tradition alone, without any reference to Scripture; just as there is not a single dogma that is derived from Scripture alone, without being explained by tradition" (ibid., 40).

76. In discussing the need for community, Congar proposes a thought experiment: "How poor our faith would be, and how uncertain, if we were really left with nothing before us but the biblical text! And who would have given it to us, where would we have gotten it, how would we have found it?" (ibid., 25).

and interprets it, using other written sources."[77] With this in view, the focal end of biblical interpretation shifts from comprehending the complexities of the biblical text or bolstering a solely personal Christian faith to an embodied living out of the gospel by the community of faith.[78]

In his treatment of biblicism, Christian Smith notes that many early Christian thinkers took for granted that bare appeals to Scripture would be inadequate for refuting heresy. Tertullian (c. 155–c. 240 CE), for example, stated that the heretics that opposed the church quoted the biblical text for their own purposes: "Though most skilled in the Scriptures, you will make no progress, when everything which you maintain is denied on the other side, and whatever you deny is (by them) maintained."[79] This difficulty led Tertullian to the conclusion that "Our appeal, therefore, must not be made to the Scriptures."[80] In other words, both Scripture and tradition are needed. For Vincent of Lérins, a fifth-century writer, tradition is also not something separate from or parallel to Scripture: "[P]erhaps someone will ask, if the canon of Scripture is complete and is in itself sufficient, and more than sufficient on all points, what need is there to join it to the authority of ecclesiastical interpretation?"[81] The answer to this question is that the church's hermeneutical judgments, or

---

77. Baptist World Alliance and Catholic Church, "The Word of God in the Life of the Church," 55.

78. There have been moments where the ecclesial location of Scripture has been elevated. For example, the report from five years of dialogue between the Baptist World Alliance and the Roman Catholic Church (2006–2010) states a unified affirmation that the "normativity of Scripture is principally located in the worship of the church, from which its life and mission grows . . . Both Catholic and Baptist patterns of worship presuppose that sacred Scripture is the source of the story of the triune God in which worshippers participate" (ibid., 50).

79. Tertullian, *Prescription Against the Heretics*; quoted in Smith, *Bible Made Impossible*, 21.

80. Ibid. Moreover, as D. H. Williams notes, "[T]he early church wasn't as concerned with establishing an authorized list of books of the Bible as modern historians have assumed" (*Tradition, Scripture, and Interpretation*, 28). For more on the early church's canonical deliberations, see Metzger, *The Canon of the New Testament*.

81. Vincent of Lérins, *Commonitorium*; quoted in Williams, *Tradition, Scripture, and Interpretation*, 77. In response to the (often Protestant) concern that Scripture take precedence over tradition, D. H. Williams notes that framing the Scripture/tradition relationship in this manner would have confused the ancient church because it presumes that "Scripture and tradition must lie in antithesis to one another." Rather, Williams states, "The ancient fathers themselves taught that the tradition was the epitome of the Christian faith, the very purport of Scripture" (*Tradition, Scripture, and Interpretation*, 23–24).

tradition, provide guidance, preventing a confusing cacophony of readings when the "depth of holy Scripture itself" produces "as many opinions as there are men."[82]

Along these lines, Irenaeus of Lyons (c. 130–c. 202 CE) revered the Scriptures as central to the transmission of the Christian faith, yet he also refused to set the Bible apart from other sources. Instead, he situated Scripture within the context of the whole apostolic tradition: "For we have known the 'economy' of salvation only through those whom the Gospel came to us; and what they then first preached they later, by God's will, transmitted to us in the scriptures so that would be the foundation and pillar of our faith."[83] However, in his opposition to the Gnostics, he did not invoke Scripture as much as the lack of tradition. That is, whereas he learned the gospel from Polycarp of Smyrna, who was taught by John the apostle, who walked with Jesus, the Gnostics—their own biblical references aside—stood as their own self-generating source: "Before Valentinus there were no disciples of Valentinus; before Marcion there were no disciples of Marcion; . . . [E]ach of them appeared as the father and mystagogue of the opinion he adopted."[84] For Irenaeus, then, naked appeals to the text of Scripture were insufficient to safeguard the truth of the gospel; tradition was needed as well, lest heresy befall the church.[85]

In the early twentieth century, French philosopher Maurice Blondel (1861–1949) addressed the relationship between Christian facts and Christian convictions in his 1904 work, *History and Dogma*. According to Blondel, both were necessary for the proper understanding of Christianity, yet each were distinct from the other. Thus, the relationship (and even the use) of historical data and dogmatic ideas confronted Blondel with an important investigation. He saw each as positioned toward the other, "a sort of coming and going passing over two obscure intervals."[86] This "double movement," as he called it, had two serious dangers—setting history over dogma and setting dogma over history—that could potentially

---

82. Vincent of Lérins, *Commonitorium*; quoted in Williams, *Tradition, Scripture, and Interpretation*, 77.

83. Irenaeus, *Against Heresies* III.1.1.

84. Ibid., III.4.3.

85. D. H. Williams cites Augustine's dispute with the subordinationist theology of Maximinus, who was "most insistent that his doctrine was derived solely from the Bible." See Williams, *Evangelicals and Tradition*, 96 n. 29.

86. Blondel, "History and Dogma," in *The Letter on Apologetics & History and Dogma*, 223.

distort both and make synthesis nearly impossible. To make this clear, Blondel sought to describe the two "incomplete, but equally dangerous" approaches to this relation, doing so with neologisms: extrinsicism and historicism.[87]

Extrinsicism subordinates historical facts to truth convictions. For the less educated or less enlightened, they "serve as signs to the senses and as commonsense proofs."[88] In other words, history helps point to the truth of dogma, but need not offer anything original to that conclusion. This is, of course, if history genuinely appears at all, since the main function of historical facts, according to extrinsicists, is authentication and confirmation of the dogmatic statement one (or one's community) has already affirmed. For instance, one would find in a miraculous healing evidence of God's activity in the world, with little or no attention given to the circumstances and context of the healing itself. Or the incarnation of the Word of God as a poor first-century Palestinian Jewish man safeguards some other doctrine (e.g., salvation) rather than revealing anything new about the world as God's creation, human beings as God's creatures, or the nature of the church as followers of Jesus.[89] As Blondel describes this perspective, "the historical facts are merely a vehicle, the interest of which is limited to the apologetic use which can be made of them; for, whether *this* or *that* miracle is involved, provided it is *a* miracle, the argument remains the same."[90] Therefore, once the historical authentication is complete, history is removed from the conversation. The external character of the relationship between history and dogma is summed up by Blondel: "[T]he relation of the sign to the thing signified is extrinsic, the relation of the facts to the theology superimposed upon them is extrinsic, and extrinsic too is the link between our thought and our life and the truths proposed to us from outside."[91]

While Blondel shows no preference for extrinsicism, he writes that his treatment of it is meant to set the stage for making sense of the

---

87. Ibid., 225.

88. Ibid., 226.

89. Blondel underscores that extrinsicism views as extraneous "the link which may exist between that miraculous character and the particular historical event invested with it, or the essential relationship which may exist between the facts and the ideas" (ibid., 227).

90. Ibid.

91. Ibid., 228.

other danger: historicism.[92] In relation to biblical criticism, this approach displayed an "insistence on studying Christian facts only according to the canons of strict historical observation."[93] For example, according to historicism, the significance of Jesus Christ can be apprehended solely by means of historical study. Thus, while historicism, with its emphasis on exercising relative autonomy in order to take facts seriously, should initially appear to manifest a legitimate alternative to extrinsicism, Blondel notes that pure history cannot provide a bridge to Christian dogma, leaving unanswered the question of whether "the tissue of critical history [is] strong enough to bear the infinite weight of the ancient faith and the whole richness of catholic dogma."[94]

Much of Blondel's discussion of history centers on the nature of the discipline's relative autonomy. While he affirms history's competence, he is clear that this does not indicate self-sufficiency, since that would mean that history would see itself as "a sort of total metaphysics, a universal vision."[95] Instead, arguing that "real history is composed of human lives; and human life is metaphysics in act," Blondel notes that the historian, because he or she is always embedded in the complex exigencies of human experience, must always be open to other vantage points and horizons. Moreover, the externalities that are available for observation do not exhaust all of reality. As Blondel writes, "What the historian does not see, and what he must recognize as escaping him, is the spiritual reality, the activity of which is not wholly represented or exhausted by the historical phenomena."[96] Thus, even though historians make seemingly totalizing claims on reality, they must always remain open to a depth that is not available for historical observation. To fail to do so, to claim that critical scientific history can offer an all-encompassing sense of reality is to make history into an abstract doctrine. Here Blondel notes that history's observational method merges with abstract determinism to form a phenomenological ontology that edges out other metaphysical claims (e.g., the final end of human beings or of creation as a whole).[97] This is the heart of the "historicism" against which Blondel warns: "the alternation

92. Ibid., 231.
93. Blanchette, *Maurice Blondel*, 196–97.
94. Blondel, "History and Dogma," in *The Letter on Apologetics & History and Dogma*, 232, 233.
95. Ibid., 234.
96. Ibid., 237.
97. Ibid., 240.

between 'real history' and 'scientific history' or the substitution of one for the other."[98]

The extrinsicism identified by Blondel lives and breathes in the biblicism discussed above. In its most extreme form, the historical character of the biblical text is avoided in order to emphasize the timeless quality of its teachings. One need not pay much attention to history, except in so far as history will confirm the veracity of the text.[99] Historicism, while taking the historical contours of the Bible seriously, reduces the Bible to those contours. It becomes an object of study that describes a world long past, cut off from any flourishing vitality in the present (let alone the future). For Blondel, only a robust sense of tradition could unite history and dogma. Yet, tradition need not be a static object that is handed on through time. Instead, Blondel writes that tradition is "linked. . . to historical facts without being absorbed into history" and "bound up. . . with speculative doctrines though. . . not completely absorbed in them."[100] Tradition, in fact, is grounded in the Incarnation (i.e., the Word made flesh), where Christ stands as a historical person who can neither be reduced to that history nor abstracted from that history.

The emphasis on tradition as grounded in the Incarnation places it alongside Scripture, which also derives its revelatory depth from the one called the Word of God, Jesus Christ. Congar makes a similar point that both tradition and Scripture sit at the intersection of the human and the divine, pointing to the fullness of the Incarnation. Indeed, this is echoed by the Second Vatican Council's Dogmatic Constitution on Divine Revelation (*Dei Verbum*):

---

98. Ibid., 239. The results of historicism are several: historical phenomena are accepted as reality itself, the external and concrete is understood to be the sum total of any given object, effects take precedence over causality, and historical moments are tied together in an organic (perhaps even evolutionary) development stripped of any final determination (ibid., 240–41).

99. In commenting on the extrinsicist approach to history, Blanchette writes, "All that counts in the Bible for extrinsicism is some external seal of the divine" (Blanchette, *Maurice Blondel*, 196). Blondel offers a scathing critique in stating what sort of biblical text emerges from extrinsicism: "[T]he ageless facts are without local colour, vanish, as the result of a sort of perpetual Docetism, into a light that casts no shadow, and disappear beneath the weight of the absolute by which they are crushed." Blondel, "History and Dogma," in *The Letter on Apologetics & History and Dogma*, 229.

100. Blondel, "History and Dogma," in *The Letter on Apologetics & History and Dogma*, 264–65.

> [T]here exists a close connection and communication between sacred tradition and Sacred Scripture. For both of them, flowing from the same divine wellspring, in a certain way merge into a unity and tend toward the same end . . . Consequently it is not from sacred Scripture alone that the Church draws her certainty about everything which has been revealed . . . Sacred tradition and Sacred Scripture form one sacred deposit of the word of God, committed to the Church.[101]

This "same divine wellspring" is the Incarnation of Christ, the unity of divine and human.[102] Both Scripture and tradition emerge from this unity, communicate the "whole Christian reality disclosed in Jesus Christ," and return to this divine-human unity, bringing the fullness of Christ to the world.[103]

In 2000, the *Baptist Faith and Message* became the central site for a sea change regarding several topics within the Southern Baptist Convention, including biblical interpretation. While moderates desired to avoid any alterations and sought to retain the 1963 version of the statement, conservatives aimed to revise the document according to their sense of faithful Baptist living. In 1963, the *Baptist Faith and Message* stated, "The criterion by which the Bible is to be interpreted is Jesus Christ."[104] Commenting on this phrase Herschel Hobbs (who chaired the 1962–63 committee) noted, "[A]ny interpretation of a given passage must be made in the light of God's revelation in Jesus Christ and his teachings and redemptive work. Indeed, the Bible is its own best interpreter as one discovers its meaning in any particular in the light of the whole."[105] In the revised statement that appeared in 2000, this phrase is replaced with "All Scripture is a testimony to Christ, who is Himself the focus of divine testimony."[106] Moderates rightly identified the problems of the

---

101. Second Vatican Council, *Dei Verbum* §§9–10.

102. Similarly, when responding to criticism that the content of apostolic preaching was not found in the original documents of Scripture, Ignatius of Antioch stated, "To my mind it is Jesus Christ who is the original documents" (*To the Philadelphians*; quoted in Williams, *Tradition, Scripture, and Interpretation*, 53).

103. Second Vatican Council, *Dei Verbum* §9. See also Dulles, foreword to *Meaning of Tradition*, ix.

104. Southern Baptist Convention, *The Baptist Faith and Message* (1963), art. i.

105. Hobbs, *Baptist Faith and Message*, 30.

106. Southern Baptist Convention, *The Baptist Faith and Message* (2000), art. i. While all forms of the *Baptist Faith and Message* (1925, 1963, and 2000) described the Bible as having "truth, without any mixture of error, for its matter," the 2000 statement

change: that it fed a growing embrace of biblicism by conservatives, even at the expense of situating Christ at the center of the Scriptures. At first glance, the language of the 1963 statement seems to resonate with *Dei Verbum*. In fact, it is common for this statement to be described as the "Christocentric criterion for interpretation of the Scriptures."[107] Curtis Freeman calls this "a fragment of the ancient rule of faith, albeit as a very slender thread."[108] However, while removing Christ from hermeneutics is a problem, locating the Christ who norms interpretation is a bit more difficult.[109] For instance, when the most prevalent language about Jesus centers on one's personal relationship with him, where does this leave biblical interpretation?[110] Indeed, does not this framing of the "Jesus as criterion" statement move from one problematic approach to the Bible (biblicism) toward another (fragmented individualism)? These concerns should push for a more robust sense of Christocentricity for Scripture, an emphasis that grounds Christ's hermeneutical priority in his true body, the church.

Toward an Ecclesially Grounded, Christocentric Sense of Scripture

Throughout the Christian tradition, the Bible was understood to be deeper than the words on the page. In his *On First Principles* (*De Principiis*), Origen of Alexandria argued that many of the problems facing the church of the second century centered on "not understanding the Scripture according to its spiritual meaning, but the interpretation of it agreeably to the mere letter."[111] Deriving a threefold pattern from Scripture,

---

also adds that "all Scripture is totally true and trustworthy."

107. Dilday, "An Analysis of the Baptist Faith and Message 2000."

108. Freeman, *Contesting Catholicity*, 112.

109. Dilday cites conservatives' concern that the Christocentric criterion provided a detour from the biblicism they had embraced (i.e., the plain meaning of the text) ("An Analysis of the Baptist Faith and Message 2000"). Numerous news stories, editorials, and blog posts underscore the conservatives' desire to set the Bible as the sole authority for Christian faith, not simply the sole written authority.

110. Dilday states as much: "[W]e are to interpret the Old Testament and the rest of the Bible in the light of the life and teachings of Jesus in the New Testament, *illuminated by our own direct experience with the living Christ*" (ibid.; emphasis added).

111. Origen, *De Principiis* IV.1.9.

Origen stated that the Bible has a body, soul, and spirit.[112] In this anthropological diagram, these latter senses (soul and spirit), while departing from the literal sense (body), still maintain a connection to the literal, though not a rigid one. Origen noted that he is not averse to the letter of the text, but that a wooden loyalty to the literal leads to absurdity.[113] In fact, to rely solely on the literal sense is actually to deny the inspiration of Scripture.[114]

Augustine's appreciation of the Bible began with the homilies of Ambrose of Milan. Drawn to the beauty of Ambrose's sermons, Augustine developed his hermeneutical sensibilities, noting that on one occasion, he heard the bishop state, "as though he were earnestly commending it as a rule of interpretation, '*The letter kills, but the spirit gives life.*'"[115] Augustine saw the Bible as enmeshed with a reporting of the past, yet not reducible to that alone: "It is a history of past things, an announcement of future things, and an explanation of present things; but all these things are of value in nourishing and supporting charity and in conquering and extirpating cupidity."[116] In this Augustine has detected a moral character to the text beyond the words on the page so that "whatever appears in the divine Word that does not literally pertain to virtuous behavior or to the truth of faith you must take to be figurative. Virtuous behavior pertains to the love of God and of one's neighbor; the truth of faith pertains to a knowledge of God and of one's neighbor."[117]

---

112. Ibid., IV.1.11. Origen sees the pattern in an older rendering (LXX and Vulgate) of Proverbs 22:20: "And do thou portray them in a threefold manner, in counsel and knowledge, to answer words of truth to them who propose them to thee" (ibid.).

113. "All these statements have been made by us, in order to show that the design of that divine power which gave us the sacred Scriptures is, that we should not receive what is presented by the letter alone (such things being sometimes not true in their literal acceptation but absurd and impossible), but that certain things have been introduced into the actual history and into the legislation that are useful in their literal sense" (ibid., IV.1.18).

114. "Ignorant assertions about God appear to be nothing else but this: that scripture is not understood in its spiritual sense, but is interpreted according to the bare letter. On this account we must explain to those who believe that the sacred books are not the works of men, but that they were composed and have come down to us as a result of the inspiration of the Holy Spirit by the will of Father of the universe through Jesus Christ. . ." Origen, *De Principiis*; quoted in Williams, *Tradition, Scripture, and Interpretation*, 125.

115. Augustine, *Confessions* VI.4; emphasis original.

116. Augustine, *On Christian Doctrine* III.10.15.

117. Ibid., III.10.14. Earlier in the same text, Augustine offered the following as

In fact, this mode of reading Scripture was prevalent throughout the Christian tradition.[118] Perhaps the most prominent was Thomas Aquinas (1225–74), who based this on the difference between the science of Christian doctrine and other scientific disciplines: "[W]hereas in every other science, things are signified by words, this science has the property that the things signified by the words have themselves also a signification."[119] Aquinas continues by detailing a fourfold sense of Scripture, with a tripartite spiritual sense (allegorical, tropological/moral, and anagogical) following from the literal:

> [T]hat first signification whereby words signify things belongs to the first sense, the historical or literal. That signification whereby things signified by words have themselves also a signification is called the spiritual sense, which is based on the literal, and presupposes it. Now this spiritual sense has a threefold division. For as the Apostle says, the Old Law is a figure of the New Law, and Dionysius says, "the New Law itself is a figure of future glory." Again, in the New Law, whatever our Head has done is a type of what we ought to do. Therefore, so far as the things of the Old Law signify the things of the New Law, there is the allegorical sense; so far as the things done in Christ, or so far as the things which signify Christ, are types of what we ought to do, there is the moral sense. But so far as they signify what relates to eternal glory, there is the anagogical sense.[120]

While the depth of Scripture blossoms from the literal sense of the text, Aquinas is clear that the literal is the essential ground of the spiritual senses.

After Aquinas, however, the fourfold sense of Scripture fell out of favor. Initially, it was attacked by fellow theologians and eventually, it was critiqued by scholars outside the church. Protestants, for their part, "came

---

something of a hermeneutical principle: "Whoever . . . thinks that he understands the divine Scriptures or any part of them so that it does not build the double love of God and of our neighbor does not understand it at all" (ibid., I.36.40).

118. Bernard of Clairvaux sees this approach embedded within the discussion of the king's rooms within his mansion in Song of Songs 1:4. Bernard of Clairvaux, "Sermons on the Song of Songs 23," in McGinn, *Essential Writings*, 27–34.

119. Aquinas, *Summa Theologiae* Ia, q. 1, art. 10. It should be noted that "science" denotes a different sort of practice in Aquinas' context, yet the use of this term may have unwittingly contributed to the later drive for an exegetical methodology that was more scientifically verifiable.

120. Ibid.

to identify the spiritual sense of Scripture with human teaching originating in the dogmas of the church rather than scriptural teaching."[121] In response, the Council of Trent reacted against the Protestant *sola scriptura*, separating Tradition and Scripture as "two sources of revelation." In the end, the text became flat, reduced to either the literal/historical sense that occurred in the past or a transhistorical sense that was grounded in an ossified conception of tradition. Historical-critical method became the prevalent mode of biblical interpretation, maintaining a seemingly unassailable objectivity.[122]

In 1950, drawing on the work of Blondel and others, Henri de Lubac wrote *Histoire et Esprit*, which exposed Origen's role in the development of multivalent readings of Scripture. Later that decade (1959), he released the first of four volumes of *Exégése médiévale* (*Medieval Exegesis*), which was ultimately completed in 1964.[123] In these texts, de Lubac extends his work on the nature-grace relationship (discussed in the previous chapter) by addressing a problematic extrinsic relationship between Old Testament promises that are flatly answered by the New Testament. Like Aquinas, de Lubac saw the two testaments as intrinsically linked, where the New does not merely answer (and thereby explain) the Old. This expands de Lubac's earlier work in *Catholicism*, where, invoking Maximus the Confessor, he uses the Incarnation to underscore the significance of the link between history and spirit (in theology and exegesis): "For 'there is a spiritual force in history' . . . [T]he reality which is typified in the Old—and even the New—Testament is not merely spiritual, it is incarnate; it is not merely spiritual but historical as well. For the Word was made flesh and set up tabernacle among us."[124] Consequently, de Lubac, following Aquinas, embraces the four senses of Scripture, opening the first volume of *Exégése médiévale* with an old Latin distich that translates as "The letter teaches events, allegory what you should believe, Morality teaches what you should do, anagogy what mark you should be aiming for."[125]

---

121. Williams, *Evangelicals and Tradition*, 104.

122. Jeffrey Morrow writes that this objectivity was an illusion, pointing to the politics underneath the rise of historical-critical methodology and the critique of the spiritual senses of hermeneutics. See "The Politics of Biblical Interpretation."

123. De Lubac was also involved in the development of *Dei Verbum*. See Bertoldi, "Henri de Lubac on Dei Verbum"; Neufeld, "In the Service of the Council."

124. De Lubac, *Catholicism*, 168–69.

125. De Lubac, *Medieval Exegesis*, 1:1.

De Lubac describes the literal/historical sense as relating to "the exterior and sensible aspect of things, as opposed to their mystic or hidden signification, which is not at all perceived by the senses but only by the understanding."[126] Each of the spiritual senses immerses the reader in the mystery of Christ. The allegorical sense presumes the omnipresence of Christ, viewing "all the Old Testament, both its history and its words, as a signification of Christ and the church."[127] The tropological sense brings a Christ-centered morality into focus, leading the church to engage Scripture as "fully *for us* the Word of God."[128] Regarding anagogy, de Lubac states that it is the sense that points to the eschatological, unifying all senses of Scripture and directing Christians toward the fullness of Christ.[129] As de Lubac points out in his study, "Each sense leads to the other as its end."[130] Thus, each transition represents a deeper attentiveness to the wisdom of Scripture. The allegorical sense, extending from the literal/historical, moves "from the letter to the spirit, from the sensible fact to the deep reality, or from the miracle to the mystery."[131] The moral sense presupposes the work of the allegorical sense: "[T]he fruits of tropology can come only after 'the flowers of allegory.'"[132] And the anagogical sense "realizes the perfection both of allegory and of tropology, achieving their synthesis . . . [T]he eschatological reality attained by anagogy is the eternal reality within which every other has its consummation."[133] The spiritual sense of Scripture, based on the hermeneutical foundation of the literal/historical sense, unites the theological virtues of faith (allegorical sense), hope (anagogical sense), and love (tropological sense), resulting in a biblical text that contains a mystical depth of wisdom for the practice of Christian discipleship.

As part of this project, de Lubac points out that the fourfold interpretation of Scripture was not unique to the medieval period, nor should it be reinstated wholesale. He notes that there certainly were excesses in the use of spiritual interpretation, but that should not prompt a halt of

126. Ibid., 2:42.
127. Hollon, *Everything Is Sacred*, 168.
128. De Lubac, *Medieval Exegesis*, 2:140.
129. Ibid., 2:187, 197.
130. Ibid., 2:203.
131. Ibid., 2:127.
132. Ibid., 2:128.
133. Ibid., 2:187.

the method entirely.[134] Instead, affirming the emergence of specialized biblical exegesis with the work of Andrew of St. Victor (d. 1175), de Lubac maintained that modern scientific exegetical methods still held some benefits for the church.[135] Viewing these methods as invaluable for understanding the literal/historical sense of the biblical text, he states, "[I]n their right and proper place, these techniques may, without undue pride, be construed as an instance of enormous progress."[136] Moreover, he sees no warrant for opposing the spiritual sense to the literal sense: "Research into the spiritual sense seems to be perfectly compatible with the most strictly critical exegesis; the latter is the work of science, while the other is exercised from within the faith and through all other ways."[137] Nonetheless, Andrew's innovation is a cause for concern. De Lubac writes that the Bible became an object of technical and scientific study, a shift that threatened to divorce science from faith when scientific exegesis exceeded its competence: "The scholar and the believer then are so well divided that the second sees himself robbed of his object."[138]

Thus, while de Lubac does not wish to return to a pre-critical period of exegesis, he is clear that contemporary exegetes stand to gain from attending to the dynamics of fourfold scriptural interpretation. For instance, while multiple senses of a text's meaning are manifested simultaneously (and in fact, coinhere), de Lubac held to the unity of the biblical text. In other words, rather than allowing the spiritual sense (that is, the allegorical, moral, anagogical) to become disengaged from the literal, de Lubac, following patristic and medieval commentators, saw them as integrally linked: "[I]n Scripture itself, one professes that there is no dissociation of the two senses. The spirit does not exist without the letter, nor is the letter devoid of the spirit. Each of the two senses is in the other . . . Each needs the other."[139] This means that a single text can offer interpretive, moral,

---

134. "[T]he mere possibility of abuse should not force us to 'dim the flame.'" De Lubac, *Scripture in the Tradition*, 16–17.

135. De Lubac, *Medieval Exegesis*, 3:271.

136. Ibid., 1:xx. For a more thorough discussion, see D'Ambrosio, "Henri de Lubac and the Critique of Scientific Exegesis," 368–72.

137. De Lubac, *At the Service of the Church*, 313. Here, de Lubac is echoing language from *Dei Verbum*.

138. De Lubac, *Medieval Exegesis*, 3:272.

139. Ibid., 2:26.

and eschatological insights, all of which are grounded and contained in the literal sense of the text.[140]

What emerges in this relationship between the literal sense of Scripture and the spiritual sense is a sacramental view of reality, where the literal sense of Scripture is completed by the spiritual. Thus, the spiritual realities of salvation and ultimate fellowship with God are not extrinsic to the literal/historical texture of the Bible. Instead, the spiritual interpretation of Scripture is, in the words of Hans Urs von Balthasar, "an instrument for seeking out the most profound articulations of salvation history."[141] However, this link is severed when that meaning occludes the literal sense of the story. Hence, the narrative of a particular story is not extraneous to its meaning. As de Lubac argues, the mystery of the spiritual sense of Scripture is not abstract or ahistorical: "[T]his mystery is entirely concrete. It does not exist in idea. It does not consist in any atemporal truth or object of detached speculation. This mystery is a reality in act, the realization of a Grand Design; it is therefore, in the strongest sense, even something historical, in which personal beings are engaged."[142]

While this method of hermeneutics may seem new and foreign to many Baptists, it does provide resources that are missing from the evangelical biblicism described above. That is to say, this rather old method of reading Scripture provides the way forward from free church problems of tearing the Bible apart. First, the fourfold sense of reading Scripture takes the Bible on its own terms. As Congar mentioned earlier, the Bible does not ground its own authority in appeals to inerrancy or verbal plenary theories of interpretation. Instead, Scripture sees itself as containing both letter and spirit, and faithful reading involves attention to both. Spiritual interpretation is employed in numerous places within the Bible (e.g., Matt 1:23; Gal 4:21–31; Heb 7:1–10). In other words, to claim the Bible as guide, as Baptists and free church Christians have aimed to do, is to own the fourfold sense of interpretation as well. As David Steinmetz writes, "Only by confessing the multiple sense of Scripture is it possible for the church to make use of the Hebrew Bible at all or to recapture

---

140. D'Ambrosio notes de Lubac's indebtedness to Maurice Blondel for this dynamic relationship: "From the letter to the spirit, . . . there is a perpetual exchange and an intimate solidarity. The letter is the spirit in action . . . If the spirit demands and evokes the letter, the true letter inspires and vivifies the spirit." Blondel, *Action (1893)*, 372–73; D'Ambrosio, "Henri de Lubac and the Critique of Scientific Exegesis," 374.

141. Balthasar, *Theology of Henri de Lubac*, 76.

142. De Lubac, *Medieval Exegesis*, 2:93–94.

the various levels of significance in the unfolding story of creation and redemption."[143]

Second, rather than grounding interpretation in only the literal sense, which either stunted theological insights gained from reading or transformed the Bible into a shallow manual, the fourfold sense of Scripture offers a way to read Scripture with the church. Since the Bible is inextricably linked with the church, we find ourselves tied to fellow Christians across space and time who have committed themselves to faithful reading and performance of the scriptural narrative. Antebellum Christians who were divided on the issue of slavery were ultimately not shaped by the shared life of the church. Other communities and other cultural forces had more influence on the formation of their convictions. The Bible simply took on the shape of each individual's views. Thus, to claim the Bible is to claim the church as the primary formative community. The fourfold sense of interpretation, which brings the riches of the Christian tradition to bear on Bible reading in the life of the church, offers a path for such communal participation.

Finally, reading Scripture within the church aims to shape the life of the church. Evangelical biblicist reading tore the Bible apart in the past because moral and theological convictions had been determined by other sources, including political party platforms and philosophical and cultural trends. Even today, attempts to find moral guidance within scripture are plagued by a cacophony of perspectives, all of which are supported by fragmented biblical readings.[144] By contrast, each of the spiritual senses corresponds to a theological virtue: faith, love, and hope.[145] These virtues are the form and substance of faithful Christian discipleship. Taken together, reading in this manner with the church aims to form Christian disciples who emulate the life of the true Word of God. Indeed, following this pattern gives greater attention to the biblical witness as the overflowing fountain of divine wisdom, ever challenging God's people to see the world rightly and live faithfully in light of the Word.

---

143. Steinmetz, "Superiority of Pre-Critical Exegesis," 32.

144. As an example of such a hermeneutical strategy, consider Rachel Held Evans's argument against selective fundamentalist readings of the biblical text: "[I]nterpretation is not a matter of *whether* to pick and choose, but *how* to pick and choose." Evans, *Year of Biblical Womanhood*, 296.

145. As Steinmetz notes, even the literal sense "could and usually did nurture the three theological virtues" as well ("Superiority of Pre-Critical Exegesis," 30).

Bible and Tradition   97

Ultimately, the fourfold sense of Scripture (or something analogous to it) is essential to the life of the church because it extends beyond the plain sense reading of the text itself (which plagued antebellum Baptists concerning slavery and confounds contemporary free church Christians). We ourselves are caught up in a story larger than our own, yet one that comprehends our own as well. As McClendon writes, the spiritual sense "meant the way the plain words bore upon readers' lives in relation to all that God had done and would do in their regard."[146] In short, the reader not only encounters the text figurally, but he or she also encounters the past figurally as well.[147] The aim of such a task is not simply the acquisition of knowledge. As Bryan Hollon writes, this hermeneutical method was central to the pursuit of "a sapiential and thoroughly christological wisdom to guide the church in its inherently social and political mission in the world."[148] That is, a sacramental quality exists as the text of the Bible (the "Word of God") serves as a sign of Christ, "conveying the Gospel so that we may live by it."[149] This reality emerges from the text, yet transcends it. In this way, Baptist interpretations might not have torn the Bible apart in the mid-nineteenth century. Instead, the fourfold sense of Scripture would have brought readings into conformity with the mystery of Christ and offered wisdom for that context.

The authors of the 1997 statement, "Re-envisioning Baptist Identity: A Manifesto for Baptist Communities of North America" offer an important suggestion about biblical interpretation as a whole: "We thus affirm an open and orderly process whereby faithful communities deliberate together over the Scriptures with sisters and brothers of the faith, excluding no light from any source."[150] Here all the saints (past and present) read the Bible across space and time. Some churches have even sought to practice this within their Sunday morning schedule.[151] Reading Scripture with the church, then, broadens the present reading community, embracing the

---

146. McClendon, *Doctrine*, 36.

147. Cf. Harvey, *Can These Bones Live?*, 159.

148. Hollon, *Everything Is Sacred*, 5.

149. Congar, *Meaning of Tradition*, 102.

150. Broadway et al., "Re-envisioning Baptist Identity," 304.

151. One method for this type of reading, which I have observed in a Baptist Sunday School class, is for class members to share in reading all four lectionary passages for the appointed Sunday, commenting as a group on the similarities, differences, resonances, and trajectories emerging from reading of these texts in close proximity. Each voice in the group is appreciated and considered, even if there is disagreement.

tradition as what G. K. Chesterton called the "democracy of the dead."[152] In this democracy, something like the fourfold sense of Scripture can flourish, opening up space for the whole church to be heard and for the pilgrim church to follow the light that emerges from Scripture.

Rather than clinging to a staunch Bible-only stance, Baptist *ressourcement* points to the importance of tradition. However, little good results from viewing tradition as one source for Christian faith and practice among others. Instead, the embrace of tradition—seen particularly (though not exclusively) in the recovery of the fourfold sense of biblical interpretation—centers on the full Word of God: Jesus Christ. This recovery of Scripture, tradition, and their intrinsic relationship extends from Christ's incarnation in the world. As the divine and human coinhere in the second person of the Trinity, so Scripture and tradition coinhere in the life of the church.[153] This provides a thicker theological context for the Bible that counters the flat "what-it-meant/what-it-means" paradigm that reduces the text to only the literal sense. As has been seen above, this sort of recovery requires more than individual readings as well. Indeed, it is the case that as *sola scriptura* led to losing the genuine christological center of the biblical text, it is also the case that it contributed to the absence of the body of Christ, the church, as well. This will become the focus of the next chapter.

152. "Tradition means giving a vote to the most obscure of classes, our ancestors... Tradition refuses to submit to the small and arrogant oligarchy of those who merely happen to be walking about." Chesterton, *Orthodoxy*, 48.

153. Williams, *Tradition, Scripture, and Interpretation*, 27.

4

Individual and Community

Beyond the Legacy of E. Y. Mullins

> In accordance with creation and by nature humanity means fellowship. This is equally true, indeed it is genuinely true, only of the humanity of the Christian. Since faith is his free human act, he cannot perform it without his neighbours, without communication with them. He cannot try to conceal it from them. Whatever may be their attitude to him, he owes this to them. To exist privately is to be a robber.
>
> —KARL BARTH[1]

BAPTISTS HAVE BEEN A tribe that values significant aspects of individual experience. The deep influence of heart-felt revivalism has left a legacy of personal encounter that can be seen by many to be the hallmark of genuine Christianity. At the same time, Baptist hymnals hail the importance of the church and the "tie that binds." While these need not work at cross-purposes, contemporary Baptist discourse has developed something of an allergic reaction to cultivating a thicker sense of the church, viewing such efforts as destructive to the personal (read: individualistic) character of Christian faith. Even communal activities such as the Eucharist are couched in individual rather than communal terms. From where does this impasse arise? What way forward, if any, can be made?

---

1. Barth, *Doctrine of Reconciliation*, 778.

Central to answering these questions within Baptist faith and practice is the influence of Edgar Young (E. Y.) Mullins (1860–1928). While Mullins is not a relatively well-known name within American religious history,[2] he certainly stands as a theological luminary for twentieth-century Baptists (especially those in the American South). Born in Mississippi in 1860, Mullins's family moved to Texas in 1869, and he eventually attended what is now called Texas A&M University as one of the institution's first students. He received further education at the Southern Baptist Theological Seminary in Louisville, Kentucky, and upon graduation, served various Baptist churches as pastor before returning to Southern Seminary in the wake of "The Whitsitt Controversy" as its fourth president in 1899.[3] Aside from his work in Louisville, which included strengthening the institution and moving its location within the city of Louisville, Mullins served wider Baptist life as president of the Southern Baptist Convention, chaired the committee that developed the *Baptist Faith and Message* in 1925, and was president of the Baptist World Alliance before his death in 1928.

The perceived importance of Mullins and his thought has not diminished over time. If anything, as the turmoil within the Southern Baptist Convention has threatened the stability of the denomination, scholarship

---

2. Mullins is only mentioned once within Sydney Ahlstrom's *A Religious History of the American People*, in order to note his contribution to *The Fundamentals*. See Ahlstrom, *Religious History*, 816; cf. Noll, *History of Christianity*, 372, 381, 488. Mark Noll briefly discusses Mullins at three points: once in association with Southern Baptists' actions with regard to evolution in the 1920s, once for his contribution to *The Fundamentals*, and once for the way in which moderate Baptists claimed Mullins's heritage after 1979.

3. Landmark Baptists (or "Landmarkers") argued that Baptist practices, particularly believers baptism and congregational church governance, were present throughout the history of Christianity (even in heterodox groups such as the Waldensians, Lollards, the medieval cathari, Donatists, and Montanists). The point of such claims (known as "church successionism") was that "Baptist" churches had existed throughout all of Christian history. See Orchard, *A Concise History of Foreign Baptists* [reprinted by Landmark leader J. R. Graves in 1855] and Carroll, *Trail of Blood*, 1931, which appears in Freeman, McClendon, and Ewell, *Baptist Roots*, 233–40. In an 1895 article and an 1896 monograph, William H. Whitsitt, then president of Southern Seminary, countered the increasingly popular sentiments of Landmark Baptists by questioning whether English Anabaptists actually practiced believers baptism by immersion before 1641 and by stating that Roger Williams (renowned for his distinction as the first Baptist in the United States) was likely "sprinkled rather than totally immersed." Ellis, *Man of Books*, 33; cf. Whitsitt, *A Question of Baptist History*. The escalated dispute threatened the seminary and the entire convention until Whitsitt resigned as president in 1899.

concerning Mullins has only increased, marking him as a site for contemporary Baptist thought.[4] After conservatives gained control of the Southern Baptist Convention in 1979, so-called moderate Baptists (those who aimed to resist the conservatives within the denomination) rallied around soul competency and people such as E. Y. Mullins to forestall conservatives' efforts.[5] The result, while not holding the SBC constituencies together, has been a heightened interest in Mullins by conservatives (as an obstacle) and by moderates (as a hero) as well as an amplification of certain aspects of his signal idea—soul competency. In this way, he is not simply one Baptist voice among many. He represents one of several theological authorities for contemporary Baptists, something of a norm for what passes as "Baptist orthodoxy." Because of this, the trajectory of Mullins's ideas after his life becomes as important as the actual ideas themselves. After discussing Mullins's thought and its reception, this chapter will evaluate his work and significance. Specifically, Mullins stands at the center of a Baptist emphasis on the individual. In this chapter, then, *ressourcement* will occur through providing a thicker account of the individual and the communal within the Christian tradition. Such work offers resources and hope for Baptist ecclesiology beyond the legacy of Mullins.

Mullins's Thought

According to William Ellis, Mullins's general intellectual outlook centered on being moderate.[6] That is, he often sought to construct "middle

---

4. In the past twenty years, for example, his magnum opus, *The Axioms of Religion* (originally written in 1908), has been reprinted twice (Mullins, "The Axioms of Religion," in *The Axioms of Religion*, ed. R. Albert Mohler Jr.; Mullins, *The Axioms of Religion* (2010), ed. C. Douglas Weaver), three issues of different Baptist journals have been dedicated to discerning his legacy ["The Mullins Legacy," *Review and Expositor* 96.1 (1999); "E. Y. Mullins in Retrospect," *The Southern Baptist Journal of Theology* 3.4 (Winter 1999); and "E. Y. Mullins and *The Axioms of Religion*," *Baptist History and Heritage* 43.1 (Winter 2008)], and innumerable Baptists have held him in high esteem, describing him in terms such as "Mr. Baptist," "Interpreter of the Baptist Tradition," and "Public Spokesperson for Baptists in America" (Maddox, "E. Y. Mullins: Mr. Baptist for the 20th and 21st Century"; Hinson, "E. Y. Mullins as Interpreter of the Baptist Tradition"; Gourley, "E. Y. Mullins: Public Spokesperson for Baptists in America").

5. For more on these developments, see Hankins, *Uneasy in Babylon*, 14–40.

6. On numerous occasions, this word is utilized to describe Mullins and his approach to a variety of topics (e.g., the Social Gospel, racial issues, interdenominational cooperation, politics, evolution).

positions" between what appeared to be significantly divergent and irreconcilable views. In short, Mullins's work is characterized by "maintaining the eternal truths of Christianity while accepting newer methods of study."[7] Early in *The Axioms of Religion*, Mullins explains this moderate mentality:

> The lines of doctrinal cleavage are as radical as at any time in the past, but the issues are new. As usual the extreme parties are doing most of the harm. On one side is the ultra-conservative, the man of the hammer and anvil method, who relies chiefly upon denunciation of opponents, and who cannot tolerate discussion of a fraternal basis; on the other is the ultraprogressive whose lofty contempt of the "traditionalist" shuts him out from the ranks of sane scholarship and wise leadership. The really safe leaders of thought, however, are between these extremes.[8]

This approach served Mullins (and, consequently, Baptists) well throughout the twentieth century. As Curtis Freeman states, Mullins's work navigated the "Southern Baptist ship" between the Scylla of fundamentalism and the Charybdis of Protestant liberalism.[9] Moreover, Bill Leonard notes that Mullins's approach was mediated to the entire denomination as he "personifie[d] the Grand Compromise that characterized the SBC throughout most of the twentieth century."[10] This moderate approach is also displayed in the intersection between the communal and the individual. Mullins sought to avoid the extremes that maximized one aspect over the other. In order to properly describe Mullins's thoughts concerning this interaction, four areas of emphasis should be discussed: personal religious experience, the doctrine of soul competency, the importance of social responsibility, and the nature of the church.

Personal Religious Experience

Regarding religious experience, while Mullins's theological positions were generally viewed as orthodox, they were also innovative and engaged with contemporary philosophical methods. Through his travels during his pastoral ministry, he had been exposed to and influenced

---

7. Ellis, *Man of Books*, 77.
8. Mullins, *Axioms of Religion*, 14.
9. Freeman, "E. Y. Mullins and the Siren Songs of Modernity," 23.
10. Leonard, *God's Last and Only Hope*, 49.

by the pragmatism of William James (1842–1910) and the personalism of Borden Parker Bowne (1847–1910), both of whom taught in Boston while Mullins resided in the area and served as pastor of Newton Centre Baptist Church. Both James and Bowne had emphasized the role of experience in human knowledge in a manner that Mullins found insightful for the Christian faith. James linked the truth of any idea to the empirical matrix of personal experience.[11] Bowne saw the personal self as the ground of knowledge and the operation of reason and personality as the fundamental modality of existence.[12]

Mullins approached Christian thought with this background. This is evident in the opening chapter of his systematic theology, *The Christian Religion in Its Doctrinal Expression*.[13] Here, Mullins developed a particular understanding of the term "religion." Noting that certain authors have described theology as "the science which treats of God," Mullins argued that more is involved.[14] In fact, what this seemingly static definition of theology requires, wrote Mullins, is to be linked with religion.[15] In other words, the Christian religion is not merely a science that relies on mechanical processes and abstracted ideas. Instead, religion is "man's relations to the divine Being . . . It is a form of experience and of life. It is an order of facts."[16]

As a result, C. Douglas Weaver rightly notes that "[m]ethodologically, [Mullins] considered religious experience to be the starting point

11. For more on James's thought and its reception, see Dorrien, *The Making of American Liberal Theology*, 218–26.

12. For more on Bowne's personalism in its historical and philosophical context, see Dorrien, *The Making of American Liberal Theology: Imagining Progressive Religion*, 373–81.

13. This book was used as the textbook for systematic theology at Southern Seminary following its publication in 1917.

14. Mullins, *Christian Religion in Its Doctrinal Expression*, 1.

15. In what appears to be an implicit reference to Thomas Aquinas's "Five Ways" (*Summa Theologiae* Ia, q. 2, art. 3), Mullins wrote, "In the past men have usually begun treatises on theology by undertaking to prove the existence of God by logical inference from nature and man. There are arguments from causation, from order and arrangement, from design, from the moral order, from the necessities of reason itself, and others . . . They are valuable in their place, and are by no means to be rejected. But they are not primary and fundamental for Christian theology." Mullins, *Christian Religion in Its Doctrinal Expression*, 38.

16. Ibid., 1–2. In another work, Mullins stated, "Religion is a personal matter between the soul and God." Mullins, *Axioms of Religion*, 54.

for theological reflection."[17] Consequently, Mullins indicated that certainty in religious conviction arises from the centrality of experiential knowledge rather than rational coherence.[18] Stating that at its best theology has tacitly embraced the experiential aspects of doctrine, he averred, "It is the principle which animates all the biblical writers of both the Old and New Testaments. It is the source of power in the writings of an Augustine, a Clement, a Schleiermacher."[19] With this in view, it is not surprising that Mullins wrote in 1905 that experience was "the holy of holies of theology."[20]

Religious experience, then, serves as a source of factual data for theological reflection. Nonetheless, Mullins is clear that experience is not the only source. His goal was to set experience as an important contributor to theological work and as a significant apologetic resource. He further described possible sources of religious knowledge, including the Bible, comparative religion, and even "the decisions of ecclesiastical courts and councils as expressed in creeds and articles of faith."[21] About the latter, though, Mullins declares:

> [T]hey are not and can never be original sources of religious knowledge . . . [T]hey are second-hand knowledge, echoes rather than original voices. They are sometimes of great value. They declare the doctrinal beliefs of the age or people who put them forth. But religious knowledge does not arise primarily by subscription to creeds. It comes rather through the presence of God in the soul.[22]

This "presence of God in the soul" clearly indicates the primacy of religious experience among the various sources for theology. Mullins even viewed experience as interwoven into Scripture, moving from experience to generate experience: "Being the literary expression of living experience in the religious life, the spontaneous and free output of that experience under the guidance of God's Spirit, it is precisely adapted to reproduce that experience in men today."[23]

17. Weaver, "Baptist Ecclesiology of E. Y. Mullins," 19.
18. Mullins, *Christian Religion in Its Doctrinal Expression*, 38–39.
19. Ibid., 3.
20. Mullins, "Theological Trend," 148.
21. Ibid., 40.
22. Ibid.
23. Mullins, *Freedom and Authority in Religion*, 402–3.

Thus, following his usual moderating position, Mullins did not set biblical revelation over religious experience; rather, he grounded the authority of the Bible in religious experience. The result is that the Bible becomes a witness to the common (yet free) experience of Christians. For Mullins, then, Christians, with both Scripture and personal encounter, have a "union and combination of the objective source and the subjective experience."[24] In this manner, it seems evident that, even though Mullins did not see experience *qua* experience as the sole determining factor for religious convictions, he did hold it as at least equal to other factors.

Soul Competency

At the first Baptist World Congress meeting in London in 1905, Mullins delivered a speech entitled, "The Theological Trend," which offered the foundation of what became Mullins's 1908 book, *The Axioms of Religion*.[25] The aim of that book was twofold. For Baptists, Mullins hoped to restate Baptist positions in order to facilitate greater clarity for other Christians, thereby inspiring further theological work among Baptists. Outside the Baptist fold, however, Mullins intended to argue for distinct Baptist contributions to the proper understanding of New Testament Christianity. That is, he wanted to declare that to embrace biblical Christianity meant in some sense to become Baptist.

Mullins's development of the substance of *The Axioms of Religion* must be understood within the context of the Whitsitt Controversy, especially the heated disputes about the historical origins of Baptists. In an attempt to carve out a moderate position, Mullins claimed that "[t]he sufficient statement of the historical significance of the Baptists is this: the competency of the soul in religion."[26] As E. Glenn Hinson notes, any claim about Baptist history entered a contentious arena: "With the Whitsitt Controversy still very much in the air, Mullins did not want to tread disputed historical ground. It was enough that he set out 'The Historical Significance of Baptists' in which he basically outlined his central thesis. Baptists were the consistent advocates of 'soul competency' throughout their history."[27] Thus, since Mullins considered soul competency the prime

---

24. Mullins, *Christian Religion in Its Doctrinal Expression*, 11.
25. Mullins, "The Theological Trend."
26. Mullins, *Axioms of Religion*, 53.
27. Hinson, "E. Y. Mullins as Interpreter," 115.

contribution of Baptists to Christian thought and practice,[28] he worked to acknowledge Baptist history (i.e., Mullins thought that Baptists have always historically embodied this principle) while also de-emphasizing the particular historical proposals for Baptist identity that characterized the Whitsitt Controversy (i.e., in effect granting soul competency the status of a first principle). Ironically, then, Mullins sought to resolve (or, at least move beyond) a significant historical debate regarding what it meant to be Baptist by setting forth a rather ahistorical theological rule.

In short, the "soul's competency in religion" refers to direct access of the individual believer to God. For Mullins, it excluded the possibility of "all human interference" such as infant baptism, the episcopacy, and "every form of religion by proxy."[29] From this theological concept, Mullins developed six "axioms" of New Testament Christianity, invoking a term with geometric etymology in order to claim that these characteristics were self-evident to all Christians and based on sound biblical texts.[30] First, the *theological* axiom stated that "the holy and loving God has a right to be sovereign."[31] Second, the *religious* axiom averred that "all souls have an equal right to direct access to God."[32] The main thrust of this axiom centered on the refutation of any proxy or middle-step between God and individual humans: "Religious privilege and religious duty subsist between men and God in the first instance in their capacity as individuals and *only secondarily* in their social relations . . . It is a species of spiritual tyranny for men to interpose the church itself, its ordinances, or ceremonies, or its formal creeds, between the human soul and Christ."[33] Thirdly, Mullins deduced from soul competency an *ecclesiastical* axiom: "All believers have a right to equal privileges in the church."[34] The *moral* axiom was fourth, affirming that "to be responsible man must be free."[35] "A free Church in a free state" made up the *religio-civic* axiom,

---

28. William Hull declares that for Mullins, soul competency is the "Magna Carta of the Baptist faith" ("Mullins and Mohler," 313).

29. Mullins, *Axioms of Religion*, 54.

30. Ibid., 73.

31. Ibid.

32. Ibid.

33. Ibid., 93–94; emphasis added.

34. Ibid., 73.

35. Ibid., 74.

and Mullins concluded with the *social* axiom, summed up as "love your neighbor as yourself."[36]

While these six axioms constitute Mullins's interpretation of what it means to be Baptist, their scope is broader than simply Baptists. Mullins saw the axioms (and the doctrine of soul competency from which they were derived) as "simply the expression of the universal elements in Christianity and thus serve as the best statement of what the religion of Christ is in its essential nature."[37] Moreover, Mullins's conception of soul competency was central to his opposition to Catholicism, which he counterposed to Baptist sensibilities: "In every particular of the ecclesiastical and religious life of the Roman Catholic, the soul's incompetency is assumed."[38] The strong emphasis on Baptist life over Catholicism is further evident in the ways that Mullins evaluates other Christian denominations, criticizing the ways in which they lack Baptist-like elements of polity and practice (which usually resulted in describing them as embracing quasi-Catholic practices) and praising them for where they seem most aligned with Baptist ideals. When seen in combination with his declaration that the six axioms are indicative of genuine Christianity, Mullins's argument for soul competency acquires a quasi-ecumenical edge.[39] Thus, his ultimate hope was that other Christian traditions would recognize and accept the truth of the Baptist position. Since he detected this hope coming to fruition, he declared, "We are approaching the Baptist age of the world . . ."[40]

These axioms, or as Mullins calls them, "the first truths of the Christian religion," all bear a great deal of family resemblance to one another, especially with regard to the individual's authority and freedom within Christianity. Indeed, as has been discussed above, Mullins placed individual religious experience at the center of Baptist life and thought (and based on the self-evident character of the axioms, at the center of Christianity as a whole). Thus, no authority other than God stands above each individual Christian. In this way, the soul's competency in religion under

36. Ibid.
37. Ibid., 50.
38. Ibid., 60.
39. Ibid., 54.
40. Ibid., 275. In another publication, Mullins wrote that as freedom spread, "Baptist life becomes the inner principle of an ongoing civilization—the formative influence of which fosters and promotes every great cause on earth." Mullins, *Soul Freedom Applied to Church Life and Organization*, 15.

God stands as Mullins's *new* interpretation of the Baptist faith, reinforcing particular Baptist practices (e.g., individual Bible readings, advocacy of religious freedom, and priesthood of every believer within congregational church polity) and placing Southern Baptists on firm footing that would seemingly last until 1979 when the Southern Baptist Convention was thrown into turmoil.

Church

Some attention has been given to Mullins's omission of a chapter or section addressing ecclesiology in his systematic theology, *The Christian Religion in Its Doctrinal Expression*.[41] While this was certainly the case, it is nonetheless true that Mullins has offered numerous insights elsewhere regarding his notion of the church.[42] In fact, one of the axioms that Mullins details, the ecclesiastical axiom, concerns the nature of the church. However, his ecclesiology was dramatically shaped by more significant convictions about the nature of salvation and the Christian life. For Mullins, the New Testament began with an individual believer's relationship with Christ.[43] Following this experience, individuals gathered together to form the church, or what he defined as "a community of autonomous individuals under the immediate lordship of Christ held together by a social bond of common interest, due to a common faith and inspired by common tasks and ends . . ."[44] The assembly of believers is certainly significant, but only as a secondary movement, not a part of the economy of salvation: "Now the individuals who thus respond to God by faith and

---

41. McClendon, *Doctrine*, 58; Freeman, "E. Y. Mullins and the Siren Songs of Modernity," 35–36. Moreover, in a work of approximately five hundred pages, only six entries for church are listed in the volume's index.

42. Weaver, echoing Fisher Humphreys, argues that Mullins's intention that the book serve as the textbook for Southern Seminary's systematic theology course is an important detail in evaluating this absence since ecclesiological questions were joined to a separate pastoral course at the seminary taught by E. C. Dargan, who used his own book as the central text. Weaver, "Baptist Ecclesiology of E. Y. Mullins," 31 n. 5; cf. Humphreys, "Edgar Young Mullins," 334.

43. Mullins was certainly concerned about excessive individualism: "[I]ndividualism alone is inadequate because man is more than an individual. He is a social being" (*Axioms of Religion*, 51). Nonetheless, it is important to highlight the relationship between the individual and Christ, where "all his dealings with his subjects are individual" (ibid., 128).

44. Ibid., 129.

who are regenerated by his grace are inevitably drawn together by spiritual affinity into fellowship with each other through Christ, the revealer of God the Father. And in this way the church arises."[45] Because Mullins grounded Christianity in the personal, this common faith was not a sharing that radiated from a singular point, but rather was assembled from an aggregate of similar experiences.[46] Mullins likens this to the process by which diamonds are formed, noting their proximity to one another. However, rather than stating that the group of diamonds shared in one experience, he focuses on the individual, stating that *each* diamond had a specific experience similar to every other diamond, placing the individual prior to the communal or the social.[47]

Moreover, discussing the nature of the church did not move Mullins away from his central idea—soul competency. In fact, he determined that whatever the church is, it must not violate the individual soul's competence, severely limiting the formative character of any ecclesiology that might be articulated. This is seen most prominently in Mullins's critique of the Catholic Church, where the soul's incompetence is displayed. Mullins continues by detailing the ways in which the seven sacraments display this incompetency.[48] By contrast, Baptist churches, according to Mullins, have embraced an institutional form of this competence that restricts all interconnection between groups to voluntary cooperation alongside the personally held voluntary faith. In other words, while Mullins did make allusions to the church as a spiritual community that extended across space and time, his primary sense of the term was to refer to a local assembly (so that Baptists are found in many local churches, not in a single translocal church). As observed above, this also governed his stance toward visible Christian unity through ecumenical efforts.[49] In the end,

45. Ibid., 35.

46. "Primarily then Christianity is a relation between persons—God and man" (ibid., 28).

47. Ibid., 35. Mullins discussed the kingdom of God in similar terms, providing the fourth "Spiritual Law of the Kingdom," which stated that "the kingdom comes always in the first instance to the individual and can only so come" (ibid., 39).

48. Ibid., 60–62.

49. When discussing ecumenism, Mullins was happy to see fellow Christians as "brethren," whether in any communion or no communion at all. Mullins, "Message of the Baptist World Alliance," 224. While this initially presents an openness to other traditions, it more primarily reflects the secondary character of the church in Mullins's theology. That is, any given church (or no church at all) merely describes the location of those who have experienced the personal relationship that is wholly constitutive of salvation.

Mullins, echoing Baptists like Augustus H. Strong (1836–1921) before him, sums up his understanding of ecclesiology by stating, "The church, therefore, is the expression of the paradoxical conception of the union of absolute monarchy and pure democracy."[50]

Thus, for Mullins, ecclesiology is dependent upon personal experience. This does not mean that he did not have an ecclesiology, but it does signify that his ecclesiology is subordinated to the central emphasis on the individual and the personal. For this reason, Mullins's notion of the church cannot be any stronger than viewing it as "the social expression of the spiritual experiences common to a number of individuals."[51] This, interestingly, resulted in a skeptical stance toward the communal and a dichotomous relationship between the individual aspects of the Christian life and the social aspects. In other words, the church is certainly important and can be helpful for promoting the kingdom of God (even if only in a secondary manner), but it can only do so if it stays out of the way.

Social Responsibility

However Mullins conceived of the church, he saw it as significant for society at large.[52] Thus, while Mullins was clear that no authority, be it a church, an ecclesiastical leader, or even a creed, stood between God and the individual Christian, he most certainly did not ignore a concern for social conditions. After describing the centrality of soul competency for Baptists and its repudiation of any "religion by proxy," he addressed the communal side of anthropology by stating, "The doctrine of the soul's competency, however, goes further than individualism in that it embraces capacity for action in social relations as well as on the part of the individual."[53] Mullins made this point clear in his description of the efforts that arise from the social axiom of religion: "To imitate Christ is to labor for equitable social conditions, just laws, and equal privileges for men that they may earn their own bread. To imitate Christ is not to take sides with labor against capital or with capital against labor in the contest

---

50. Mullins, *Axioms of Religion*, 129. Cf. Strong, *Systematic Theology*, 3:903.

51. Mullins, *Axioms of Religion*, 35.

52. "The church is the dynamo whose task it is to charge all departments of life with righteousness" (ibid., 209).

53. Ibid., 55.

for rights, but rather to teach capital and labor to perform their respective duties."[54] Clearly, then, for Mullins, one's unmediated relationship with God should have implications for how one inhabits and shapes the world; one has a responsibility to work for better social conditions.[55]

Moreover, Mullins understood community to play a role in influencing the individual. For instance, at several points, he emphasized the impact of context on the development of children, noting the necessity for "an environment of the child which will predispose it to Christ and the church."[56] Mullins stated that even Jesus received the awakening in his soul that came from an environment that lifted him "to a new stage in his career under God's blessing."[57] It is perhaps because of the influence of this environment that Mullins claimed, "We may assume that the child will become a Christian, but we dare not assume that he is a Christian prior to his own choice."[58]

At the same time, Mullins reiterated that the relationship between the individual and the social begins with the individual: "To regenerate the individual is the sole condition of permanent moral progress in the social sphere."[59] That is, rather than viewing a symbiotic link between the two, Mullins was clear that a Christianity that first focuses on the social (whether within the church or in society at large), has extinguished itself by "abandon[ing] its doctrine of 'regenerate individualism.'"[60] With this in view, the communal or the social, while certainly important, is subordinated to the individual. In other words, Christians who care about societal conditions should be aware of how their tasks should be prioritized: "The best service which Christianity can render to society is to produce righteousness in individual character and at the same time set the man

---

54. Ibid., 208. It should be noted that, aside from the major differences in their larger projects, Mullins's sentiment resonates at this point with that of Pope Leo XIII in the encyclical *Rerum novarum*, where he stated, "Each needs the other: capital cannot do without labor, nor labor without capital. Mutual agreement results in the beauty of good order, while perpetual conflict necessarily produces confusion and savage barbarity" (§19).

55. "The Christian who understands the meaning of his religion, therefore, will be a force for civic, commercial, social, and all other forms of righteousness." Mullins, *Axioms of Religion*, 207.

56. Ibid., 181.
57. Ibid., 182.
58. Ibid., 174.
59. Ibid., 204.
60. Ibid.

free as an agent of righteousness in society at large."[61] Thus, the church does not mediate any formation to individuals, and it "cannot become the organ of social reform save indirectly."[62]

Baptists' Reception of Mullins

Evaluation of Mullins is not complete with the details of his life and writings. Equally important are the ways in which his thought has been received and employed by his Baptist descendants. Below, the reception of Mullins's work will be traced, describing how his most notable contribution to Baptist theological discourse—soul competency—has been used throughout the twentieth century. This story of reception will center on two post-World War II figures, Herschel Hobbs and Douglas Hudgins, both of whom were Southern Baptist pastors in the 1950s and 1960s and both of whom drew deeply from the well of Mullins's thought. Despite these similarities, however, they move in different directions on several significant issues and describe their distinct positions as extending from Mullins's thought. What will emerge, then, are diverging theological paths from Mullins that contribute to deep fragmentation within Baptist life.

Herschel Hobbs

In 1963, the Southern Baptist Convention revised the *Baptist Faith and Message*, which had remained unchanged since Mullins's contributions in

---

61. Ibid., 210.

62. Mullins, *Baptist Beliefs*, 77. Mullins's views seem to presuppose (and perhaps require) a substantial community that forms individuals prior to exercising their direct access to God. Curtis Freeman elaborates upon this sentiment, stating, "[Mullins] might have done well to delineate the qualities of character that constitute competency: the habits and skills which a competent soul would need to possess in order to read the Bible wisely. He could also have indicated the sort of community and spiritual formation that are necessary to initiate and sustain converted souls in the Christian life . . . [P]erhaps he says nothing because the safeguards of character and community were givens, part of the evangelical consensus of his day, constitutive elements of the Baptist understanding of the Christian life that he thought needed no explanation to his readers." Freeman, "E. Y. Mullins and the Siren Songs of Modernity," 34. Because such a community is never explicitly addressed and examined, it would seem that the formative character of Southern culture on Baptists fills the void (a formation that cannot be presumed as given in the present context).

1925, under the chairmanship of then-president of the Southern Baptist Convention, Herschel Hobbs. After the revision was completed, Hobbs, who was also pastor of the First Baptist Church of Oklahoma City from 1949 until 1972, wrote an exposition of the document, describing the significance of each article. In the introduction to the book, he turned to Mullins in order to address "The Rock From Which We Are Hewn." While Hobbs largely stood in agreement with Mullins, he did argue that soul competency is found in the Old Testament, bound up with the creation of humanity in the image of God.[63] Moreover, Hobbs clarified some of the implications of Mullins's ideas when he wrote,

> In reality Baptists are the most broad-minded of all people in religion. They grant to every man the right that he shall be free to believe as he wants. But they insist upon the same right for themselves . . . This does not mean that Baptists believe that one can believe just anything and be a Christian or a Baptist. The competency of the soul in religion entails the authority of the Scriptures and the lordship of Jesus Christ. The priesthood of believers grants to every Christian the right to read and interpret the Scriptures for himself as he is led by the Holy Spirit.[64]

As the center of Hobbs's understanding of Baptist identity (signaled by his appropriation of it at the outset of his exposition of the Southern Baptist confession of faith), soul competency opens Baptists to other faith traditions while also establishing some sense of authority found in the New Testament and Jesus Christ.

Other treatments of soul competency were also produced in this period,[65] with a revised edition of Mullins's *The Axioms of Religion* in 1978 as one of the more prominent. Despite the fact that Mullins had been deceased for nearly fifty years, Hobbs and Mullins "co-wrote" this edition, which meant that Hobbs utilized portions of approximately half of the original chapters and added his own contributions, mixed with Mullins's original words, for explaining their importance for that context, with no distinct textual markings to indicate where Mullins ends and Hobbs begins. In fact, Hobbs's voice occasionally impacted the shape and tone of Mullins's original words. For instance, following the introduction of soul competency as the historical significance of Baptists (which comes

---

63. Hobbs, *Baptist Faith and Message*, 8.
64. Ibid., 9–10.
65. See, e.g., Hinson, *Soul Liberty*.

directly from Mullins), Hobbs intensifies the force of Mullins's statement by adding: "This is not a creed; Baptists are not a creedal people. To the contrary, it stands as a safeguard against coercion with respect to solidifying one's faith in the form of a written creed."[66]

Furthermore, in the chapter regarding the social axiom of religion, Hobbs inserted an evaluation of the social gospel movement, which was still nascent when Mullins originally wrote *The Axioms of Religion*. Hobbs held that the social gospel brought to light the need for social concern on the part of regenerated individuals, but any idea that the goal of the gospel was solely to effect a change in social conditions is wrong.[67] At the same time, Hobbs pointed to the role of the Southern Baptist Christian Life Commission in fulfilling the duty to social responsibility that is bound up with the gospel, calling it "the *social conscience* of the Southern Baptist Convention."[68] Thus, while much of Mullins's original work remains intact (at least that which is included in the revised edition), Hobbs's additions and revisions intimate a move away from some of Mullins's initial ideas and toward a more robust individualism with an intensified notion of soul competency at the center. This in some sense leaves behind what Mullins might have originally presumed, a largely Christian (perhaps even Baptist) culture that would play a significant formative role in persons who claim to have competent souls.

Douglas Hudgins

Douglas Hudgins, pastor of the First Baptist Church of Jackson, Mississippi, from 1946 to 1969, was no less involved in Southern Baptist life, having faithfully attended annual meetings and served as the vice-chairman of the revision committee for the *Baptist Faith and Message*.[69] Nonetheless, he displayed a use of soul competency that diverged from

---

66. Hobbs and Mullins, *Axioms of Religion*, 48. Mullins's original statement, which can be seen as leaving open the question as to whether Baptists can have creeds, was "I am not stating a Baptist creed . . . It is the historical significance of the Baptists I am stating, not a Baptist creed" (*Axioms of Religion*, 53).

67. Hobbs and Mullins, *Axioms of Religion*, 150. It should be noted that Mullins's chapter on Christian nurture is not present in this revised edition of *The Axioms of Religion*.

68. Ibid., 155.

69. Southern Baptist Convention, *Annual of the Southern Baptist Convention*, 281.

Hobbs in several places. Leading a prominent church in the Deep South during the struggle for civil rights, Hudgins unwaveringly "preached a gospel of individual salvation and personal orderliness, construing civil rights activism as not only a defilement of social purity but even more as simply irrelevant to the proclamation of Jesus Christ as God. The cross of Christ . . . has nothing to do with social movements or realities beyond the church; it's a matter of individual salvation."[70]

This sharp division between the individual and the social contributed to the lack of support by Baptists for the civil rights of African-Americans.[71] Charles Marsh frames Hudgins's posture as a concern for purity, so that, for Hudgins, "If the Christian admits other concerns into the event of salvation—like good works, doctrinal or creedal confession, or mediations like church traditions and hierarchy—then the purity of the soul's intimacy with God becomes threatened."[72] Such sentiments diminish the importance of events in the physical world (and even particular groups of people within that world), interiorizing the faith to such an extent that political and social changes in line with the gospel are neglected. That is, while remaining faithful to the full theological force of soul competency,[73] Hudgins's use of the term effectively allowed him to neglect part of creation (in this case, the bodies of certain people in the South).[74] Using Mullins's words, Hudgins avoided all "religion by proxy,"

70. Marsh, *God's Long Summer*, 89. Hudgins's story, though not recounted in great detail here, figures prominently in Marsh's book, with Hudgins positioned as the theologian of the closed Southern society in the 1960s.

71. Hudgins even employed the Baptist ecclesiological principle of the autonomy of the local church to argue that his congregation was not bound to follow the 1954 Southern Baptist Convention resolution supporting the Supreme Court's decision in *Brown v. Board of Education*: "'Let me remind you that every Baptist congregation in the world—if it be truly Baptist in its position—is a democratic entity, and is responsible to no other body or individual, but is under the leadership of the Lord'" (ibid., 99–100). Herschel Hobbs, while not serving on the committee proposing the resolution, was a member of the Southern Baptist Convention executive committee from 1954 until 1956. Thanks to Richard Cheek of Oklahoma Baptist University's Mabee Learning Center Library for his help in obtaining this information.

72. Ibid., 106.

73. See Hankins, *Uneasy in Babylon*, 242. Hudgins himself stated in a 1947 sermon entitled "Baptists and the Bible," "[T]he 'competency of the individual soul' sets the policy and the polity of Baptists" (quoted in Marsh, *God's Long Summer*, 111–12).

74. On one particular Sunday in 1963, seventeen African-Americans were refused admission at four churches in Jackson, Mississippi, including five at First Baptist Church. See "Churches Turn Away Negroes," 2. While Hudgins is not mentioned and may not have been directly involved, his neglect of the concerns of African-Americans

that is, any sort of mediation of God's presence to humanity.[75] Moreover, Hudgins developed three principles of religion that functioned as a distillation of Mullins's six. First, the New Testament is the only rule of faith. Second was the emphasis on individuality in matters of religion. Third, Hudgins focused on the autonomy of the local church.[76] Consequently, according to Marsh, Hudgins's views resulted in an "unmediated harmony with God" that turned "racial homogeneity into a theological—if not a metaphysical—necessity."[77]

Further, the atomization of individual Christians under the banner of soul competency (each with their own personal social responsibility) left little, if anything, for the creation of a common ecclesial identity. As a result, Marsh rightly notes that "accidents of race, class, and custom" fill the void and provide form to the social framework of the competent soul's existence.[78] Moreover, even though Mullins himself might have questioned the actions of Southern Baptist pastors such as Hudgins (Mullins did, after all, advocate some measure of social responsibility and even aided African-Americans on certain issues), Hudgins' appeal to soul competency as the basis for the individuality of religious belief and the unmediated nature of the Christian faith and his divergence from Hobbs's use of Mullins uncovers a more ambiguous character of soul competency. That is, the disparity between Hobbs and Hudgins regarding their use of soul competency reveals the tension within the concept itself, as well as the ways in which the two trajectories of the concept align with the social disputes concerning race in the South, calling the idea's usefulness into question, especially as the basis for ecclesiology.

Where Do We Stand Now?

While soul competency has been well received throughout twentieth-century Baptist thought, it has also contributed to an individualistic emphasis among Baptists and a concomitant "growing irrelevance for

---

in his community and region certainly shaped his congregation and had profound consequences.

75. Marsh writes, "When salvation is interiorized to the soul's competency before God, every reality outside this encounter, which is to say all worldly reality, is stripped clean of sacramental consequence" (*God's Long Summer*, 108).

76. Ibid., 107.

77. Ibid., 112.

78. Ibid., 109.

any attempt to explain church life theologically or historically."[79] Moreover, this indifference toward the church has contributed to an "abiding mistrust and fear of institutions that might transgress the boundaries of individual or congregational prerogatives."[80] Winthrop Hudson, an American Baptist, correctly identified the deeply problematic character of soul competency and the danger this "highly individualistic principle" posed to Baptists. Recognizing the ways in which this twentieth-century Baptist doctrine emerged through the mediation of radical individualism via the general influence of evangelical revivalism and through the thought of Isaac Backus, John Leland, and Francis Wayland, Hudson declared, "It has become increasingly apparent that this principle was derived from the general cultural and religious climate of the nineteenth century rather than from any serious study of the Bible."[81]

The problems associated with soul competency were not just its individualism, which distracted from the necessity of Christian sociality. Indeed, Hudson argues that, because the concept is the basis of virtually any Baptist description of their ecclesial life in the early twentieth century, the competency of the soul does not merely lack certain positive characteristics, but embodies negative ones as well:

> Not only did [soul competency] fail to provide detailed guidance for questions of church order beyond such generalized corollary axioms as "all believers have a right to interpret the Bible for themselves" and "all believers have a right to equal privileges in the church"; but also it served to dissolve any real concept of the church, for it interpreted faith as a one-to-one relationship between God and the individual.[82]

By locating virtually all authority within the individual, this solitary soul is placed over and above church, tradition, and even the Bible itself. That is, the individual is endowed with the power of arbitrating the parameters of a genuine encounter with the divine, meaning that any experience has the potential to carry the fullness of God's presence, not based on any analogous relationship with an external norm, but based on the judgment of the individual. Hudson drives home this point by memorably stating that "the practical effect of the stress upon 'soul competency' as

---

79. Goodwin, *Baptists in the Balance*, 15.
80. Ibid., 17.
81. Hudson, *Baptists in Transition*, 142.
82. Ibid.

the cardinal doctrine of Baptists was to make every[one's] hat [their] own church."[83]

At best, a church in this framework is an association of individuals that is not a necessary feature of the Christian life, and each congregation is equally competent and independent from other congregations and other overseeing authorities.[84] In other words, the individualism seen in soul competency also isolates particular communities of believers. Treatment of ecclesiology centers largely on discussion of polity and sociological study rather than a theological account of the church or its mystical ties that bind Christians together.[85] This individualized ecclesiology, grounded within a metaphysic of soul competency, places the individual and the social in a dualism such that to speak of one is to neglect the other. Thus, contemporary defenses of Mullins's ecclesiology ironically end up focusing primarily on his emphasis on the individual.[86] Thus, the metaphysic of soul competency has much in common with the nominalism discussed earlier in this book. That is, an emphasis on voluntaristic freedom leaves the church as an entity that can only be named as the aggregate of individuals. The result is a zero-sum game between the communal and the individual.

Contemporary moderate Baptist thought finds itself very much indebted to Mullins's ideas, especially soul competency. Baptist historian Bill Leonard sees soul competency as synonymous with freedom, stating that it results in a "radical and dangerous ideal: the people can be trusted, the individual 'soul' is competent in matters religious."[87] This is meant to open up the ecclesial polity to dissent that will challenge authority within the church.[88] Fellow historian Walter Shurden expands this notion of freedom, tying it more closely to the individual:

83. Ibid.

84. "Every local church is held to be competent in and of itself, to bear the whole witness of Christ to the whole world. It has no need of commission or authority save that received from Him who dwells in the church and is its only Head and Lord." McNutt, *Polity and Practice*, 26.

85. In fact, many twentieth-century Baptist ecclesiology texts, including Dargan's, spend much more time and effort attending to questions of polity and sociological relationships than discussing a theology of the church.

86. See Weaver, "The Baptist Ecclesiology of E. Y. Mullins."

87. Leonard, "Varieties of Freedom," 11.

88. Leonard writes of two sides of Mullins that must be held in tension: "Dr. Mullins the inerrantist, and Dr. Mullins the prophet of soul liberty" (*God's Last and Only Hope*, 76). However, literary critic Harold Bloom sees this tension as so unstable that

> Freedom is such an important ingredient in the human enterprise that one could philosophically justify freedom for freedom's sake. Baptists had more in mind, however, than simply breaking free from chains that held them back. Freedom had purpose for Baptists. They wanted freedom from a state-enforced religion because they thought that the freedom of the human spirit was worth saving. They rebelled against the priority of institutionalism because they believed that the priority of the individual was worth saving.[89]

In light of Hudson's critique, Shurden also fails to deploy a substantive ecclesiology, reducing Baptist significance to the individual: "The Baptist word for the world is that each individual is free to answer and is responsible for answering."[90] James Dunn, former director of the Baptist Joint Committee on Public Affairs, responded to Winthrop Hudson's concerns by pointing to Mullins's interaction with "much of the best available Baptist writing on social justice."[91] Furthermore, Dunn draws from Mullins's optimism concerning soul competency as an influence on societal progress:

> The principle of the competency of the soul in religion under God, along with the axiomatic spiritual principles rooted in it, can show a vital connection with all the great lines of human progress. Intellectual liberty, or the right to think; aesthetic liberty, or the right to self-expression in the realm of art; economic liberty, or the right to work and a fair wage; political liberty, or the right to vote; religious liberty, or the right to worship—all

soul competency will eventually eclipse biblical authority or redefine it in terms of the former: "If soul competency is simply a description of an absolutely unmediated and intimate relationship with Jesus, then what precisely is the function of reading and interpreting Scripture? . . . If you reject the Catholic idea that the Church is the mystical body of Christ, then why cannot you be free of congregation, preacher, and text, and so be wholly alone with Jesus, walking and talking, spirit with spirit, spirit to spirit?" (*American Religion*, 207). The result of the unraveling of this tension is that the individual soul is situated epistemically prior to and free from any authority, whether it be a church, a priest or minister, a creed or confession, or the Bible itself.

89. Shurden, *Baptist Identity*, 27.

90. Ibid., 28.

91. Dunn, "Church, State, and Soul Competency," 66. It seems, though, that simply positioning Mullins's concern for the social alongside the individual does not fully answer Hudson's concerns, i.e., the necessity of Christian sociality and a more developed understanding of ecclesiology. Moreover, one can observe Mullins's legacy becoming more like a late-twentieth-century moderate Baptist when Dunn describes him as "creedless" (ibid., 68).

these are the fruit of the direct revelation of men [and women] to God.[92]

While these freedoms are noteworthy and not to be taken for granted, they are negative freedoms that serve to separate individuals from one another, looking with suspicion on any communal tie that binds. Therefore, Dunn is clear that "The only Baptist creed is, 'Ain't nobody but Jesus goin' to tell me what to believe.'"[93] The result is an insufficient theological account of the church. As William Roy McNutt states, the individual Christian "has no inescapable need of church to bring him salvation or mediate to him divine grace . . ."[94] By splitting the gifts of supernatural grace from the texture of ecclesial life, Mullins and his descendants have created a "chasm between salvation and history."[95]

Toward *Ressourcement*

H. Wheeler Robinson, principal of Regent's Park College in England, quoted Mullins in 1927 in order to write that Mullins's identification of the soul's competency in religion as the significance of Baptists would be acceptable to most Baptists.[96] At the same time, there were points where Robinson understood that soul competency needed to be tempered by a stronger sense of community than one finds in Mullins. Noting the strengths and weaknesses of Baptist theology, he points out that Baptists have an "eighteenth-century philosophy of society, disguised under their traditional interpretation of Scripture":

> That pronounced individualist, Jean Jacques Rousseau, discussed the social forms of life as if they were the arbitrary and voluntary creation of a number of unitary individuals, instead of being the cradle in which the individual life is nurtured and the breast at which it sucks . . . But this ignores the fact that there are two elements of individuality and sociality growing side by

92. Ibid., 70.

93. Woodward, "Sex, Sin and Salvation." Curtis Freeman sees this negative freedom extending one more step, arguing that soul competency can easily become *sole* competency. Freeman, "E. Y. Mullins and the Siren Songs of Modernity," 41.

94. McNutt, *Polity and Practice*, 22. Along similar lines, Augustus Strong disputes Cyprian's declaration that whoever does not have the church as mother does not have God as father. Strong, *Systematic Theology*, 3:901.

95. Freeman, "E. Y. Mullins and the Siren Songs of Modernity," 36.

96. Robinson, *Life and Faith of the Baptists*, 18.

side from the very beginning, and not less in religious than in biological and cultural and moral development.[97]

Robinson directs his concern to the formation of a church as a cohesive whole that is more than an aggregate of individuals. That is, despite his praise for Mullins, Robinson invokes him as an example of the dualism within Baptist thought that allows the social to be eclipsed by the individual: "The family is already a social environment, and without it there could be no individual life, yet it is possible for a Baptist to write, 'fatherhood and sonship are relations expressive of individual and not of corporate experiences.'"[98]

With this concern at the fore, Robinson argued that "Baptists need an 'Oxford Movement' *of their own order*, so as to give their truth of an individual relation to God its complementary truth of a social relation to Him."[99] Robinson stated that this Baptist Oxford Movement would certainly bring about changes in liturgy and church polity, but it would not graft new ideas onto an old tradition. Rather, it would be realizing "true changes of a living development in which the unity is not lost."[100] This Oxford Movement, like its Anglican predecessor led by John Henry Newman and Edward Pusey, would attend much more closely to its forebears within the Christian tradition. Like the *ressourcement* impulse, it would embrace an organic ecclesial connection extending from the apostles through the texture of the church's sojourn throughout the centuries.[101]

Central to the work necessary to bridge the gap between the individual and the social with a view to reintegration is a thick account of the church. However, twentieth-century Baptist thought has displayed a reticence to offer such an account. This is seen clearly in the three versions of the *Baptist Faith and Message*, two of which (1925 and 1963) were developed by Mullins and Hobbs, respectively. In 1925, following the language of the 1833 *New Hampshire Confession of Faith*, the church is only described as "a congregation of baptized believers."[102] In 1963, this

97. Ibid., 172.
98. Ibid., 172–73. Cf. Mullins, *Axioms of Religion*, 39.
99. Robinson, *Life and Faith of the Baptists*, 174; emphasis original.
100. Ibid.
101. Mullins saw John Henry Newman and the Tractarians, with their quest for organic ecclesial unity and external authority (even for interpreting the Scriptures) as a move away from the soul's competency in religion. See Mullins, *Axioms of Religion*, 23–24, 42–43, 142.
102. Southern Baptist Convention, *Baptist Faith and Message* (1925), art. xii. Cf.

is expanded to state that a church is "a local body of baptized believers" that operates as an "autonomous body." At the end of this section of the confession, there is a reference to the church as "the body of Christ which includes all of the redeemed of all the ages."[103] In the most recent revision (2000), descriptions similar to 1963 are given, with the only significant change being the restriction of the office of pastor exclusively to men.[104] For the purposes of this chapter, while it is notable that only the latter two statements stated that the church extends beyond the local congregation, what is entirely absent is any sense of how these two conceptions of the church are related.[105]

This confusion, however, is deeper than terminology or a lack of clarity. Mullins's thought begins with the human person and extends observations from there to God: "We infer that God has will, intelligence, consciousness, from the possession of these qualities by men. That is, we argue God's personality from our own."[106] Here univocal language is invoked within Mullins's theological discourse, where God-talk is employed in a manner like that used for humans. That is, not only is analogical language—which preserves the intrinsic link between Creator and creature and their simultaneous ever-greater dissimilarity—eschewed, but the anthropological bridge to the divine invoked by Mullins is the individual person. This gives credence to James McClendon's claim that a "metaphysical individualism" extends from Mullins's thought and results in congregations that are ontologically fragmented from one another and from the wider Body of Christ, and individual Christians that are divided from one another within local congregations.[107]

The proper treatment for this ailment is not simply a renewed emphasis on the communal against the individual. Though this sort of refocusing may be needed at times (as Robinson argues), one cannot find

---

"New Hampshire Confession of Faith," art. xiii, in Lumpkin, *Baptist Confessions of Faith*, 365–66.

103. Southern Baptist Convention, *Baptist Faith and Message* (1963), art. vi.

104. Southern Baptist Convention, *Baptist Faith and Message* (2000), art. vi.

105. Mikael Broadway notes that these twentieth-century Baptist confessions of faith differ from their earlier sixteenth- and seventeenth-century counterparts in their meager language with regard for the church, including sparse use of the word *body* in describing it. See Broadway, "Come Now, Let Us Argue It Out," 62–63.

106. Mullins, *Christian Religion in Its Doctrinal Expression*, 192.

107. McClendon, *Witness*, 218.

the correct treatment by merely "balancing the two."[108] Such a stance at best produces a juxtaposition of the individual and the social and at worst reconstitutes the same dualism currently in view. In fact, any attempt to view this chapter's argument in this light is to profoundly misunderstand the problem and to reproduce its symptoms.[109] Instead, the problem is an ontological one and, as Robinson indicates, what is necessary is a reconceived understanding of the relationship between the individual and the social, so that each shapes the other and both can be present within the church and the Christian life. In short, Baptists need a more robust sense of catholicity.

Baptists have rarely embraced the term *catholic*. In fact, it often receives a negative assessment due to association with Roman Catholicism. Nevertheless, this term refers to the sense of the whole that appears in hymns sung within Baptist worship such as "The Church's One Foundation":

> Elect from every nation, yet one o'er all the earth,
> Her charter of salvation, one Lord, one faith, one birth;
> One holy name she blesses, partakes one holy food,
> And to one hope she presses, with every grace endued.[110]

With Mullins's contempt for "religion by proxy," a substantive ecclesial role is lost, crippling his and much of twentieth-century Baptist thought. What is left instead is an emphasis on the individual, often set over the communal or the catholic.[111] Even when the church is mentioned, it is

---

108. This "attempt to balance" is seen in numerous well-meaning treatments of Baptist life and thought, such as Goodwin, *Baptists in the Balance*. One might also view Walter Shurden's response to the Baptist Manifesto, with its aim to balance the individual/communal polarity, as an example of this approach. See Shurden, "The Baptist Identity and the Baptist *Manifesto*."

109. One version of this dualism is found in Al Mohler's introduction to a 1997 reprinting of Mullins's *Axioms of Religion*, where the internal is set against the external (not only in Mullins, but for all of theology): "Either personal experience will be submitted to revelation, or revelation will be submitted to personal experience. There is no escape from this theological dilemma, and every theologian must choose between these two methodological options." Mohler, introduction, to *Axioms of Religion*, 25.

110. Samuel S. Wesley, "The Church's One Foundation," in McAfee, *Celebrating Grace Hymnal*, #246.

111. "For me, one of those [Baptist convictional] genes has to do with the centrality of the individual, the individual's religious experience with God, the individual's freedom from God, the individual's freedom of conscience." Shurden, "The Baptist Identity and the Baptist *Manifesto*," 339.

local (i.e., individual) communities situated in opposition to any sense of the broader ecclesial unity shared by churches across space and time.

In his 1938 book, *Catholicism*, Henri de Lubac articulated the manner in which the church was catholic. Not aiming to write a book about Roman Catholicism or the papacy or the Catholic Church, de Lubac discussed aspects of the whole that characterizes the body of Christ itself.[112] Here, *Catholic* is "social in the deepest sense of the word . . . in the heart of its mystery."[113] *Catholic* means that the communal dimensions of the Christian faith are not add-ons, but are essential for understanding the significance of the gospel. Along these lines, de Lubac refers to Maximus the Confessor, who elaborated on the idea of original sin as separation by viewing it as "an individualization it might be called, in the depreciatory sense of the word."[114] Elevation of the individual over the whole (i.e., the catholic), therefore, is a mark of the effects of sin. For this reason, the incarnation of the Word is not merely the appearance of one human being who is also divine. Rather, it is the reinstantiation of humanity within the incarnation.[115] Jesus's mission consists of more than redeeming individuals; it centers on the creation of a people.

In this light, the church becomes something of a picture of the whole, though not as "a mere federation of assemblies" nor as a "simple gathering together of those who as individuals have accepted the Gospel."[116] Instead, the church has a shared calling prior to being gathered together.[117] In other words, taking seriously that the church (*ekklesia*) is a collective term that refers to "the called-out ones," becoming a Christian is more than a personal choice or significant moment for a solitary individual. As Barry Harvey writes, "According to the New Testament, the principal site of the Spirit's activity is not the individual believer, but the gathered community of disciples who form a distinctive commonwealth in the world . . . Who Christians are as individuals, therefore, is the product of their involvement in this communion, this *community*."[118] Thus, in the

---

112. De Lubac, *Catholicism*, 17–18. The word *Catholic* is sometimes translated "universal," though this does not properly describe its meaning, which in a basic sense, is "of the whole."

113. Ibid., 15.

114. Ibid., 33.

115. Ibid., 37–38.

116. Ibid., 63.

117. The church is "a *convocatio* before being a *congregatio*" (ibid., 64).

118. Harvey, *Can These Bones Live?*, 251–52.

church a person is called along with everyone else within the church to the whole—the body of Christ. In this manner, with the original unity of humanity and the designated end of humanity united in the incarnation, something different than metaphysical individualism is presented here. Human beings are first and foremost caught up in a community that is in relationship with the Triune God.

To be certain, the catholic does involve holding shared theological convictions. Vincent of Lérins stated three characteristics of what is truly catholic—universality, antiquity, and consent:

> [A]ll care must be taken, that faith which has been believed everywhere, always, by all . . . We shall follow universality if we confess that one faith to be true, which the whole Church throughout the world confesses; antiquity, if we in no wise depart from those interpretations which it is manifest were notoriously held by our holy ancestors and fathers; consent, in like manner, if in antiquity itself we adhere to the consentient definitions and determinations of all, or at the least of almost all priests and doctors.[119]

Vincent continues by noting that if a new challenge faces the church, the way forward would involve consultation with the ancient and established voices of the tradition.[120] Because of this, any discussion of faith is also caught up with the church's shared profession of faith.[121] This transcends the individual/communal boundary by extending personal aspects of this faith to the corporate, as both the Roman Catholic de Lubac and Protestant Karl Barth make clear: "faith's interior quality is deepened and developed only within the ecclesial communion."[122] Thus, while theological diversity and creativity is welcome, seeking to be a "theological maverick" (or inadvertently becoming one through lack of care for the communal dimensions of the Christian faith) will leave one in danger of heresy by standing against the shared faith of the church.

These reflections on the nature of the church and its catholicity certainly require a thicker notion of salvation. Twentieth-century Baptist thought, expressed prototypically by Mullins, has viewed salvation as an

119. Vincent of Lérins, *Commonitorium* 2.6.

120. Ibid., 2.7–8.

121. "All authentic faith is bound up with the faith of the Church." De Lubac, *Christian Faith*, 191.

122. Ibid., 198. Barth: "With his personal faith, [the Christian] is a member of this body of Christ" (*Doctrine of Reconciliation*, 751).

individual matter between the person and God. Even his attempts to situate the individual within a community place the individual prior to that community. As an alternative, *ressourcement* of ecclesiology necessitates a *ressourcement* of soteriology as well. In other words, salvation needs to dynamically link the personal and the communal. Such a notion of salvation was present in the church fathers and mothers, who saw the Christ event as establishing new possibilities for humanity. As Athanasius of Alexandria stated, "[God], indeed, assumed humanity that we might become God."[123] This concept, derived in part from a scriptural description of humanity's end as becoming "participants of the divine nature" (2 Pet 1:4), has received the label *theosis* (or divinization) and understands Christ's redemptive work not to occur solely at the individual level, with mere social implications (e.g., working for justice, serving the poor) added afterward. Instead, the ties that bind the church together were initiated at the moment that the Word became flesh, inaugurating the transformation of humanity along with all of creation.

Thus, even the resurrection, which for Baptists is often couched in individualistic terms, takes on the character of this thicker ecclesiology. Instead of individual souls who are separately joined to God in heaven one-by-one, we have a robust image of the revivified bones of Israel in Ezekiel 37. While in the vision, the bones of individual skeletons are put together, Harvey writes that the body of the whole itself—the covenant people of God—is also re-membered.[124] In similar fashion, the church is a gathering of its members, but through the breath of God, it is made into one whole, a *catholic* body that is in relationship with the Triune God. This community, also named the Body of Christ (1 Cor 12:27), maintains an intrinsic link with Jesus. The locality of Christ's presence opens out to that which is beyond the local. As John Inscore Essick and Mark Medley state, "The presence of the risen Christ is the place where love abides in vulnerability and generosity; it is a 'locale.'"[125] In other words, Christ does not merely visit places where "two or three are gathered," but he is the local itself. Here we find resonance with Hans Urs von Balthasar's declaration that Jesus is the "concrete universal," the place where the local and the catholic meet and mutually inform one another.[126] In short, as

123. Athanasius, *On the Incarnation of the Word* §54.
124. Harvey, *Can These Bones Live?*, 29–31.
125. Essick and Medley, "Local Catholicity," 55.
126. "[T]he two are identical in God, and in the incarnation of Christ, God is brought into the world. Christ is neither one individual among others, since he is God

Ignatius of Antioch stated, "Wherever Jesus Christ is, there is the catholic church."[127]

What emerges from this discussion of the "Catholic" is not an individual vs. communal dualism, nor a mere juxtaposition of individual and communal that must be "balanced." Instead, there is an intrinsic dynamism that allows the individual and the social to coinhere so that where one is found, so is the other (though not in the same form as the deficient alternatives or counterweights). This notion of a church catholic that serves as more than an aggregate of redeemed individuals is not entirely foreign to Baptist life and thought. In 1678, General Baptists approved the *Orthodox Creed*, which offers a contrast to ecclesiological statements found in twentieth-century Baptist confessions:

> There is only one holy catholick [sic] church, consisting of, or made up of the whole number of the elect, that have been, are, or shall be gathered in one body under Christ, the only head thereof, which church is gathered by special grace, and the powerful and internal work of the spirit, and are effectually united unto Christ their head, and can never fall away.[128]

Indicating that the unity of Christians moves beyond simply the togetherness of living Christians, the General Baptists saw all Christians across time as bound together in the church. The concept of catholicity receives attention as well, with the addition of a key ecclesiological declaration: "[W]e believe the visible church of Christ on earth, is made up of several distinct congregations, which make up that one catholick [sic] church, or mystical body of Christ."[129]

The use of the phrase "mystical body of Christ" highlights a church that is tied together across space and time. Drawing from the scriptural witness of 1 Corinthians 12:12–27 and Ephesians 2:19–22, the individual members of this community do not vanish into the whole but participate in it, and this participation simultaneously forms them into the one body. Joseph Ratzinger echoes this: "The idea of the Catholic, the all-embracing, the inner unity of I and Thou and We does not constitute one chapter

---

and so not susceptible of comparison, nor is he the norm in the sense of a universal, since he is an individual." Balthasar, "Characteristics of Christianity," 170; cf. Essick and Medley, "Local Catholicity," 55.

127. Ignatius of Antioch, *Smyrnaeans* 8.

128. "Orthodox Creed (1678)," art. xxix, in Lumpkin, *Baptist Confessions of Faith*, 318.

129. Ibid., art. xxx, in Lumpkin, *Baptist Confessions of Faith*, 318–19.

of theology among others. It is the key that opens the door to the proper understanding of the whole."[130]

Harvey notes that re-membering of the body of Christ occurs through thick constitutive practices. These practices will do more than remind Christians of their link to other Christians; they will form in them an identity as one singular body.[131] The Eucharist, the remembrance of Christ's death, serves as the paradigmatic practice of this sort.[132] William Cavanaugh explains that the shared performance of this act by numerous local congregations does not signal that multiple Eucharists are performed; there is one celebration of the Eucharist shared by all.[133] Drawing on de Lubac's statement that the Eucharist makes the church, by extension, these same local bodies of believers are not plural churches.[134] As Cavanaugh states, "Each particular church is not an administrative division of a larger whole, but is in itself a 'concentration' of the whole."[135] Thus, instead of an ecclesiology of autonomy that fragments individual congregations from one another, we find one church, in which all localities participate as "the whole" without closing themselves off from "the whole" in other local settings.[136] In 1926, British Baptists articulated an ecclesiology of this sort:

> We believe in the Catholic Church as the holy society of believers in our Lord Jesus Christ, which He founded, of which He is the only Head, and in which He dwells by His Spirit, so that though made up of many communions, organized in various modes, and scattered throughout the world, it is yet one in Him.

---

130. Ratzinger, foreword to *Catholicism*, 11.

131. De Lubac states as much about the sacraments: "Just as redemption and revelation, even though they reach every individual soul, are none the less fundamentally not individual but social, so grace which is produced and maintained by the sacraments does not set up a purely individual relationship between the soul and God or Christ" (*Catholicism*, 82).

132. De Lubac described the Eucharist as the sacrament of ecclesial unity (*sacramentum unitatis ecclesiasticae*) (ibid., 89).

133. "The Eucharist celebrated in the scattered local communities is . . . gathered up into one." Cavanaugh, "World in a Wafer," 190.

134. De Lubac, *Corpus Mysticum*, 88.

135. Cavanaugh, "World in a Wafer," 190.

136. Or, in the words of *Called to Be the One Church*, a 2006 statement by World Council of Churches: "Each church is the Church catholic and not simply part of it. Each church is the Church catholic, but not the whole of it." World Council of Churches, *Called to Be the One Church*, II.6.

> We believe that this holy society is truly to be found wherever companies of believers unite as churches on the ground of a confession of personal faith. Every local community thus constituted is regarded by us as both enabled and responsible for self-government through His indwelling Spirit who supplies wisdom, love, and power, and who, as we believe, leads these communities to associate freely in wider organizations for fellowship and the propagation of the Gospel.[137]

Here, believers are always already situated within a community that is bound together across space and time "where two or three are gathered" (Matt 18:20). And this place is none other than Christ himself, affirming the local gathering, but always opening the particular assembly to participate in the fuller communion with all other gatherings and in the divine fellowship of the Triune God.

—

A dualistic understanding of the relationship between the individual and communal is problematic in Christian theology. That is, both are required, and yet not simply in juxtaposition to one another, as though they have no intrinsic relationship to each other. Despite his perceived historical significance in helping Baptists negotiate the challenges of the fundamentalist-modernist crisis of the first three decades of the twentieth century, Mullins and his ideas—most notably soul competency—leave a troubling present legacy for Baptists' potential for understanding and embracing the church catholic, and they create a practiced ecclesiology that is underwhelming at best and nonexistent at worst. If the church is truly to be the body of Christ, the vision for recognizing this Christ in the visible church has been seriously impaired. Of Mullins, even though he led the Baptist watercraft on "a route through the narrow straits between the crushing rock of common sense rationality and the threatening swirl of experiential religion," Freeman notes that "he made the journey on a calm day." Unfortunately, as he continues, "The seas on which we sail, however, are more turbulent, and the currents are more treacherous."[138] Rougher seas require a more robust vessel (i.e., the church) than that left by soul competency. This means a *ressourcement* that provides a deeper

---

137. "The Baptist Reply to the Lambeth Appeal, adopted by the Annual Assembly, May 4, 1926"; quoted in Payne, *Fellowship of Believers*, 143.

138. Freeman, "E. Y. Mullins and the Siren Songs of Modernity," 37.

understanding of the relationship between the local and the communal, and a quest for that which is genuinely catholic. In the next chapter, we will discuss what this theological *ressourcement* would mean for a significant Baptist conviction like religious liberty.

5

Truth and Freedom

Making Theological Sense of Religious Liberty

> Alyosha had listened in silence; towards the end he was greatly moved and seemed several times on the point of interrupting, but restrained himself. Now his words came with a rush. "But . . . that's absurd!" he cried, flushing. "Your poem is in praise of Jesus, not in blame of Him—as you meant it to be. And who will believe you about freedom? Is that the way to understand it? That's not the idea of it in the Orthodox Church . . . [I]t's false."
>
> —FYODOR DOSTOEVSKY[1]

ONE OF THE SIGNATURE Baptist theological convictions is religious freedom, considered by many to rest at the heart of genuine Baptist life and faith.[2] Indeed, from their beginnings in the seventeenth century, Baptists have held that religious faith should be freely embraced and not coerced. Nonetheless, when pursuing theological renewal, convictions such as religious liberty must be (re)considered under a specifically theological lens. That is, with the rise of democratic institutions and constitutionally granted religious freedom, it is worthwhile to revisit this conviction in its more recent context, especially compared to its Baptist origin. Thus, while religious liberty has appeared in Baptist confessions

---

1. Dostoevsky, *The Brothers Karamazov*, 241.

2. An earlier version of this chapter was published as "George W. Truett and *Dignitatis Humanae*: Searching for a Theological Account of Religious Freedom" in the *Pacific Journal of Baptist Research*.

of faith throughout the centuries, additional attention is needed in order to ensure that it finds its proper theological place within a life of discipleship to Jesus Christ.

In this chapter, Baptists' arguments for religious liberty, exemplified by George W. Truett, will be examined and placed in conversation with the breadth of the Christian tradition. This includes the categories of nature and grace, terms which point to the relation between the created order and God's economy of grace and will clarify the promises and perils of Truett's defense of religious freedom. However, despite this complicated picture, religious liberty remains an important theological conviction, one that can also be retained after (and because of) *ressourcement*. Therefore, after evaluating Truett's account of religious liberty in connection with other twentieth-century conceptions of this idea, a more theological alternative will be found among the documents of the Roman Catholic Church's Second Vatican Council.

Baptists' Struggle for Religious Liberty

In many ways, religious liberty is not only a signature Baptist concept, but it also stands at the heart of their genesis as a tribe. The threat of religious persecution drove a Separatist congregation from Gainsborough, England, to flee to the Netherlands in 1607 under the leadership of John Smyth (c. 1570–1612). Two years later, the church was reconstituted on the basis of believers baptism.[3] In 1611, when Smyth was moving the group closer to a merger with the Waterlanders (Mennonites), Thomas Helwys (1575–1616) led a small remnant back to England to establish in Spitalfields what is usually called the first Baptist church on English soil. In the next year, Helwys published *A Short Declaration of the Mystery of Iniquity*, a copy of which was sent to King James I with a personal note on the flyleaf. In the text of this document, Helwys argued that the king was only an earthly authority who had no control in religious matters since "Christ is King alone."[4] Significantly, Helwys's concern was not merely the

---

3. See McBeth, *Baptist Heritage*, 34–35. Interestingly, in order to have the congregation baptized by someone who had been baptized as a believer, Smyth baptized himself first and then baptized the church (ibid., 36).

4. Helwys, *Short Declaration*, 34. As part of this allegiance to Christ as king, Helwys notes that Jesus rebukes the disciples who wish to call down fire on those who reject Christ: "Here is no sword of justice at all required or permitted to smite any for refusing Christ. Then let not our lord the king suffer his sword of justice . . ." (ibid., 35).

religious convictions of his church, but of all religious faith. Thus, he even defended Roman Catholics by stating that "our lord the king has no more power over their consciences than over ours, and that is none at all."[5] As a result, Helwys understood that "men's religion to God, is between God and themselves. The King shall not answer for it. Neither may the King be judge between God and man. Let them be heretics, Turks, Jews, or whatsoever, it appertains not to the earthly power to punish them in the least measure."[6] Helwys, likely in response to such bold critique of the crown, was imprisoned, where he died in 1616.

In the United States, religious liberty emerged as a central concern for Baptists. Roger Williams (c. 1603–83), though not a Baptist for long, separated from the Puritan-led Massachusetts Bay Colony and founded the first Baptist church on American soil in what is now Providence, Rhode Island in 1639.[7] While still a supporter of compulsory public worship and restrictions on specific religious groups (e.g., Catholics), Isaac Backus (1724–1806) became a staunch opponent of religious taxation (even when granting exemptions for certain religious groups) in Massachusetts as the lead agent for the Grievance Committee of the Warren Association in New England.[8] In Virginia, John Leland (1754–1841) presented a similar case for Baptists in support of religious liberty. In "The Rights of Conscience Inalienable," he argued that "Every man must give an account of himself to God, and therefore every man ought to be at liberty to serve God in a way that he can best reconcile to his conscience ... [R]eligion is a matter between God and individuals."[9] Like his Baptist forebears, Leland extended religious liberty to everyone, noting that

> Government has no more to do with the religious opinions of men, than it has with the principles of mathematics. Let every man speak freely without fear, maintain the principles that he believes, worship according to his own faith, either one God, three Gods, no God, or twenty Gods; and let government

---

5. Ibid., 53.
6. Ibid.
7. Though no longer a Baptist when he wrote them, Williams's views of religious liberty were published in *The Bloudy Tenent of Persecution* (1644) and *The Bloudy Tenent Yet More Bloudy* (1652).
8. See Bebbington, *Baptists Through the Centuries*, 204.
9. Leland, "Rights of Conscience Inalienable," 179.

protect him in so doing, i.e., see that he meets with no personal abuse, or loss of property, for his religious opinions.[10]

Leland's strong stance in this text and others fed and grew from events of the period. The Virginia Declaration of Rights (1776) granted free exercise of religion and the Virginia Statute on Religious Freedom (1786) broadened this right to full liberty of worship, all of which shaped the contours of the First Amendment in the United States Bill of Rights (1791).[11]

In the twentieth century, Baptists have seen religious liberty as a "distinctive" Baptist characteristic, with several Baptist groups combining their efforts to create the Baptist Joint Committee on Public Affairs in 1946 (since 2005, the Baptist Joint Committee on Religious Liberty). While there have been many Baptist advocates for religious freedom, perhaps George W. Truett (1867–1944) can be hailed as its most prominent voice. Indeed, along with the Baptist Joint Committee's J. M. Dawson and James M. Dunn, Truett, who spent his entire career as a pastor, stands as the face of this distinctive Baptist emphasis.[12] The details of Truett's life, including his fundraising efforts to save Baylor University, his dedication to the founding of Baylor Hospital in Dallas, and his long pastorate at First Baptist Church in Dallas, have been masterfully narrated in two biographies, one by his son-in-law, Powhatan James, and a recent volume by Keith Durso.[13] Of course, no event cemented George W. Truett's legacy in Baptist and even American life more than his speech on the United States Capitol steps on May 16, 1920,[14] which occurred during that year's Southern Baptist Convention annual meeting.[15] Historian

---

10. Ibid., 180.

11. See Bebbington, *Baptists Through the Centuries*, 204–6.

12. For more on Dawson, see his *Baptists and the American Republic*; for more on Dunn, see Weaver, *James M. Dunn and Soul Freedom*.

13. James, *George W. Truett*; Durso, *Thy Will Be Done*.

14. Cf. Gambrell, "A Historic Address"; Truett, "Baptists and Religious Liberty." This sermon has been reprinted several times. See Truett, "Baptists and Religious Liberty (1998)"; Truett, "Baptists and Religious Liberty," in Shurden, *Proclaiming the Baptist Vision*, 61–84. References here will come from the original version.

15. This moment was re-enacted on June 29, 2007 at the Baptist Unity Rally for Religious Liberty at Fountain Plaza of Upper Senate Park, near the Capitol Building in Washington D.C. The event, sponsored by the Baptist Joint Committee on Religious Liberty, included some remarks by several United States Congressmen and the recitation of portions of the 1920 sermon by nine Baptists. See Pierce, "Truett's Famed Religious Liberty Sermon Celebrated by Baptists in Nation's Capital."

Walter Shurden notes that this address is "one of the most often quoted Baptist statements on religious liberty of the twentieth century."[16] In this way, without forgetting his primary vocation in the pastorate, Truett's influence extends beyond his ecclesial role to the life of Baptists throughout the United States, as is indicated by the numerous buildings and institutions throughout the United States that bear his name.[17] This can also be readily observed in the number of references to Truett when one broaches the subjects of religious freedom and separation of church and state. He becomes, then, an important site for Baptist life and thought on the subject of religious liberty and worthy of further attention.

Truett and Religious Liberty

After a rousing corporate singing of "My Country, 'Tis of Thee," Truett delivered that 1920 address, entitled "Baptists and Religious Liberty," to a tremendous audience.[18] One of his most memorable statements from the speech was that "the supreme contribution of the new world to the old is the contribution of religious liberty. This is the chiefest [sic] contribution that America has thus far made to civilization. And historic justice compels me to say that it was pre-eminently a Baptist contribution."[19] Truett's speech remains one of the hallmarks of Baptist advocacy in this area. Virtually all articles and book chapters on the subject of Baptists and religious liberty at least mention this speech, and several treatments are relatively lengthy. In a note at the conclusion of the 1998 reprinting of Truett's address, an editor of *Baptist History and Heritage* declared that Truett's words from the Capitol steps are "a powerful statement of Baptist beliefs," and that they "[remind] Baptists of foundational principles and [defend] them eloquently and passionately."[20] Thus, Truett is generally remembered as a prominent exemplar of this "Baptist distinctive," one that has increasingly been elevated by some Baptists. Not surprisingly,

---

16. Shurden, introduction to *Proclaiming the Baptist Vision*, 5.

17. For example, Truett-McConnell College in Cleveland, Georgia; Truett Auditorium at Southwestern Baptist Theological Seminary in Fort Worth, Texas; and George W. Truett Theological Seminary on the campus of Baylor University in Waco, Texas.

18. James, *George W. Truett*, 1–2. Cf. Dawson, *Baptists and the American Republic*, 22; Stephens, "At Washington with the Southern Baptists."

19. Truett, "Baptists and Religious Liberty," 32.

20. See editor's note in Truett, "Baptists and Religious Liberty (1998)," 85.

Truett's address is congruent with several aspects of Baptist discourse at that time. Within the speech itself and Truett's thought as a whole, a love of democratic freedom emerges as paramount, one that dovetails nicely with Truett's (and prevailing Baptist) thought about personal salvation.[21]

For Truett, personal salvation places the focus on the individual who privately believes. He saw this emphasis as grounded in the Bible, stating, "When we turn to this New Testament, which is Christ's guidebook and law for His people, we find that supreme emphasis is everywhere put upon the individual."[22] Moreover, Truett elevated the individual's ability to read and interpret for him or herself, describing this as a right that was anthropologically and christologically grounded: "The right to private judgment is the crown jewel of humanity, and for any person or institution to dare to come between the soul and God is a blasphemous impertinence and a defamation of the crown rights of the Son of God."[23] Ultimately, along with fellow Southern Baptist E. Y. Mullins, Truett advocated for a direct approach to God: "Everyone must give account of himself to God. There can be no sponsors or deputies or proxies in such a vital matter."[24] Consequently, religious liberty was firmly grounded in the freedom of the individual's conscience to pursue voluntary and uncoerced belief (or lack of belief), a point that Truett makes in contrasting absolute liberty to toleration.[25]

Spurning any ecclesiology that produced a hierarchy of authority, Truett saw democracy as the hope of the church: "Christ's church is not only a spiritual body but it is also a pure democracy, all its members being equal."[26] Viewed through his focus on individualism in religion, Truett underwrites a form of political atomism, where each person and his or her actions are to be isolated as much as possible. In this way, liberty of conscience indicates that no other person can determine the truth for

---

21. See Canipe, "Echoes of Baptist Democracy," 418.

22. Truett, "Baptists and Religious Liberty," 38.

23. Ibid., 39.

24. Ibid., 38. Truett stated in 1939: "The late President Mullins . . . affirms the competency of the individual, under God, in matters of religion . . . Religion is a matter of personal relationship between the soul and God, and nothing extraneous may properly intrude here" ("Baptist Message and Mission," 113).

25. "Toleration implies that somebody falsely claims the right to tolerate. Toleration is a concession, while liberty is a right. Toleration is a gift from man, while liberty is a gift from God." Truett, "Baptists and Religious Liberty," 33.

26. Ibid., 42.

another, which is why toleration of others' religious beliefs is insufficient. Thus, Truett labeled the Protestant Reformation as an "arrested development," because the Reformers "turned out to be persecutors like the Papacy before them."[27] For him, then, the United States, despite retaining some of the remnants of church-state union, became a truly remarkable site where genuine religious and civil liberty could take root and flourish as the fruits of democracy. This, according to Truett, was "pre-eminently a Baptist achievement."[28]

Truett understood separation of church and state to produce two separate realms with different functions.[29] After dividing the functions of church and state, he notes the implications of this division for Christians: "We are members of the two realms, the civil and the religious, and are faithfully to render unto each all that each should receive at our hands."[30] Consequently, each person has responsibilities to fulfill in both the religious and the civil realms. According to Truett, one does not supersede the other. Moreover, he does not indicate that these two realms will ever conflict with one another. That is, once separated, the state will never tread on the church's liberty.

With his emphasis on democracy over autocracy, both the civil and the religious arenas are constituted by individuals who participate in two different democracies, one for citizens and the other for believers. Truett's argument for the separation of church and state resonates quite strongly with the work of English philosopher John Locke (1632–1704). That is, even though no evidence can be provided that Truett actually read Locke, when viewed alongside one another, Locke clarifies and sharpens Truett's argument for religious liberty, perhaps standing far in the background of Truett's thought (i.e., influencing those whom Truett did read).

Locke argued that church and state should be understood as separate entities: "There is a twofold society, of which almost all men in the world are members, and that from the twofold concernment they have to attain a twofold happiness: viz. that of this world and that of the other: and hence there arises these two following societies, viz. religious and

27. Ibid., 48.
28. Ibid., 50.
29. Ibid., 43. To make this point, Truett references Matthew 22:21 ("Give therefore to the emperor the things that are the emperor's, and to God the things that are God's") and John 18:36 ("My kingdom is not from this world").
30. Ibid., 53.

civil."[31] Following this statement, Locke systematically details the difference between "religious society, or the church" and "civil society, or the state," linking the civil sphere to the operations of the state and the religious sphere to the church.[32] In addition, Locke argues that the political point of departure (i.e., the state of nature) was one of individuality. Society, then, is constructed when "individuals come together on the basis of a social *contract*, each individual entering society in order to protect person and property."[33]

Two important points emerge from this discussion. First, civil government cannot decide on the truth of various religious claims since they are internal to each individual.[34] Second, religion is grounded in the individual who has been convinced of the truth of a particular tradition.[35] Because of this, churches serve as associations of like-minded people, choosing to assemble with one another for worship, an understanding which serves to undercut any substantive social nature of the church.[36] Finally, Locke's political philosophy offers a body/soul dichotomy,[37] articulating church/state separation so as to locate all genuine political activity in the state-centered public arena (i.e., as statecraft), leaving the church as an (apparently) apolitical, private entity concerned only for the salvation of souls.[38]

---

31. Locke, "Civil and Ecclesiastical Power," 300.

32. Ibid.

33. Cavanaugh, *Theopolitical Imagination*, 17. Cavanaugh notes that a less palatable, though logically similar, description of this state of nature comes from Thomas Hobbes, who argues for individual freedom and equality of all human beings by stating that human beings are in a state of "war of all against all" (ibid.).

34. Locke did, however, argue against religious toleration for Catholics and atheists.

35. "All the life and power of true religion consists in the inward and full persuasion of the mind." Locke, "Letter Concerning Toleration," 219.

36. "A church . . . I take to be a voluntary society of [people], joining themselves together of their own accord in order to the public worshipping of God" (ibid., 220).

37. "The care of souls cannot belong to the civil magistrate, because his power consists only in outward force, but true and saving religion consists in the inward persuasion of the mind . . ." (ibid., 219).

38. Locke exhibited confidence that this separation would preclude any conflicts between the civil and religious realms: "[I]f each of them [i.e., church and state] would contain itself within its own bounds, the one attending to the worldly welfare of the commonwealth, the other to the salvation of souls, it is impossible that any discord should ever have happened between them" (ibid., 251).

Echoing Locke, Truett argues that church and state must never be joined because the individual's liberty of conscience would be violated. He also employs a separation between body and soul, implying that responsibilities to the state are bodily while those of religion relate to the soul. For instance, while he consistently writes of the soul's uninhibited relation with God, Truett also identifies the causes worthy of giving one's physical life: "The sanctity of womanhood is worth dying for. The safety of childhood is worth dying for . . . The integrity of one's country is worth dying for. *And, please God, the freedom and honour of the United States is worth dying for.*"[39] Curiously, Truett does not mention the Christian faith as worthy of similar bodily sacrifice.

With this divide between the body and soul, the church is left with no concerns for external (i.e., "worldly") affairs, only with saving souls. The church, as seen with Locke, is constituted as an association of like-minded individuals. Not surprisingly, Truett views Baptists as remarkably good citizens: "Happily, the record of our Baptist people toward civil government has been a record of unfading honour. Their love and loyalty to country have not been put to shame in any land."[40] Indeed, Truett does not seem to allow for the possibility that church and state might be counterposed, that love for country could come into conflict with love for Christ. Thus, rather than viewing them as opponents, he discusses the missions of church and state by using the same terminology, setting them up as parallel entities: "Democracy is the goal toward which all feet are travelling [sic], whether in state or in church."[41] Freedom, then, is the rhetorical link between the civil and religious spheres, as one scholar has noted: "Baptists stood for freedom in the spiritual realm, America stood for freedom in the political realm."[42] In other words, Truett was fully Baptist and fully American, indicating that the temporal and spiritual realms were separate, even if they were also parallel.

---

39. Truett, "Baptists and Religious Liberty," 57; emphasis added.

40. Ibid., 53.

41. Ibid., 65. In another sermon, he writes that democracy "is the goal for this world of ours—both the political goal and the religious goal." Truett, "Prayer Jesus Refused to Pray," 43.

42. Canipe, "Echoes of Baptist Democracy," 420.

John Courtney Murray and Religious Liberty

Despite the observed problems with Truett's understanding of religious liberty, this does not mean that the concept need be abandoned altogether. Rather, a path toward an alternative might require additional conversation partners, such as American Jesuit John Courtney Murray (1904–1967). At first glance, however, placing Truett in conversation with a Catholic thinker might seem strange. In fact, as discussed in chapter 2, Truett and many of his Baptist (and Protestant) coreligionists were suspicious of Catholicism. That is to say, while his ideas cannot be reduced to mere anti-Catholicism, Truett was certainly representative of the pervasive Baptist anti-Catholic sentiments of the nineteenth and twentieth centuries.[43] Therefore, before discussing Murray's account of religious liberty, it is necessary to briefly describe the attitudes about Catholics shared by Truett and most Baptists of his time.

Extending from his emphasis on individualism, which he positioned against "absolutism," Truett saw democracy as opposed to what he considered to be autocracy, with little possibility for compromise. Even within the famous 1920 address, Truett saw the Catholic Church as antithetical to Baptist and even American ideals: "The Roman Catholic message is sacerdotal, sacramentarian and ecclesiastical . . . The Baptist message is non-sacerdotal, non-sacramentarian and non-ecclesiastical."[44] Consequently, Truett counterposed the Catholic dogma of papal infallibility to individual interpretation of the New Testament.[45] According

---

43. For more information, see Canipe, *Baptist Democracy*, 138–39.

44. Truett, "Baptists and Religious Liberty," 36; such words were repeated in 1939 at the Sixth Baptist World Congress. See Truett, "Baptist Message and Mission," 112.

45. "You recall that in the midst of all the tenseness and tumult of that excited assemblage [at the First Vatican Council], Cardinal Manning stood on an elevated platform, and in the paper just passed, declaring for the infallibility of the Pope, said, 'Let all the world go to bits and we will reconstruct it on this paper' . . . But what is the answer of a Baptist to the contention made by the Catholic for papal infallibility? Holding aloft a little book, the name of which is the New Testament, and without any hesitation or doubt, the Baptist shouts his battle cry: 'Let all the world go to bits and we will reconstruct it on the New Testament.'" Truett, "Baptists and Religious Liberty," 37–38. It should be pointed out that the First Vatican Council did not initiate the Catholic understanding of papal infallibility; it dogmatically defined it. Further, the definition issued requirements that restrict the papal statements that are considered to be infallibly promulgated. That is, the definition of papal infallibility of 1870, while it was intended to solidify the papacy as an authoritative arbiter of ecclesial disputes, actually made it possible for Catholics to better distinguish between infallible statements and those that were authoritative to a lesser degree.

to Truett, not only did papal infallibility threaten unimpeded individual access to God by solidifying the place of the pope and the episcopal hierarchy as obstacles between the individual and God, but it also stood as a constituent part of the barrier to democratic religious freedom presented by the Catholic Church. Thus, Catholicism stands as the prime example of autocracy (of a spiritual variety) that is to be avoided.

In a 1939 speech in Atlanta, Truett elaborated: "Baptists are in conscience compelled to reject and oppose sacerdotalism that puts a priest between a soul and Christ; and sacramentarianism that makes external ordinances in themselves vehicles of grace; and ecclesiasticism that puts a church between a sinner and salvation."[46] In short, even though Truett (echoing his Baptist forebears) defended Catholics' ability to practice their faith without imposing it on others, he saw Catholicism as in error and viewed Catholics as an "other" that stood on the fringe of (American) society.[47]

Further, Truett's views were not unique. They were also represented by the work of his friend J. M. Dawson and the Baptist Joint Committee on Public Affairs (BJCPA), where opposition to Catholicism was a prime concern during the first half of the twentieth century. According to Baptist historian Robert Torbet, the offices of the BJCPA were "strategically located where there is need for Baptists to defend religious liberty by raising their voices against encroachments of the state upon the church, and against what Baptists regard as Roman Catholic aggression in behalf of sectarianism in education and political favor."[48] Truett and many of his Baptist contemporaries held suspicions about Catholics in the United States, wondering if they "really believed" in the separation of church and state, concerns that some Catholics constantly felt obligated to refute,[49]

46. Truett, "Baptist Message and Mission," 112.

47. Recent Baptist scholars have attempted to distance themselves from Truett's apparent anti-Catholic sentiments. See the editor's note in Truett, "Baptists and Religious Liberty (1998)," 85; and Shurden, introduction to *Proclaiming the Baptist Vision*, 5–6. While Canipe is dubious of these attempts to "decontextualize Truett's remarks in the name of ecumenism" ("Echoes of Baptist Democracy," 430 n. 34), J. David Holcomb has offered a more sustained defense of Truett. See "A Millstone Hanged about His Neck?"

48. Torbet, *History of the Baptists*, 455. Much of the concerns in this era centered on two Supreme Court cases, *Everson v. Board of Education* (1947) and *McCollum v. Board of Education* (1948). For more on these cases, see McGreevy, *Catholicism and American Freedom*, 183–85.

49. John Courtney Murray seemed to know this experience well: "It is customary

and some stated that those who did not hold to strict separation had "failed to become thoroughly Americanized."[50]

With this background, engagement with Murray may proceed. Educated both in the United States and in Rome, he taught dogmatic theology at Woodstock College in Maryland from 1937 to 1967. During much of this time, he was the editor of *Theological Studies*, the Jesuit theological journal.[51] A prolific writer, Murray was subjected to suspicion in the United States and in Rome for his positions concerning church and state. In 1955, his Jesuit superiors asked him to cease writing on the topic.[52] Ultimately, he and his legacy were perceived as vindicated when he was welcomed as a theological expert at the Second Vatican Council.[53] Interestingly, in contrast to Truett, Murray argued for engagement with the American sense of separation of church and state in a manner that was structured similarly.

Murray attempted to shift Catholic conversations about the relationship between church and state. Previously, church teaching had preferred an established union between church and state. In the *Syllabus of Errors* (1864), Pope Pius IX condemned the idea that church and state should be separate from one another.[54] The situation in Europe in the nineteenth century contributed to such a stance by the Catholic Church. Disestablishment of church and state in France resulted in radical anticlerical sentiment that challenged any sizeable presence of the church in the region. Meanwhile in Germany, Chancellor Otto von Bismarck's Kulturkampf brought restrictions on Catholic activities in that country. In light of these challenges, what developed among Catholic scholars was an understanding of church/state relations where the ideal construal, or the "thesis," was an established church/state union, but certain, limited historical circumstances could produce an acceptable alternative, or

---

to put to Catholics what is supposed to be an embarrassing question: Do you really believe in the first two provisions of the First Amendment?" (*We Hold These Truths*, 62).

50. Dawson, "Temptations of the Churches," 6.

51. Komonchak, "Murray, John Courtney (1904–67)."

52. McGreevy, *Catholicism and American Freedom*, 208.

53. For a sympathetic and more detailed account of Murray's life and work, see Pelotte, *John Courtney Murray*.

54. Pius IX, *Syllabus of Errors* §55.

"hypothesis."[55] Murray, in no way straying from his Catholic training,[56] argued that different philosophical and historical influences stood behind the intellectual traditions of various forms of non-Catholic states. As Joseph Komonchak notes,

> [Murray] distinguished an Anglo-Saxon liberal tradition whose roots he found in the medieval tradition and whose distinction between the *duo genera* of societies, the church and the civil order, was quite compatible with the Catholic insistence on the public significance and necessity of religion. Continental liberalism, on the other hand, was the heir of the absolutism of the *ancien régime* and understood the separation of church and state to imply the irrelevance of religion to the public order and the sole right of the state to control all aspects of public life.[57]

Thus, based on philosophical differences as well as historical factors (e.g., the United States did not have or shed an established church in the same manner as France or Germany), the United States' liberal philosophy was not the same as that of Europe. Popes and prelates were right to be worried about the European context, but "failed to take note of the quite different philosophy underlying the liberal tradition that inspired the American political experiment."[58] In other words, concerned that democracy in its American form was wrongly demonized because of abuses in European countries, Murray argued that democratically based separation of church and state need not always present a danger to the church.

---

55. William Portier notes that this distinction originated with Félix Dupanloup (1802–78), a French bishop, in response to the *Syllabus of Errors*, an interpretation that was commended by Pius IX. Portier, "Theology of Manners," 85.

56. Philip Gleason states that Murray was "thoroughly Catholic, for though he applied the resources of Neoscholasticism in new and creative ways, his thinking was steeped in the Thomism that had been the official Catholic philosophy since Leo XIII's *Aeterni Patris* of 1879" ("American Catholics and Liberalism, 1789–1960," 66).

57. Komonchak, "Vatican II and the Encounter between Catholicism and Liberalism," 85–86.

58. Ibid., 86. For example, in commenting on a portion (§6) of Pope Leo XIII's *Longinqua Oceani* (1895) where he discusses the American system of church/state separation ("[I]t would be very erroneous to draw the conclusion that in America is to be sought the type of the most desirable status of the Church, or that it would be universally lawful or expedient for State and Church to be, as in America, dissevered and divorced."), Murray argues that Leo maintains a distinction, based on a dyarchy established by Pope Gelasius I, that there are two forms of authority, spiritual and temporal (or divine and human law). See Murray, "Leo XIII and Pius XII," 86–89.

Murray's primary text on issues of church and state, *We Hold These Truths: Catholic Reflections on the American Proposition* (1960), was a collection of Murray's work gathered from the 1950s (though some articles were later revised). In the second chapter, originally published as "The Problem of Pluralism in America,"[59] Murray avers that the First Amendment of the American Constitution should be read as "Articles of Peace" rather than "Articles of Faith." To read the First Amendment as "Articles of Faith" is to see it as "dogmas, norms of orthodoxy, to which one must conform on pain of some manner of excommunication . . . It is necessary to believe them, to give them a religiously motivated assent."[60]

In contrast, an "Articles of Peace" reading of the First Amendment declares that "these constitutional clauses have no religious content . . . [T]hey are not invested with the sanctity that attaches to dogma, but only with the rationality that attaches to law . . . [I]t is not necessary to give them a religious assent but only a rational civil obedience."[61] In other words, an "Articles of Peace" reading of the First Amendment would offer something like a "public discourse" that would not seek to restrict the activities of various groups in the name of freedom. In a claim directed toward the positions of people like Truett and Dawson, Murray states that the "Articles of Faith" reading has historical roots in free church Protestantism. In many ways, Murray can be seen as mounting a historical argument against those, such as Baptists, who would hold up someone like Roger Williams as the "original theologian of the First Amendment."[62] To do so, in Murray's eyes, would insert a free church ecclesiology into the United States Constitution and allow "an outstanding Baptist spokesperson" to speak of public schools as agents of "the Americanization of the churches," tacitly placing Baptist life and thought at the heart of being American.[63]

Much of Murray's argument involved what he perceived to be the difference between the American and French contexts, essentially

---

59. Murray, "The Problem of Pluralism in America."
60. Murray, *We Hold These Truths*, 62.
61. Ibid.
62. Ibid., 68.
63. In "The Problem of Pluralism in America," Murray names "the Reverend Joseph Martin Dawson" as this spokesperson (189). Dawson stated this in *America's Way in Church, State, and Society*, 15–16. For more on Murray's criticism of Dawson, see Hughson, "From James Madison to William Lee Miller," 23–28.

stating that their revolutions were godly and godless, respectively.[64] In fact, Murray states that the American Revolution was "less a revolution than a conservation" of the liberal tradition of politics.[65] Murray notes that hostility toward religion characterized French society under Jacobin rule.[66] Beginning with the 1905 Act of Separation of Church and State, the French Third Republic inaugurated a period known as *la separation*, creating a sharp divide not only between religion and the state, but also between Catholicism and culture as well as faith and reason.[67]

Within the United States, however, political unity and stability were maintained, even as democratic processes and institutions were embraced:

> [T]he American Republic was rescued from the fate, still not overcome, that fell upon the European nations in which Continental Liberalism, a deformation of the liberal tradition, lodged itself . . . There have never been "two Americas," in the sense in which there have been, and still are, "two Frances," "two Italys," "two Spains." Politically speaking, America has always been one.[68]

Murray rightly identifies crucial differences between the American and French contexts, even commenting on the divergent philosophical foundations of both places: "The Jacobin tradition proclaimed the autonomous reason of man to be the first and the sole principle of political organization. In contrast, the first article of the American political faith is that the political community, as a form of free and ordered human life, looks to the sovereignty of God as the first principle of its organization."[69] As a result, by beginning with the formative ground of the community rather than the autonomous individual person, Murray distinguishes

---

64. "The first truth to which the American Proposition makes appeal is stated in that landmark of Western political theory, the Declaration of Independence . . . I mean the sovereignty of God over nations as well as over individual men. This is the principle that radically distinguishes the conservative Christian tradition of America from the Jacobin laicist tradition of Continental Europe." Murray, *We Hold These Truths*, 44.

65. Ibid., 46.

66. Jaime Balmes offers a similar contrast between the American and French revolutions. Cf. *European Civilization*, 389.

67. Joseph Komonchak has described these circumstances as theology being in exile, drawing on Marie-Dominique Chenu's term, a Christianity of émigrés. See "Returning from Exile."

68. Murray, *We Hold These Truths*, 47.

69. Ibid., 44.

the United States from other countries, pointing out that America has not historically experienced the "militant atheism" found elsewhere, despite the fact that the United States has been populated by a significant number of non-Christians.[70] Moreover, even though what Murray calls "sectarian liberalism" animated continental European countries that held anti-religious views, Murray argued that it actually put forth a theological argument.[71] By contrast, the American system is "simply political."[72]

In the end, Murray views the United States as constituted by a consensus that binds together the American political community, so that the First Amendment does not underwrite any form of quasi-religious establishment (i.e., the "Articles of Faith" rendering of the First Amendment) and is directed toward the good of social peace. Moreover, while for Murray church and state were separate, church and society were not. Murray pointed to the religious character of the United States as evidence that the church was unencumbered by establishment issues there.[73] That is, separation of church and state (as constructed in the United States) does not silence the church, but actually accomplishes the same goals as concordats with national governments, namely, the founding of a stable place for the church within society and the independence of the church to pursue its mission.[74] Indeed, Murray writes that Catholics should not merely accept American ideas of religious freedom and the separation of church and state, but they should welcome them as a breath of fresh air: "For Catholics this fact [the American distinction between church and state] is of great and providential importance for one major reason. It serves sharply to set off our constitutional system from the system against which the Church waged its long-drawn-out fight in the nineteenth century, namely, Jacobinism, or . . . totalitarian democracy."[75] Thus, for Murray, the separation of church and state cannot be seen as an idol, an object of faith, or even an ecclesiology (as in the "Articles of Faith"

---

70. Ibid., 45.

71. Ibid., 77. "The Jacobin thesis was basically philosophical; it derived from a sectarian concept of the autonomy of reason. It was also theological, as implying a sectarian concept of religion and of the church" (ibid., 78).

72. Ibid.

73. Ibid., 73.

74. Ibid., 79.

75. Ibid., 77.

interpretation), but it certainly (in its American instantiation, at least) provides the possibility for the church to thrive.[76]

Murray's understanding of separation of church and state within the American context maintains natural law as crucial. While only a few Catholics were among the founders of the United States, Murray—echoing the Third Plenary Council of Baltimore (1884)—argued that the predominantly Protestant founders of the American constitution were "building better than they knew,"[77] constructing a political context that was thoroughly informed by Catholic natural law, even if that influence was unacknowledged.[78] This providential development enabled Catholics to give an account for the existing American consensus in which they could participate.

Furthermore, Murray counters the notion that natural law cannot be employed within the American context if one does not accept its Catholic underpinnings by arguing for a form of natural law without Catholic presuppositions that is aimed at developing and maintaining a public consensus.[79] The United States is unique in its ability to foster this consensus by not arguing about final ends:

> In America, we have been rescued from the disaster of ideological parties . . . It has been remarked that only in a disintegrating society does politics become a controversy over ends; it should be simply a controversy over means to ends already agreed

---

76. Ibid., 86.

77. This phrase and its variants have a significant role in American Catholic history, though this trajectory begins with Ralph Waldo Emerson's 1839 poem, "The Problem" ("builded better than he knew", ln. 23). American Catholic convert Orestes Brownson invoked the phrase in his 1856 essay, "The Mission of America," stating that the founders of the United States "did not follow their Protestantism. They were bravely inconsequent, and 'builded better than they knew'" (569). In the pastoral letter of the Third Plenary Council of Baltimore in 1884, a variant of the phrase was used, again emphasizing a providential fit between the United States and the Catholic Church: "We consider the establishment of our country's independence, the shaping of its liberties and laws as a work of special Providence, its framers 'building wiser than they knew,' the Almighty's hand guiding them" ("Pastoral Letter of the Third Plenary Council of Baltimore," 20).

78. "[T]he American political community was organized in an era when the tradition of natural law and natural rights was still vigorous." Murray, *We Hold These Truths*, 46. Murray goes as far as calling Thomas Aquinas "the first Whig" (ibid., 47).

79. The only presuppositions of Murray's conception of natural law are (1) human beings are intelligent, (2) reality is intelligible, and (3) when reality is grasped by intelligence, it imposes the obligation that it be obeyed on the will (ibid., 111).

on with sufficient unanimity. The Latin countries of Europe have displayed this spectacle of ideological politics, a struggle between a host of "isms," all of which pretend to a final view of man and society, with the twin results of governmental paralysis and seemingly irremediable social division. In contrast, the American experience of political unity has been striking . . . To this experience of political unity the First Amendment has made a unique contribution; and in doing so it has qualified as good law.[80]

In other words, Murray understands substantive discussions about final ends to threaten the fabric of a society. The United States has structurally avoided such problems while, according to Murray, pursuing a public peace. In *We Hold These Truths*, he calls this "the common good in its various aspects."[81]

Reading Murray, Reading Truett

Despite the ways that Murray is helpful in pointing out the deficiencies in Truett's position, Murray's stance is problematic as well, though for different reasons.[82] Murray was positioned against the leading neo-scholastic theologians of the day, but when one looks at Murray's work in its broader theological context, one discovers that "[his] project was fundamentally an exercise in the distinction of realms; as such, it assumed the traditional dualities of nature and grace, secular and sacred, temporal and spiritual."[83] In other words, Murray, like many neo-scholastics, maintained an extrinsic relationship between nature and grace that held both realms apart from one another. Drawing on a Suarezian interpretation of Aquinas, Murray writes, "Grace perfects nature, does not destroy it—this is the central point of emphasis. There is indeed a radical discontinuity between nature and grace, but nature does not therefore become irrelevant to grace."[84]

---

80. Ibid., 82.

81. Ibid., 73.

82. In this section, I am indebted to the work of David L. Schindler for his pointed critique of Murray. See Schindler, *Heart of the World, Center of the Church*.

83. Gleason, "American Catholics and Liberalism, 1789–1960," 67.

84. Murray, *We Hold These Truths*, 176–77. Cf. Aquinas, *Summa Theologiae* Ia, q. 1, art. 8, ad. 2.

This "radical discontinuity" moves beyond simply distinguishing the orders of nature and grace and granting each a sense of relative autonomy. Indeed, Murray writes that the Second Vatican Council's *Dignitatis Humanae* (Declaration on Religious Freedom) establishes the idea that "the aim and object of the action of the Church in the world today" is "[n]ot nostalgic yearnings to restore ancient sacralizations, not futile efforts to find new forms of sacralizing the terrestrial and temporal order in its structures and processes, but the purification of these processes and structures and the sure direction of them to their *inherently secular ends*."[85] The church, then, is not tasked with pursuing a supernatural end within society, but only natural ends. David L. Schindler explains how this positions nature and grace extrinsically by contrasting Murray with Henri de Lubac:

> For Murray, grace's influence on nature takes the form of assisting nature to realize its own finality; the ends proper to grace and nature otherwise remain each in its own sphere. For de Lubac, on the contrary, grace's influence takes the form of directing nature from within to serve the end given in grace; the ends proper to grace and nature remain distinct, even as the natural end is placed *within*, internally subordinated to, the supernatural end.[86]

The emphasis here must be placed not on the number of ends or *teloi*, but on their relationship. Murray's argument situates the temporal and spiritual realms with distinct ends that are parallel to one another, creating dual final ends. Recall that de Lubac never stated that humanity only had one end; rather, he argued that there was one *final* end—communion with God. Schindler points out as much, underscoring the intrinsic and ordered relationship between the role of citizen and the role of believer: "For de Lubac . . . the call to sanctity 'comprehends' the call to citizenship. The eternal end 'comprehends' the temporal ends."[87]

While helpful for Murray's argument for church/state separation, this dualism threatens to undermine his gains since a dichotomy between the spiritual and temporal realms (and their corresponding ultimate and penultimate ends) results in a duality between citizen and believer. That is, as Schindler argues, instead of one integrated civilization (which is,

---

85. Murray, "Declaration on Religious Freedom," 193; emphasis added.
86. Schindler, *Heart of the World*, 79.
87. Ibid.

in fact, Murray's aim by invoking the American consensus and focusing on civil society), two civilizations exist: "One is a civilization wherein citizenship is to be suffused with sanctity; the other, a civilization wherein sanctity is always something to be (privately/hiddenly) added to citizenship."[88] Murray's argument for natural law without Catholic presuppositions reinforces this extrinsic construal of the relationship between nature and grace. The result is what one scholar describes Murray's natural law as a "kind of separate, free-standing philosophical position to which grace or theology is superadded."[89]

Murray's goal was to theoretically establish space for public consensus. This is why he admired the United States' lack of controversy (and discourse) concerning ultimate ends. According to Michael Baxter, Murray viewed American constitutionalism, founded on a separation of the spiritual and temporal realms, as "cultivat[ing] a distinctively non-ideological form of politics, one in which Catholics, Protestants, Jews, and members of other religious or secular groups, are able to unite in order to develop a public discourse concerning the common good of society as a whole."[90] This was intended to free Catholics in the United States to enter into dialogue with their fellow countrymen (and women) about what was best for their homeland. However, because it is devoid of any reference to final ends (e.g., the formative role of society, the purpose of the state), it is unclear whether the common dialogue is heard in the same manner by all participants, or if all are in fact able to participate.

Additionally, Murray's argument for public consensus employs terms (e.g., common good, peace, and natural law) that originally had Catholic underpinnings and were directed toward and shaped by a supernatural end. Murray's new formulations of these terms removed any supernatural teleology. Instead, society pursues a public peace or a common good that is completely natural. Thus, because Murray wanted to affirm public peace as a good, though not one informed by final ends or ordered in any supernatural direction, he was left with the mere absence of conflict as a significant portion of the substance and goal of such "peace." Consequently, Murray's specific political arguments are sometimes indistinguishable from American public and foreign policy.[91]

88. Ibid., 80.
89. Portier, "Theology of Manners," 101.
90. Baxter, "Writing History in a World Without Ends," 445.
91. For example, in chapter 11 of *We Hold These Truths*, Murray, as he aims to promote appropriate uses of military technology, addresses the use of force in global

What emerges from Murray's construal of the public sphere is a conception of freedom that is "non-confessional." In other words, it is not intended to achieve any specific goal other than non-interference. Schindler describes this notion of freedom as juridical-negative (i.e., freedom *from*), coinciding with Murray's development of natural law as disconnected from any confessional (i.e., Catholic) foundation.[92] Murray himself states as much:

> Religious freedom is obviously not the Pauline *elutheria*, the freedom wherewith Christ has made us free (Gal 5:1). This is a freedom of the theological order, an empowerment that man receives by grace. In contrast, religious freedom is an affair of the social and civil order; it is an immunity that attaches to the human person within society, and it has its guarantee in civil law.[93]

One wonders at this point what sort of freedom is gained for the church within American constitutionalism. That is, does the church, as Murray claimed, have social and political space to pursue its mission or is it reduced to virtual silence by having its theological content (because it inherently concerns final ends) excluded from the public discourse? Schindler rightly thinks the latter is the case: "Murray's (putative) purely juridical definition of religious freedom serves, notwithstanding his explicit intention to the contrary, to dispose society logically toward an 'indifferent' nature and away from a nature always-already positively oriented toward God."[94]

In the end, what are lost in Murray's understanding of freedom are the culture-forming aspects of grace. Even as he is sympathetic to Murray's goals, Komonchak posits,

---

politics, including the utilization of "ABC warfare" (atomic, biological, and chemical weapons), noting that "force is still the *ultima ratio* in human affairs, and that its use in extreme circumstances may be morally obligatory *ad repellendam iniuriam*. The facts assert that today this *ultima ratio* takes the form of nuclear force, whose use remains possible and may prove to be necessary, lest a free field be granted to brutal violence and lack of conscience" (244).

92. Schindler, *Heart of the World*, 60–71.

93. Murray, "Problem of Religious Freedom," 141.

94. Schindler, *Heart of the World*, 65. Schindler also notes that, similar to Murray in the United States, in France a logical connection existed between a nature/grace dualism and "the cultural exile of theology in the modern era" (ibid., 64 n. 18).

> The issue is whether the construction of society is possible simply on the basis of a formal notion of freedom, as "freedom from," which leaves in suspense or perhaps even considers unresolvable the question of "freedom for." This is the question not only of the purposes for which freedom of conscience is being used, but also of the cultural, ethical, and even religious presuppositions which underlie the very choice of a liberal political order. Put most simply, does the *constitutional* indifference of the state imply *substantive* cultural indifference to questions of truth and value?[95]

The question of indifference and its scope is crucial to how Murray's public peace unfolds for the theological (and no less public) claims of the church. If grace does not play a significant role in forming culture, then one is left with a marginalized church with a virtually private faith (which is ironically similar to the Lockean position Murray hopes to avoid).[96] Schindler points out that Murray's stumbling blocks at this point may arise from the way in which he argues against formal church/state union:

> [Murray] hesitates to affirm the need for Christianizing "the terrestrial and temporal order in its structures and processes" because Christianizing entails "juridicalizing," which in turn entails a renewed integralism. To put it another way, Murray backs away from any strong affirmation of the culture-forming dimension of grace, because "forming" for him would immediately imply the *juridical* sort of form(ing) indicated by the legal-magisterial structure of the Church.[97]

Though Truett is not the intended target of this critique, much of it would also apply to him. Most importantly, Truett's thought reflects a dualism between nature and grace similar to that found in Murray. That is, without discussing the categories of nature and grace specifically, Truett tacitly segregated the sacred from the secular, the temporal from the spiritual. This manifests itself in a variety of ways. First, Truett deploys a

---

95. Komonchak, "Vatican II and the Encounter between Catholicism and Liberalism," 90.

96. Murray critiques Locke's "state of nature" as atomistic and "the law of individual nature" such that the "common good consists merely in the security of each individual in the possession of his property . . . [T]he social end differs from the individual end only quantitatively." Murray, *We Hold These Truths*, 276, 275. Instead, Murray aims to conceive of Americans as bound together as a cohesive body politic that shares a consensus concerning important (i.e., public) judgments.

97. Schindler, *Heart of the World*, 85 n. 39.

dichotomy between citizen and believer, using the words of Jesus to justify this dualism. As he stated on numerous occasions, the separation of church and state is predicated upon a sharp divide between the religious and the civil realms. Even though he envisioned both arenas as democracies, they were never to be intertwined. Each governed one aspect of human existence in separation of the other (e.g., body divided from soul).

Second, Truett's extrinsic relationship between nature and grace is most clearly evident in his notion of freedom. As Murray argued for a form of freedom that emphasized non-interference, Truett did likewise, linking his understanding of freedom to concepts such as soul competency and individualism, which urge caution toward other entities (e.g., church) that might usurp the autonomy of the individual. This bears closer resemblance to liberal democratic concepts of freedom than a positive (i.e., more teleological) view of freedom. That is, both Murray and Truett maintained a concept of freedom that was more oriented toward freedom *from*, namely a juridical-negative form of freedom, than freedom *for*, a more theological form of freedom.

Third, for Truett, the goal was to safeguard the freedom of individual conscience by removing any obstacles to the individual soul's relationship with God, but while Truett argued for a "free church in a free state," his understanding of the church as an association of like-minded individuals actually left the church rather "un-free" as a non-public entity. In other words, Truett's emphasis on individual salvation, combined with liberty of individual conscience, undercuts any freedom for the church to be a formative community for followers of Jesus. Instead, other sociopolitical institutions (e.g., schools, American political processes, economic structures and practices) and their respective ends (e.g., citizenship, profitability) garner virtually all influence of this sort. Thus, not only is citizen divided from believer, but in the temporal realm (which has rather expansive boundaries), the role of citizen (and even consumer) supersedes that of believer.

Therefore, Truett's (and Murray's) arguments for the separation of church and state lead Baptists (and Catholics) to look to the nation-state as the arena of genuine political activity and ultimate guarantor of religious freedom. The church, while not entirely eliminated, is left without a politics, except insofar as it can facilitate the civil realm's achievement of its natural, political ends. In the end, then, despite his critique of Dawson and Blanshard, Murray is not entirely successful in extricating himself from a Baptist (or free church ecclesiology) reading of the First Amendment, leaving him with the same problems.

As has been argued, Truett and Murray would both benefit from a theological notion of freedom. That is, what they lack is a sense of the purpose of freedom (i.e., freedom *for*). Such an understanding of freedom would address the nature/grace relationship by treating the culture-forming aspects of grace that both Murray and Truett neglect. Moreover, the church could play a significant role within that culture, forming the lives of Christians into conformity with the life and witness of Jesus. While this problem is serious and requires thorough remedy, it will suffice to gesture toward resources for developing a theological account of freedom that maintains an affirmation of religious liberty (i.e., non-coercion in matters religious) but also attends to the gaps in the arguments of Murray and Truett.

Dignitatis Humanae: Searching for a Theological Account of Religious Liberty

John Courtney Murray was not the only Catholic voice supporting religious freedom in the twentieth century. On December 7, 1965, Pope Paul VI promulgated *Dignitatis Humanae*, the Second Vatican Council's Declaration on Religious Freedom, which emerged from several years of tense discussions and heated debates. In light of the Roman Catholic Church's prior history with religious liberty (especially in the *Syllabus of Errors*), the Declaration was viewed as a monumental achievement that signaled to many that a new day for the church had dawned. The first half of the document (§§1–8), with one exception, frames religious freedom within a constitutional argument, discussing the proper function of government and religious freedom as part of that role. Here, in language reminiscent of the First Amendment, the "free exercise of religion" is supported, and non-interference on the part of civil government is enjoined so that individual rights can be protected.[98] Religious communities have freedom within society, then, to educate their adherents (including children) accordingly, with no danger of infringement by the state, except in cases where the public order is violated.[99] The goal of such a defense of

---

98. Second Vatican Council, *Dignitatis Humanae* §§3, 6.
99. Ibid., §§4–7.

religious freedom as a right is the protection of the "common welfare" and "genuine public peace."[100]

The second half of the Declaration is clearly more theological and notes the ways in which religious freedom aligns with the Christian tradition broadly and orthodox doctrine in particular. As the document states, "Religious freedom in society is entirely consonant with the freedom of the act of Christian faith."[101] This act of faith, though, is situated within the context of the believing church, countering any move to privatize free exercise of faith.[102] More importantly, the second half of the document proclaims that religious freedom is grounded in the life and witness of Jesus and the apostles, making faithful discipleship the primary way to embody this liberty.[103] Indeed, "the Church is following the way of Christ and the apostles when she recognizes and gives support to the principle of religious freedom as befitting the dignity of man and as being in accord with divine revelation."[104] Finally, religious freedom underscores the fact that the church has freedom to work for the "fulfillment of her divine mission" in the world,[105] which may result in martyrdom when the powers of the world do not receive the church's witness favorably.[106]

While *Dignitatis Humanae* stands as a single declaration, these two halves of the document actually present two different arguments for religious liberty, both of which are evident in the history of its composition.[107] The first was represented by Murray and other Catholics from the United States. This American group put forth an account of religious liberty that was juridical, constitutional, and linked to American-styled arguments for negative freedom. Because of the spread of religious liberty across the known world, Murray thought *Dignitatis Humanae* was "a

---

100. Ibid., §7.
101. Ibid., §9.
102. Ibid., §10.
103. Ibid., §§9, 11.
104. Ibid., §12.
105. Ibid., §§13–14.
106. Ibid., §11.

107. For more about this process, see Dreuzy, "*Dignitatis Humanae* as an Encounter Between Two 'Towering Theologians.'" Many theologians have offered evaluations of the structure of *Dignitatis Humanae*. Stanley Hauerwas has described the Declaration as problematically having a distinctly divided mind (*Better Hope*, 110). William Portier views the Declaration as perhaps performing an extrinsic relationship between nature and grace "in the double-decker theological universe of modern Catholic theology" ("Theology of Manners," 102).

significant event in the history of the Church" but of minor importance within human history as a whole.[108] After the Declaration was promulgated, though, Murray further worked to ensure that the juridical perspective was given primacy in reading the document. In 1966, Murray participated in an interfaith conference at the University of Notre Dame regarding the developments of the Second Vatican Council. Murray's task was to discuss *Dignitatis Humanae*:

> [T]he Declaration presents the content or object of the right to religious freedom as simply negative, namely immunity from coercion in religious matters. Thus the Declaration moves onto the solid ground of the constitutional tradition of the West, whose development, in what concerns religious freedom, was first effected by the Constitution of the United States in 1789 and by the First Amendment in 1791.[109]

This was consistent with Murray's other remarks about the Declaration after the Second Vatican Council. Commenting on the text of the document elsewhere, Murray wrote, "[I]n assigning a negative content to the right to religious freedom (that is, in making it formally a 'freedom from' and not a 'freedom for'), the Declaration is in harmony with the sense of the First Amendment to the American Constitution."[110]

Truett's argument for religious liberty, with its own emphasis on juridical freedom, certainly has distinct resonances with the American half of *Dignitatis Humanae* represented primarily by Murray. However, as has been noted, the juridical/constitutional argument for religious freedom is not the only one found in *Dignitatis Humanae*. The theological argument of the second half of the document was represented by Dominican Yves Congar and other French participants, who emphasized that religious freedom was grounded in revelation (and teleology). This approach employed Scripture much more (fourteen total references) than its constitutional counterpart (only one reference). Specifically, "Congar suggested that after a short introduction there should be a section on the biblical concept of freedom, starting with the idea of the original freedom given by God to humanity and of the development of the history of salvation."[111]

---

108. Murray, "Religious Freedom," 673.
109. Murray, "The Declaration on Religious Freedom," 568.
110. Murray, "Religious Freedom," 678 n. 5.
111. Alberigo and Komonchak, *History of Vatican II*, 4:535.

French-speaking theologians, such as René Coste, continued their work following the Second Vatican Council, attempting to either invert the arguments within the Declaration or move beyond the document altogether.[112] These theologians, while sharing Americans' displeasure with church/state union, had a much different experience within France than Murray in the United States. Komonchak has described theology in France during the early twentieth century as a discourse in exile.[113] Thus, theologians who emerged from this context (including Congar, Coste, and de Lubac) had to navigate the church/state union proposed by the pro-fascist French nationalist movement *Action française* and the radical division between church and state advocated by the anti-clerical Third Republic. Murray, having only experienced the favorable conditions for religion in the United States (under church/state nonestablishment), was not able to conceive of the dangers of certain forms of church/state division in the same way as his French coreligionists. In a similar manner, Truett, whose advocacy for religious liberty in the United States goes so far as to situate both church and state along parallel tracks of freedom, does not acknowledge the potential pitfalls to his account of church/state separation.

Thus, rather than the negative freedom of the first half of *Dignitatis Humanae*, a more theological account of freedom must be embraced. The foundation of this account can be founded upon section 11 of the Declaration, which grounds non-coercion in discipleship to the life of Jesus. This, as intended by the French-speaking theologians at the Council, initiates the discussion of religious liberty within Christocentric biblical revelation. In many ways, this resonates with the affirmation of the Second Vatican Council's *Gaudium et Spes* (Pastoral Constitution on the Church in the Modern World): "Christ, the final Adam, by the revelation of the mystery of the Father and His love, fully reveals man to man himself and makes his supreme calling clear."[114] In other words, Christ displays what it means to be authentically human, providing a *telos* for human existence. As the Declaration states, "God has regard for the dignity of the human person who He himself created."[115] Thus, efforts to ground religious freedom in anthropology and nature without a link to a

112. See Coste, *Théologie de la liberté religeuse*. For more on some of the efforts of these French-speaking theologians, see Rico, *Legacy of "Dignitatis Humanae,"* 41–51.
113. See Komonchak, "Theology and Culture at Mid-Century."
114. Second Vatican Council, *Gaudium et Spes* §22.
115. Second Vatican Council, *Dignitatis Humanae* §11.

christologically shaped doctrine of creation are deficient and disordered. Therefore, in terms of nature and grace, an extrinsic link between the two is rejected by underscoring the ways in which revelation speaks to the truth of nature and the relationships found therein. Put differently, religious freedom cannot be established on the merits and dignity of the human person or society alone. Rather, the content of revelation discloses the true reality of both nature and grace, with religious freedom's shape and significance illuminated by the intrinsic relationship between the natural and the supernatural.

Religious Liberty, Nature/Grace, and the Baptist Dilemma

Once this theological form of freedom, based on an intrinsic construal of nature and grace, is embraced, markedly different cultural results are produced without compromising Truett's initial goal of resisting formal union between church and state.[116] Of course, establishment of a state church is still rightly avoided, guaranteeing non-coercion in religious matters. Moreover, the church is still enabled to pursue its mission, but this will involve a more critical, though no less engaging, role within the world. That is, discourse concerning freedom will not be viewed as outside the church's competence (i.e., it is not simply a juridical, constitutional issue). With Truett, the church's freedom was restricted in the temporal realm by a dualistic relationship between nature and grace. The parallel trajectories of citizen and believer left the church as an apolitical entity, resting on statecraft as the only avenue for a viable political voice within society. By contrast, when nature and grace, while distinct, maintain an intrinsic relationship, the political is not disconnected from the theological. In other words, rather than simply establishing the church as *free from* state control, the church is *free for* embodying a way of life faithful to Christ. Along these lines, de Lubac writes,

> The authority of the Church is entirely spiritual and is exercised only on consciences. But it does not follow that there are areas of thought or human activity that ought to be, a priori, closed to it. Because there is no activity, however profane it may appear, where the Faith and morality guarded by the Church cannot in one way or another, one day or another, be involved. Christianity

116. Cf. Schindler, *Heart of the World*, 84.

is universal not only in the sense that all men have their Savior in Jesus Christ but also in the sense that *all of man* has salvation in Jesus Christ . . . And it is hard to see why "politics" should be an exception to this principle.[117]

Therefore, theology can and should have purchase on contemporary sociopolitical concerns within the communal witness of the church. For example, the justification of a war (or the condemnation of a particular military action) would not be offered simply on the basis of national goals and interests. Instead, the means and ends of particular moments of military action should be examined and evaluated through a theological lens that, among other questions, asks whether violence is part of the church's discipleship to the crucified Lord.

Moreover, as evident from the quote by de Lubac, conscience retains an important role within theological anthropology, though it is not the virtually unfettered individual conscience found in Truett's thought. Instead, through the formative influence of the church, conscience is ordered toward the good and subject to supernatural direction.[118] Along with the corporate political witness of the church, individual Christians, fashioned in the church and inhabiting society, act as a leavening influence that shapes political structures and decisions, enacting social renewal more subtly and imaginatively (e.g., a church offering micro-loans in order to aid people in need who might otherwise be exploited through payday lending establishments). In this manner, de Lubac notes that the church has power "in temporal matters," without ascribing to it any form of power over the temporal. The church is not privatized, but formal church/state union is also avoided.

Further, closer contextual examination reveals de Lubac and his French co-religionists to be a timely resource for Baptists arguing for religious liberty. Truett's assessment of the United States' political landscape, even if it accurately reflected his own era, does not best fit the present circumstances of late modernity. In other words, the appeals to consensus and parallel trajectories of freedom found in Truett's thought no longer have the same relevance. Instead, fragmentation and hyperdiversity characterize American society, with clear problems even for constitutional interpretation, let alone ecclesial consensus and discernment. The French Catholic context that gave rise to the second half of *Dignitatis*

117. De Lubac, "The Authority of the Church in Temporal Matters," 230.
118. Cf. ibid., 213.

Humanae, however, has much more resonance with ecclesial existence in late modernity. France, in the first half of the twentieth century, was hostile to Christianity through legal acts to separate church and state, even to the point of exiling Jesuit institutions of theological education from mainland France to England.[119] Moreover, Catholics' theological positions had significant bearing on de Lubac's context during the Second World War. For instance, because of his theological convictions, de Lubac participated in what he called "spiritual resistance to nazism."[120] Through this and his previous work, de Lubac theologically criticized political options such as *Action française* and Nazism itself, noting how the extrinsic relationship between nature and grace had made these political movements possible and further enabled their designs.[121] The emphasis, then, is not on whether theology and politics intertwine, but the precise nature of that entanglement and whether it coheres with the shape of Christocentric politics within the church.

Baptists today face a pluralistic context that, while different in key ways, more closely resembles the situation of the French Third Republic than that of Truett's United States. That is, contemporary Baptists are more likely to encounter indifference and hostility regarding the public significance of the Christian faith than consensus and acclaim. Accordingly, it is not uncommon to describe the church's position within late modern American society as one of exile. Likewise, Baptists would do well to temper the use of Truett's voice on matters of religious liberty and learn from twentieth-century French Catholics (such as de Lubac and Congar) who have navigated the Scylla of overt and formal church/state union and the Charybdis of complete privatization of the Christian faith. Because they have inhabited and interacted with a context such as this, their experiences are instructive for Baptists as they present particular insights for living as what Pierre Colin has called "the presence and exercise of a spiritual power in a pluralist society."[122]

---

119. The Act of Separation of Church and State, passed in December 1905, formally ended the concordat between the Catholic Church and the French Third Republic, effectively establishing secularism (or *laïcité*) in France. Schloesser, *Jazz Age Catholicism*, 53.

120. For more on this period in de Lubac's life and his contributions to *Cahiers du Témoignage catholique*, see de Lubac, *At the Service of the Church*, 50–55, and de Lubac, *Christian Resistance to Anti-Semitism*, 131–45.

121. Schindler, *Heart of the World*, 64 n. 18.

122. Colin, *L'audace et le soupçon*, 267; cited and translated in Talar, "Swearing Against Modernism," 547. While these words by Colin describe the Modernist crisis

Baptists have been advocates for religious liberty since their birth. However, this has been part of a broader call to Christian discipleship within the church. As a distinct *polis*, the church offers a counter-formation to that found in the state or the market. Truly, such formation is crucial to being "in the world, but not of it" (cf. John 17:14–18). As this chapter has described, Truett's rhetoric, at one time helpful in solidifying Baptist claims to religious liberty, is now problematic. These issues are visible most clearly when Baptist life and thought is first situated within the broader Christian tradition, linking Baptists with the communities of Christians who preceded their four-hundred-year history. Thus, this return to the sources (especially non-Baptist ones) cultivates the necessary vision for Baptists to see what is truly at stake in their own convictions, as well as how they might stay true to those beliefs within the context of the entire tradition. In the conclusion of this volume, we will bring together the efforts at Baptist *ressourcement* seen throughout its pages and discuss the ways in which this theological revitalization can take root among Baptists within the church catholic.

---

of the early twentieth century, he also notes that this crisis is the matrix of modern Catholic theology, underscoring its staying power for describing the contemporary context.

Conclusion

The Liturgical Ground of Ressourcement

> To be a Christian means to be in the world in a certain way and not in another way because one's relationships are constituted by the primary relationship of what it means to be united to the Father through the Son in the Spirit. To be a Christian is to be transformed according to the patterns of the liturgy.
>
> —SUSAN WOOD[1]

IN THE FOURTEENTH CHAPTER of John's Gospel, Jesus declares that he is "the way, and the truth, and the life," and that no one comes to the Father except through him (John 14:6). Baptists, like many Christians, take this centrality of Jesus seriously. In fact, much of Baptist theology has declared this as its aim. Yet, even this phrase has occasionally lost its luster as some Baptists' zeal for Christ has prompted them to invoke him over the church catholic and the Christian tradition. Throughout this book, *ressourcement* has been embraced as the path for renewing Baptist theology, for (re)centering Baptist life and thought on Jesus. However, this "return to the sources" is not something disconnected from church and tradition, but part and parcel of each (or perhaps better stated, each is part and parcel of Christ). In other words, to place Jesus at the center of the Christian life is to recognize that peculiar life as inextricably bound up with the depth of the Christian tradition and the practices of the church.

This centrality of Jesus has been crucial to the argument of this book, but especially in the three previous chapters. In chapter three, the Bible was not only described as the church's book, but it was also

---

1. Wood, "The Liturgy," 109.

situated as the record of the primary revelation of God—in Jesus Christ. In other words, the Bible, as read by the church, points to the fullness of the one known as "Word of God." In the fourth chapter, the body of Christ was invoked as an image of the seamless union of the personal and the communal, highlighting the ways in which an individual/communal dichotomy (even while attempting to "properly balance" the two) betrays the unity of the church as an extension of Christ's presence in the world. Finally, in chapter five, religious liberty was discussed not as a defense of a priori individual rights within a liberal democratic state. Rather, it was situated within the broader call to Christian discipleship, where religious freedom is ingredient in the rhythm of following Jesus within the politics of the church. When seen in this light, it is clear that *ressourcement* enables renewed Baptist life and thought to take shape. Moreover, Baptist contributions to the wider Christian tradition can be better received as well. For instance, dissent, a practice cherished by many Baptists, is not lost. In fact, it is bolstered and exemplified by many non-Baptist figures within the tradition, such as de Lubac, who remained faithful to his theological convictions and to the church even while silenced by his Jesuit superiors. In this manner, *ressourcement* can help Baptists learn how to offer their distinct gifts to the wider body of Christ.

A significant question, certainly pastoral yet no less theological, concerns how a central emphasis on Christ is to be developed or cultivated. That is, since Jesus Christ stands at the theological center of the life of the church, what will form Christians to embrace this Christ as center and what will nurture a theological vision around him (or, what will enable us to see a particular or particular set of expressions as more faithful to Jesus than others)? By way of concluding this book, the primary answer to this question will be found in liturgy. In other words, the worship life of the church is crucial to the development of the theological vision described earlier in this volume. For some Baptists, this may seem odd since most conversations about worship have either focused on stylistic preferences (and mainly about music) or the historical themes, such as the differences between the Sandy Creek and Charleston traditions of Baptist practice in the United States.[2] Therefore, in order to draw out the

---

2. The Charleston strand of Baptist life in the United States emphasized theological and liturgical order and ministerial training, while the Sandy Creek strand was more revivalistic with less emphasis on formal ministerial training. For more information, see McBeth, *Baptist Heritage*, 234. For an excellent summary of the Baptist liturgical landscape, see Harmon, *Towards Baptist Catholicity*, 152.

theological insights provided by liturgical practices, the most prevalent emphasis seen in contemporary evangelical worship will be juxtaposed to a more robust treatment of liturgy provided by a Catholic liturgical reformer, with the hope of offering light for precisely the sort of theological revitalization sought in *ressourcement*.

Liturgy as Technique

While worship is a central activity of the church, in the United States its purpose has sometimes aimed elsewhere. The fervor of the Second Great Awakening, and the broader revivalistic impulses that emerged from it, attracted many people to Christianity. No one understood this better than Charles Grandison Finney (1792–1875), a lawyer-turned-preacher in western New York who in the 1830s instituted what some of his contemporaries pejoratively called the "New Measures." These liturgical innovations were used in Finney's revival meetings and involved focused attention on the moment of decision. Finney boasted that he had borrowed these ideas from successful politicians who did everything possible to attract the gaze of the masses, the object of which was "to get up an excitement, and bring the people out."[3] Churches needed similar methods, he argued, to invite popular attention and ultimately bring more people to Jesus. As Finney stated, the church would lose potential converts "unless we . . . wisely adopt such new measures as are calculated to gain attention of men [sic] to the gospel of Christ."[4] Many of these methods, such as the use of an altar call at the end of the service, were not necessarily created by Finney, but they were regularized as an expected part of the liturgical pattern. To pursue Finney's aim of gaining people's attention, the altar call had flexibility that allowed the revival preacher the option to extend the duration of the service if he felt that someone needed to obey the Spirit of God and "come to Jesus" at that precise moment.[5] If more time was needed, this was not a problem either. Finney also popularized the protracted revival meeting, which meant that he

---

3. Finney, *Lectures on Revivals of Religion*, 181.

4. Ibid., 272.

5. This is not to take away from Finney's strong interest in efforts to reform society. For more on Finney and his "New Measures," see Hatch, *Democratization of American Christianity*, 196–201; Noll, *History of Christianity*, 174–78.

could also wait even longer for these decisions, perhaps staying in one town for several days, or weeks, if necessary.

Finney also employed what he called the "anxious bench," a place to sit near the front of the service where "the anxious may come and be addressed particularly, and be made subjects of prayer, and sometimes be conversed with individually."[6] For Finney, this seating area served as an indicator that a person was indeed willing to do anything to demonstrate his or her dedication to Christ, an act that Finney paralleled with the early church's use of baptism: "The gospel was preached to the people, and then all those who were willing to be on the side of Christ were called on to be baptized. It held the precise place that the anxious seat does now, as a public manifestation of their determination to be Christians . . . This is as much setting up a test as the other."[7] While the anxious bench ostensibly appeared to be a marker of God's activity, in actuality, it undergirded the role of freedom as choice. That is, the person sitting on the bench was, in the words of a popular invitation hymn, deciding whether to follow Jesus.[8]

Finney's methods were remarkably successful, meaning that he had numerous converts at his revival meetings. He considered this a mark of the validity of the New Measures. In short, according to Finney, they were good and acceptable because they worked. Not surprisingly, these methods are virtually ubiquitous in contemporary evangelical worship services to such an extent that their absence is notable and occasionally a cause for alarm. Historian Ted A. Smith has commented on their prevalence: "Practices like seeking to be effective, trying to hold the congregation's attention, calling for individual decision, addressing hearers as a mass of equals, purposefully displaying sincerity, and telling stories seem so obvious that they rarely merit explicit discussion except in the most rarefied homiletical circles."[9] With this in view, several observations should be made. First, the New Measures placed worship in service of evangelism. The primary goal of worship (and virtually all collective Christian activity) was to save souls through whatever methods presented themselves. Worship was merely one more avenue for producing conversions. Second, with the emphasis on personal decision and the relegating

6. Finney, *Lectures on Revivals of Religion*, 267.

7. Ibid., 268–69.

8. Reynolds, "I Have Decided to Follow Jesus," in Forbis, *The Baptist Hymnal*, #305.

9. Smith, *New Measures*, 9.

of discipleship and spiritual formation to the solitary Christian's personal life, Finney's New Measures left an individualistic legacy in their wake that highlighted the moment of decision and choice as paramount. Like Joshua speaking to the Israelites at Shechem, they were to "choose this day whom you will serve" (Josh 24:15). Third, the emphasis on "what works" transformed liturgical practices into a technique with an external end. The liturgy itself did not have an internal *telos*. In other words, a minister's task was not to search for the contextually appropriate way to worship the Triune God. Instead, he or she aimed to find the right button to push or lever to pull (liturgical or otherwise) that would bring about the desired result (conversion of outsiders). From where those buttons or levers came was of little importance as long as they worked. This is demonstrated by the mid-nineteenth century publication and popularity of several instructional (or "how to") manuals concerning revivalistic methods, including one by Finney himself in 1834.[10]

This emphasis on technique was heightened in the post–Civil War evangelistic revivals of Dwight L. Moody (1837–99), who is described by one historian as a "salesman of salvation."[11] Further, in the twentieth century, the influence of Finney's methods can be seen in the efforts of preachers such as Billy Sunday (1862–1935) and, even to some extent, Billy Graham (b. 1918), but also in the popularity of the church growth movement, symbolically led by evangelical church researcher George Barna. Through his Barna Research Group (now Barna Group, owned by David Kinnaman), churches have learned of the developing sociological and cultural issues related to the contemporary Christian faith. As with Finney, the underlying emphasis is effectiveness or relevance—in other words, "what works." In Barna's case, "what works" are marketing methods that are interested in doing whatever will draw people to churches. As businesses re-brand themselves (we might think of Apple Computer's transition to Apple, Inc.), the church should do likewise.[12] Furthermore,

---

10. Finney, *Lectures on Revivals of Religion*. Smith also lists Beecher and Skinner's *Hints to Aid Christians*, Ebenezer Porter's *Letters on the Religious Revival*, and Calvin Colton's *History and Character of American Revivals of Religion* (*New Measures*, 67).

11. Hofstadter, *Anti-Intellectualism in American Life*, 111.

12. This example has itself evolved. In his 1988 book, *Marketing the Church*, Barna invokes Apple Computer as an example of shifting market focus from individual homes to businesses and educational settings (13). In 2007, Apple Computer refocused again, changing its name to Apple, Inc. and shifting toward a broader array of consumer electronic devices (e.g., portable music players, smartphones, television services, and watches).

like any business, a church has a "product" to sell and must, according to Barna, "impact a growing share of its market area."[13] This "market area," though, cannot include every person, for this is far too broad. A church that embraces these techniques must therefore find their population niche—that is, their specific target audience—and cater to their needs and wants. These needs, including but not limited to, children's activities and programs, married adult programs, and varying degrees of comfort, serve as the path for a church to reach their niche (i.e., gain more attendees). Thus, despite caveats to the contrary, within the church growth movement, numerical growth is the ultimate goal of discussions about liturgy and its shape.[14]

The results of this emphasis on church growth are staggering. One such church, which is also one of the fastest growing churches in the United States, has swelled from attendance of one hundred fifty in 1989 to approximately twenty thousand currently, scattered across eight campuses. However, despite the visible efficacy of the methods, their deeper ramifications are equally surprising. In other words, while these methods do "work," there is more to the story. One prominent North American megachurch was founded on the research of a door-to-door marketing survey of those who did not regularly attend church. According to survey participants, they were bothered by constant appeals for money, boring church services, and reliance on outdated (i.e., ancient) religious symbols. The church that emerged from this data, which currently holds three weekend services in an auditorium that seats over seven thousand people, has become the prototype for other so-called seeker churches. It has no religious icons or symbols (including crosses or crucifixes), provides to visitors a very professional product, and requires very little of the audience in the way of participation. Another popular church has directed its marketing attention to liturgical music. In discussing his church's deliberations concerning what music is appropriate, the pastor asks, "How does this tune make me feel?"[15] He answers this question by underscoring the need for an upbeat celebratory mood within a worship service. Consequently, seemingly oblivious to the significant presence of

---

13. Barna, *Marketing the Church*, 14.

14. Marva Dawn observes that Barna distinguishes between numerical growth and spiritual development, yet he is oblivious to the ways in which these characteristics "compete more than they complement one another" (*Reaching Out Without Dumbing Down*, 63).

15. Warren, *Purpose Driven Church*, 286.

lament and doubt within Scripture, he writes, "We rarely sing a song in a minor key."[16]

The same individualism that lurked beneath Finney's methods is found in these churches as well. Despite the size of their crowds, individual religious consumers are the emphasis for church growth models of megachurches and their imitators. Even without the aforementioned pastor's conclusion that somber tunes have no place in worship, he begins with a question that focuses on individual feelings. The centrality of perceived (yet uninterrogated) needs or desires to the shape of a congregation's life and liturgy is problematic as it leaves little room for transporting people from their present emotional status. Moreover, as the New Measures underscored, worship exists for evangelism, for drawing a large crowd with the hopes that they will individually decide to follow Jesus.[17] This is the goal, and everything within worship is dedicated to reaching that goal. Attention to liturgy for its own sake is considered to be insular and perhaps akin to navel-gazing, a serious distraction from more important work. Even the word *liturgy* itself is avoided as a symbol of such misdirected effort.

Liturgy and the Mystical Body of Christ

Worship need not be construed as a lever pulled or a button pressed to gain a specific end. Conversations about worship that often center on stylistic preferences betray an exclusive emphasis on the personal, or display a felt need to do whatever is necessary to be "relevant."[18] In contrast, the vast majority of the Christian tradition has understood (and does understand) liturgy in a different manner—as participation in the mystical body of Christ. This perspective not only adds immense theologi-

---

16. Ibid., 287.

17. Those who critique church growth methods are likely to be accused of opposing evangelism, as was the case with theologian Stanley Hauerwas when his North Carolina United Methodist congregation aimed to learn from Willow Creek Community Church "how a church that utilized these methods works." When he questioned his pastor about this, she accused him of not wanting to bring people to Jesus (*Hannah's Child*, 258–59). Among Baptists, the focus on evangelism has even determined the frequency of sacramental practices. According to Nathan Hatch, Virginia Baptist John Leland seldom administered the Eucharist within his congregations, arguing that "in thirty years of practical experience he had never seen the ordinance move a single sinner to conversion." Hatch, *Democratization of American Christianity*, 100.

18. For more on these debates, see York, *America's Worship Wars*.

cal depth to the worship activity of the church, but it also counters the adverse aspects of liturgy as technique that endanger liturgical habits and theological reflection. In what follows, a brief discussion of the work of Benedictine priest and liturgist Virgil Michel will present significant insights regarding how granting greater attention to liturgy will contribute to the theological renewal sought by Baptists.

Initially a Pauline concept, the mystical body of Christ developed within late-nineteenth- and early twentieth-century Catholic theology into a central theological idea. Through the work of Johann Adam Möhler and Emile Mersch, among others, the doctrine of the Mystical Body of Christ gained traction, resulting in its affirmation as part of a hierarchical ecclesiology in Pius XII's 1943 encyclical *Mystici Corporis Christi*.[19] With all these contributions, we find within the Mystical Body of Christ a soteriological emphasis ("ineffable participation in the knowledge and love of God") as well as an ecclesiological one ("the visible, concrete, and tangible life of the ecclesial communion").[20] Michel encountered this concept when studying in Europe in the 1920s. His conversations with Lambert Beauduin and other Benedictine monks involved in European liturgical renewal inspired Michel to undertake a parallel effort in the United States.[21] This renewal, like the similar Catholic efforts for *ressourcement*, would be a return to the sources—that is, a return to "active contact with the living sources of life in Christ."[22]

When Michel discussed the Mystical Body of Christ, he referred to the church as "all the faithful being the members that makes [sic] up this body, with Christ as the head."[23] This "common fellowship of souls in Christ" does not simply come together on its own; instead, it is developed through the Spirit-infused work of the liturgy.[24] Because of this, Michel observed that in the liturgy, we find the nexus of the communal and the personal. In a short article published in the liturgical periodical *Orate Fratres* (which was founded by Michel in 1926), he tackled the question of whether the liturgy depersonalizes and even annihilates individual piety. His response denied such a claim, noting that while the liturgy does

19. For more on the history of this concept within Catholic theology, see Pecklers, *Unread Vision*, 29–34.
20. Groppe, *Yves Congar's Theology of the Holy Spirit*, 119.
21. Pecklers, *Unread Vision*, 21.
22. Quoted in ibid., 33.
23. Michel, *Liturgy of the Church*, 47.
24. Ibid.

offer an immensely personal dynamic (e.g., in the presentation of a candidate for baptism and in the distribution of the eucharistic elements), the individual is not cut off from the life of Christ and his body: "It [Liturgy] is also related to the Church as the wider Christ, and to the continuous indwelling and activity of Christ in His Church."[25] Concerns about collective action obliterating the individual are then mistaken. Instead of annihilation of the individual, Michel wrote that liturgy facilitates "the losing of one's life in order to find it on a higher level. It is an ennobling of the self, a sort of divinization of self, in which the best characteristics of the self are not destroyed but transformed into a higher supernatural richness of being."[26] Therefore, as Michel stated, "The religious experience of the liturgy . . . is calculated to enrich the individual for the sole reason that it brings him into such intimate real contact with Christ, the true way and life."[27]

While the individual is certainly entwined in the liturgical drama, there is also something larger than the individual at work. Elsewhere, Michel noted, "The liturgy, uniting all members in Christ, is then not the prayer or activity of isolated individuals united by a common bond. The liturgy is above all corporate activity, a fellowship in action."[28] This communal task transcends the individual, drawing her into the depth of union with Christ but also with others in a local community. Thus, the parish becomes a microcosm of the mystical body of Christ, a visible and concrete expression of the unity of the church. Additionally, the boundaries of this community extend to the church catholic as well. The liturgy is not only an incorporation into Christ, but a concorporation, a gathering together of the communion of saints across space and time.[29]

The "work of the people" found in worship forms a community whose life bears witness to the fullness of Christ. Unlike liturgy as technique, worship is not forced to serve evangelism. However, with an emphasis on divinization and partaking of the divine nature (2 Pet 1:4),

25. Michel, "Religious Experience," 493.
26. Ibid., 494.
27. Ibid., 493–94.
28. Michel, *Liturgy of the Church*, 53.
29. Michel, "The Social Nature of Communion"; quoted in Baxter, "Reintroducing Virgil Michel," 506. De Lubac, in discussing the act of baptism, similarly states, "As the water flows over our foreheads it does not merely effect a series of incorporations, but there takes place at the same time a 'concorporation' of the whole Church in one mysterious unity" (*Catholicism*, 85).

Michel certainly saw salvation as intimately involved in the practice of the liturgy. In a later article (also in *Orate Fratres*), Michel discusses the relationship between mysticism and the liturgy. Rejecting any notion that the two are opposed to one another, the mystic who has "an immediate experience of God's presence to the soul" must still be grounded in the sacramental action of the liturgy, wherein all participants are drawn into the church, outside of which there is no salvation.[30] Eternal life, then, is not merely a possession gained by capitalizing on the moment of decision; it is participation in a lifelong pilgrimage toward union with God in the fellowship of the church. The result of this, according to Michel, is a "liturgical type" of sanctity nurtured by worship as "the indispensable source of the Christian spirit for all men."[31]

The emphasis on liturgy as participation in the mystical body of Christ, however, does not leave the church looking inwardly. Indeed, Michel understood that liturgy was far from navel gazing or a distraction from mission, evangelism, or social justice. Instead, he saw the liturgy as the ground of those efforts. Following the Apostle Paul's notion that all Christians are tied together so that "if one member suffers, all suffer together with it; [and] if one member is honored, all rejoice together with it" (1 Cor 12:26), Michel stated that all Christians "live and breathe this supernatural social unity of all members of Christ."[32] In other words, the liturgy not only draws individuals together with Christ and with one another, but it also serves as the basis for what he called "social regeneration." Refuting the extreme positions of collectivism and individualism, Michel articulated a vision of the liturgy that opens out into active participation in the life of God and is welcoming of others into the same participation. As Michael Baxter comments, "For Michel, the liturgy is always already social; it is itself the prototype and paradigm of any genuine conception of the social; and it therefore does not need to be linked to an independently established, extra-ecclesial entity called 'society.' In short, for Virgil Michel, the liturgy constitutes society."[33] Because of this emphasis, Michel supported lay efforts for Catholic Action generally and

---

30. Michel, "Mysticism and Normal Christianity," 546. "If there is no salvation outside the Church, then there is none outside the liturgy" (ibid., 547).
31. Ibid., 548.
32. Michel, "Liturgy the Basis for Social Regeneration," 430.
33. Baxter, "Reintroducing Virgil Michel," 506.

the mission of the Catholic Worker and the National Catholic Rural Life Movement in particular.[34]

For Baptists, the mystical body of Christ, while not a part of their regular vocabulary, is witnessed in the New Testament. Ephesians, for example, declares that "There is one body and one Spirit, just as you were called to the one hope of your calling, one Lord, one faith, one baptism, one God and Father of all, who is above all and through all and in all" (Eph 4:4–6). These organic links bind together all Christians and make it possible for Paul elsewhere to discuss the gifts of the Spirit in a collective manner as intended for "building up the church" (1 Cor 14:12). As Michel observed, the problem is not whether one chooses the individual or the communal, but precisely the setting of the individual over the communal to the detriment of each. To do so fails to take seriously that "just as the body is one and has many members, and all members of the body, though many, are one body, so it is with Christ. For in the one Spirit were all baptized into one body—Jews or Greeks, slaves or free,—and we were all made to drink of one Spirit" (1 Cor 12:12–13).

On the Road Toward *Ressourcement*

Baptist theologian Christopher Ellis has noted that worship, as "embodied theology," is "an encounter in which God and humanity are active participants and in which 'something' happens."[35] This "something" highlights the fact that liturgy unfolds the mystery of who God is, what God is doing in the world, and who the people of God are—questions that lie at the heart of theological renewal. To be sure, Virgil Michel initially stands as a strange interlocutor for Baptists since his references to the church and its liturgy are directed toward the Roman Catholic Church and its performance of the Mass. However, his voice is no stranger than that of Henri de Lubac, Yves Congar, and the rest of the Christian tradition that has guided the discussion of this book, and his work should be similarly

---

34. Dorothy Day, cofounder of the Catholic Worker Movement, commented on the shared outpouring of grief at the execution of Italian anarchists Nicola Sacco and Bartolomeo Vanzetti in 1927, stating, "All the nation mourned. All the nation, I mean, that is made up of the poor, the worker, the trade unionist—those who felt most keenly the sense of solidarity—that very sense of solidarity which made me gradually understand the doctrine of the Mystical Body of Christ whereby we are the members one of another" (*Long Loneliness*, 147).

35. Ellis, *Gathering*, 2, 7.

instructive to Baptists. Indeed, since Michel claimed that "The Protestant breakoff from the progressive Christian tradition of many centuries was in great part also a rejection of much of the Christian liturgy," Baptists and other free church pilgrims will need to attend to voices like Michel's and reconsider aspects of this earlier "breakoff" if they have any hope for theological revitalization through the liturgy.[36] The beginnings of such work might involve careful readings of documents from the Second Vatican Council, including *Sacrosanctum Concilium* (Constitution on the Sacred Liturgy), which describes the presence of Christ in the liturgical celebration in four ways: (1) in the person of the minister as the vicar of Christ, (2) in the eucharistic elements which become, by transubstantiation, the body and blood of Christ, (3) in the reading of the Scriptures within the community of faith, and (4) in the church's prayers and singing.[37] This last point should especially resonate with free church Christians, since it is highlighted by Christ's promise to be present "where two or three are gathered together" in his name (Matt 18:20).

The contours of this theological renewal are found within the texture of the liturgy as well. The Bible, when properly understood as the church's book, highlights that the primary reading of Scripture (i.e., the one around which all other readings orbit) is performed by the church in the context of worship. Moreover, the dichotomy between the individual and the communal is transcended by the body of Christ drawing together all Christians across space and time to worship the Triune God known through Jesus.[38] Finally, while religious liberty should be situated within discipleship to Jesus, as Michel states, the church is most robustly understood and experienced as a genuine *polis* when tied to the depth of liturgical formation.[39] In short, theological *ressourcement* unavoidably requires liturgical *ressourcement*. Accordingly, Baptists will need to hear the liturgical voices of the entire tradition, including Michel, Anglican theologian Gregory Dix, free church Protestant theologian Marva Dawn,

---

36. Michel, *Liturgy of the Church*, 1–2.

37. Second Vatican Council, *Sacrosanctum Concilium* §7.

38. "When we are thus united in mind and heart in the liturgical worship, the actual realization of the mystical body of Christ is at its highest, the realization of the fullness of Christ at its best, Christ himself is most intimately present in his body." Michel, *Liturgy of the Church*, 55.

39. "The liturgy alone is the official, primary means of transforming men into Christians, of putting off the old man and putting on 'the new man, who according to God is created in justice and holiness of truth,' of following the behest of St. Paul, 'Put ye on the Lord Jesus Christ'" (ibid., 52).

and Eastern Orthodox theologian Alexander Schmemann, among others.[40] This work will most certainly explore multiple aspects of worship. Some of this important work has already begun and even now offers wisdom for liturgical and theological renewal to Baptist churches, especially through attention to the ways in which the dramatic progression of the liturgical calendar rehearses the life of Christ and through the quest for tangible and bodily liturgical gestures that point to the significance of the Incarnation.[41]

For Michel, the liturgy, literally "the work of the people," was more than crowd-gathering. He states that its function is to "assimilate us unto Christ, to make us partakers of the Christ-life, of the eternal life of God."[42] Elsewhere, in detailing how this incorporation into Christ is expressed in the vertical relationship between humanity and God, he writes, "The liturgy is filled with the spirit of divine love, of God's love reaching down to man, and of man's steeping himself in this love and living by it as an adopted child of God and a very sharer in the divine nature."[43] At the nexus of theology and liturgy, therefore, are not simply new ideas to consider. Rather, the mystery of the love of God is found there, shaping the people of God as they travel through the world. The result of such attention to liturgy is a deeper appreciation of and participation in Paul's notion that we are the body of Christ and individually members of it (1 Cor 12:27). This love of Christ animates all Christian action, especially liturgical action, such that human beings exist as lovers, or what James K. A. Smith calls *homo liturgicus*.[44]

This book has argued that Baptists and other free church Protestants are in desperate need of theological renewal, of *ressourcement*. However, such work will necessarily require liturgical renewal as well. James Mc-Clendon, who opened the book's discussion of theology by pointing

---

40. See Dix, *The Shape of the Liturgy*, and Schmemann, *Introduction to Liturgical Theology*, as well as Fagerberg, *Theologia Prima*.

41. See, e.g., Ellis, *Gathering*; Harmon, *Towards Baptist Catholicity*, 151–77; and the excellent essays in Kennedy and Hatch, *Gathering Together*.

42. Michel, *Liturgy of the Church*, 46.

43. Michel, "Religious Experience," 495.

44. Smith, *Desiring the Kingdom*, 39–51.

out a dearth of Baptist contributions, noted that theology is by nature self-involving, so that a theologian must be an active participant in the shared life of the community.[45] In other words, active participation in the worship of the church is crucial for theological reflection. In the same way that contemporary worship music and practices have shaped the resurgent Calvinistic convictions discussed at the outset of this book, the ongoing shape of the liturgy matters. Indeed, what is clear is that the church's ancient axiom, *lex orandi, lex credendi* ("the law of worship is the law of belief"), is more true than ever. The habits and practices of Christian worship give shape and voice to the church's theological declarations. For Baptists, this means that concerns such as maintaining the Trinitarian form of the Christian faith will require liturgical witness to such (e.g., the use of Trinitarian formulae and observance of Trinity Sunday as well as explicit teaching about these matters). Moreover, cultivating faithfulness to Jesus necessitates shared activities in worship that reveal what that faithfulness looks like and facilitates the community's move toward that goal. Along these lines, Michel stated, "The liturgy is *par excellence* the mediatorial action of Christ in the Church. It is in this sense that the term *Christo-centric* has been applied to the liturgy, that is, centering in Christ."[46] Thus, Christocentric liturgy is the gateway to theological renewal grounded in the Incarnate Word desperately needed in Baptist life and thought.

As one Catholic theologian has stated, "The church assembled by God for worship is in a very real sense the *verum corpus*, the true body of Christ."[47] In short, in the liturgy, the diverse gatherings of Christians are transfigured into the one mystical body of Christ. For Baptists, then, *ressourcement* is both theological and liturgical, drawing our hearts, minds, and bodies into the pattern of the whole body. And yet, this renewal is about far more than Baptists alone, for this *corpus* includes all Christians across space and time and the saints throughout the ages. It truly is a *catholic* body. Thus, *ressourcement* has an ecumenical horizon as we reflect on the nature of our participation, through Jesus Christ, in the life of the Triune God, being drawn into the reality of Jesus's high priestly prayer that all those who have believed and would believe in him would be one as he and the Father are one (John 17:22). Such participation in

---

45. McClendon, *Ethics*, 39.
46. Michel, *Liturgy of the Church*, 31.
47. Portier, "Assembly Required," 13.

liturgical and theological renewal embodies the refrain of John B. Foley's eucharistic hymn:

> One bread, one body, one Lord of all,
> One cup of blessing which we bless.
> And we, though many, throughout the earth,
> We are one body in this one Lord.[48]

---

48. John B. Foley, "One Bread, One Body," in Batastini, *Gather*, #830.

Bibliography

Acting Board of the General Missionary Convention. "Reply of the Foreign Mission Board to the Alabama Convention." In *A Sourcebook for Baptist Heritage*, edited by H. Leon McBeth, 258–59. Nashville: Broadman, 1990.
Ahlstrom, Sydney E. *A Religious History of the American People*. 2nd ed. New Haven: Yale University Press, 2004.
Alberigo, Giuseppe, and Joseph A. Komonchak, eds. *History of Vatican II*. 5 vols. Maryknoll, NY: Orbis, 2003.
American Baptist Home Mission Society. "Minutes." In *A Sourcebook for Baptist Heritage*, edited by H. Leon McBeth, 257. Nashville: Broadman, 1990.
Aquinas, Thomas. *Summa Theologiae*. Translated by Fathers of the English Dominican Province. 2nd ed. New York: Benziger Bros., 1920.
Athanasius. *On the Incarnation of the Word*. http://www.ccel.org/ccel/athanasius/incarnation.pdf.
Augustine. *The City of God*. Translated by Gerald G. Walsh et al. Edited by Vernon J. Bourke. Garden City, NY: Image, 1958.
———. *The Confessions of St. Augustine*. Translated by Hal M. Helms. Brewster, MA: Paraclete, 1986.
———. *On Christian Doctrine*. Translated by D. W. Robertson Jr. New York: Macmillan, 1958.
———. *On Free Choice of the Will*. Translated by Anna S. Benjamin and L. H. Hackstaff. Upper Saddle River, NJ: Prentice Hall, 1964.
———. *On the Trinity: Books 8–15*. Edited by Gareth B. Matthews. Translated by Stephen McKenna. New York: Cambridge University Press, 2002.
"An Autocrat's Democracy." *The Baptist Standard* 31, no. 4 (January 23, 1919) 10–11.
Balmes, Jaime. *European Civilization: Protestantism and Catholicity Compared in Their Effects on the Civilization of Europe*. Edited by Robert Kershaw and C. J. Hanford. Baltimore: Murphy, 1850.
Balthasar, Hans Urs von. "Characteristics of Christianity." In vol. 1 of *Explorations in Theology*, translated by A. V. Littledale and Alexander Dru, 161–80. San Francisco: Ignatius, 1989.
———. *The Theology of Henri de Lubac: An Overview*. San Francisco: Ignatius, 1991.
———. *The Theology of Karl Barth: Exposition and Interpretation*. Translated by Edward T. Oakes. San Francisco: Communio, 1992.

Bibliography

Baptist World Alliance and Catholic Church. "The Word of God in the Life of the Church: A Report of International Conversations between the Catholic Church and the Baptist World Alliance." *American Baptist Quarterly* 31 (2012) 28–122.

Barna, George. *Marketing the Church: What They Never Taught You about Church Growth*. Colorado Springs: NavPress, 1988.

Barron, Robert. *The Priority of Christ: Toward a Postliberal Catholicism*. Grand Rapids: Brazos, 2007.

Barth, Karl. *The Doctrine of Reconciliation, Part 1*. Vol. IV/1 of *Church Dogmatics*, translated by G. W. Bromiley, edited by G. W. Bromiley and T. F. Torrance. Edinburgh: T. & T. Clark, 1956–1975.

Batastini, Robert J., ed. *Gather: Comprehensive*. 2nd ed. Chicago: GIA, 2004.

Baxter, Michael J. "Reintroducing Virgil Michel: Towards a Counter-Tradition of Catholic Social Ethics in the United States." *Communio* 24 (1997) 499–528.

———. "Writing History in a World Without Ends: An Evangelical Catholic Critique of United States Catholic History." *Pro Ecclesia* 5 (1996) 440–69.

Bebbington, David W. *Baptists Through the Centuries: A History of a Global People*. Waco, TX: Baylor University Press, 2010.

Beilby, James K., and Paul R. Eddy, eds. *Divine Foreknowledge: Four Views*. Downers Grove, IL: IVP Academic, 2001.

Bell, Rob. *Love Wins: A Book about Heaven, Hell, and the Fate of Every Person Who Ever Lived*. San Francisco: HarperCollins, 2011.

Bertoldi, Francisco. "Henri de Lubac on Dei Verbum." Translated by Mandy Murphy. *Communio* 17 (1990) 88–94.

Billings, J. Todd. *Calvin, Participation, and the Gift: The Activity of Believers in Union with Christ*. New York: Oxford University Press, 2007.

Bireley, Robert. *The Refashioning of Catholicism, 1450–1700: A Reassessment of the Counter Reformation*. Washington, DC: Catholic University of America Press, 1999.

Blanchette, Oliva. *Maurice Blondel: A Philosophical Life*. Grand Rapids: Eerdmans, 2010.

Blanshard, Paul. *American Freedom and Catholic Power*. Boston: Beacon, 1949.

———. *Communism, Democracy, and Catholic Power*. Boston: Beacon, 1951.

Blondel, Maurice. *Action (1893): Essay on a Critique of Life and a Science of Practice*. Translated by Oliva Blanchette. Notre Dame: University of Notre Dame Press, 1984.

———. *The Letter on Apologetics & History and Dogma*. Translated by Alexander Dru and Illtyd Trethowan. Grand Rapids: Eerdmans, 1994.

Bloom, Harold. *The American Religion: The Emergence of the Post-Christian Nation*. New York: Simon & Schuster, 1992.

Boersma, Hans. *Heavenly Participation: The Weaving of a Sacramental Tapestry*. Grand Rapids: Eerdmans, 2011.

———. *Nouvelle Théologie and Sacramental Ontology: A Return to Mystery*. New York: Oxford University Press, 2009.

Bonhoeffer, Dietrich. *Letters and Papers from Prison*. Translated by Reginald Fuller. New ed. New York: Touchstone, 1997.

Bonino, Serge-Thomas. "Foreword: The Conception of Thomism after Henri de Lubac." In *Surnaturel: A Controversy at the Heart of Twentieth-Century Thomistic Thought*, edited by Serge-Thomas Bonino, translated by Robert Williams and Matthew Levering, vii–xii. Ave Maria, FL: Sapientia, 2009.

Boring, M. Eugene. *Disciples and the Bible: A History of Disciples Biblical Interpretation in North America*. St. Louis, MO: Chalice, 1997.

Boyce, James Petigru. *Abstract of Systematic Theology*. Philadelphia: American Baptist Publication Society, 1887.

Brackney, William Henry. *The Baptists*. New York: Greenwood, 1988.

———. *Doing Baptism Baptist Style: Believer's Baptism*. Brentwood, TN: Baptist History & Heritage Society, 2001.

Broadway, Mikael. "Come Now, Let Us Argue It Out." *Review & Expositor* 112 (2015) 60–70.

Broadway, Mikael N., et al. "Re-envisioning Baptist Identity: A Manifesto for Baptist Communities in North America." *Perspectives in Religious Studies* 24 (1997) 303–10.

Brownson, Orestes A. "The Mission of America." In vol. 11 of *The Collected Works of Orestes A. Brownson*, edited by Henry F. Brownson, 551–84. Detroit: T. Nourse, 1884.

Bryant, Barry E. "Molina, Arminius, Plaifere, Goad, and Wesley on Human Free-Will, Divine Omniscience, and Middle Knowledge." *Wesleyan Theological Journal* 27.1–2 (1992) 93–103.

Burrell, David. *Faith and Freedom: An Interfaith Perspective*. Malden, MA: Blackwell, 2004.

Calvin, John. *Institutes of the Christian Religion*. Edited by John T. McNeill. Translated by Ford Lewis Battles. Philadelphia: Westminster, 1977.

Camp, Ken. "Troubled Waters: Baptists Watering Down Commitment to Baptism?" *Baptist Standard* 118, no. 13 (June 26, 2006) 1, 7.

Campbell, Alexander. "Address to the Readers of the Christian Baptist—No. I." *The Christian Baptist* 1, no. 5 (December 1, 1823) 32–33.

———. *The Christian System*. New York: Arno, 1969.

Canipe, Lee. *A Baptist Democracy: Separating God from Caesar in the Land of the Free*. Macon, GA: Mercer University Press, 2011.

———. "The Echoes of Baptist Democracy: George Truett's Sermon at the U.S. Capitol as Patriotic Apology." *American Baptist Quarterly* 21 (2002) 415–31.

Carroll, James M. *The Trail of Blood*. Lexington, KY: American Baptist, 1931.

Cary, Jeffrey W. *Free Churches and the Body of Christ: Authority, Unity, and Truthfulness*. Eugene, OR: Cascade, 2012.

Cavanaugh, William. *Theopolitical Imagination: Discovering the Liturgy as a Political Act in an Age of Global Consumerism*. London: T. & T. Clark, 2002.

———. "The World in a Wafer: A Geography of the Eucharist as Resistance to Globalization." *Modern Theology* 15 (1999) 181–96.

Cessario, Romanus. *A Short History of Thomism*. Washington, DC: Catholic University of America Press, 2005.

Chandler, Matt. *The Explicit Gospel*. Wheaton, IL: Crossway, 2012.

Chesterton, G. K. *Orthodoxy: The Romance of Faith*. 1908. Reprint, New York: Doubleday, 1990.

"Churches Turn Away Negroes." *Baptist Standard* 75, no. 25 (June 19, 1963) 2.

Clendenin, E. Ray, and Brad J. Waggoner, eds. *Calvinism: A Southern Baptist Dialogue*. Nashville: B&H Academic, 2008.

Colin, Pierre. *L'audace et le soupçon: la crise moderniste dans le catholicisme français (1893–1914)*. Paris: Desclee de Brouwer, 1997.

Colter, Sharayah. "Patterson Delivers Sermon on Inerrancy of Scripture." News Release for Southwestern Baptist Theological Seminary, April 8, 2013. http://www.swbts.edu/news/releases/patterson-delivers-sermon-inerrancy-scripture.

Congar, Yves. *The Meaning of Tradition*. Translated by A. N. Woodrow. 1964. Reprint, San Francisco: Ignatius, 2004.

Conner, W. T. *Christian Doctrine*. Nashville: Broadman, 1937.

Conway, Joe. "Pastor Task Force Addresses Declining Baptism Rates." *NAMB News*, May 2014. https://www.namb.net/news/pastor-task-force-addresses-declining-baptism-rates.

Coste, René. *Théologie de la liberté religieuse: Liberté de conscience, liberté de religion*. Gembloux: J. Duculot, 1969.

D'Ambrosio, Marcellino. "Henri de Lubac and the Critique of Scientific Exegesis." *Communio* 19 (1992) 365–88.

Dawn, Marva J. *Reaching Out without Dumbing Down: A Theology of Worship for This Urgent Time*. Grand Rapids: Eerdmans, 1995.

Dawson, Joseph Martin. *America's Way in Church, State, and Society*. New York: Macmillan, 1953.

———. *Baptists and the American Republic*. 1956. Reprint, New York: Arno, 1980.

———. "Temptations of the Churches." *Baptist Standard* 67, no. 30 (July 25, 1955) 6.

Day, Dorothy. *The Long Loneliness: An Autobiography of the Legendary Catholic Social Activist*. San Francisco: HarperSanFrancisco, 2010.

De Lubac, Henri. *At the Service of the Church: Henri de Lubac Reflects on the Circumstances That Occasioned His Writings*. Translated by Anne Elizabeth Englund. San Francisco: Communio, 1993.

———. *Augustinianism and Modern Theology*. Translated by Lancelot Sheppard. New York: Crossroad, 2000.

———. *A Brief Catechesis on Nature and Grace*. Translated by Richard Arnandez. San Francisco: Ignatius, 1984.

———. *Catholicism: Christ and the Common Destiny of Man*. Translated by Lancelot C. Sheppard and Elizabeth Englund. San Francisco: Ignatius, 1988.

———. *The Christian Faith: An Essay on the Structure of the Apostles' Creed*. Translated by Richard Arnandez. San Francisco: Ignatius, 1986.

———. *Christian Resistance to Anti-Semitism: Memories from 1940–1944*. Translated by Elizabeth Englund. San Francisco: Ignatius, 1988.

———. *Corpus Mysticum: The Eucharist and the Church in the Middle Ages*. Translated by Gemma Simmonds, Richard Price, and Christopher Stephens. Notre Dame: University of Notre Dame Press, 2007.

———. *Medieval Exegesis: The Four Senses of Scripture*. Translated by Mark Sebanc and E. M. Macierowski. 3 vols. Grand Rapids: Eerdmans, 1998–2009.

———. *The Mystery of the Supernatural*. Translated by Rosemary Sheed. 1967. Reprint, New York: Herder & Herder, 1998.

———. *Paradoxes of Faith*. Translated by Paule Simon, Sadie Kreilkamp, and Ernest Beaumont. San Francisco: Ignatius, 1987.

———. *Scripture in the Tradition*. Translated by Luke O'Neill. New York: Crossroad, 2000.

---. *Theological Fragments*. Translated by Rebecca Howell Balinski. San Francisco: Ignatius, 1989.

Dilday, Russell H. "An Analysis of the Baptist Faith & Message 2000." *Christian Ethics Today* 40 (June 2002) 4. http://www.christianethicstoday.com/cetart/index.cfm?fuseaction=Articles.main&ArtID=582.

Dix, Dom Gregory. *The Shape of the Liturgy*. New ed. New York: Bloomsbury T. & T. Clark, 2005.

Dorrien, Gary. *The Making of American Liberal Theology: Idealism, Realism, and Modernity, 1900–1950*. Louisville: Westminster John Knox, 2003.

---. *The Making of American Liberal Theology: Imagining Progressive Religion, 1805–1900*. Louisville: Westminster John Knox, 2001.

Dostoevsky, Fyodor. *The Brothers Karamazov*. Translated by Constance Garnett. New York: Barnes & Noble, 2004.

Dreuzy, Agnes de. "*Dignitatis Humanae* as an Encounter between Two 'Towering Theologians': John Courtney Murray, SJ, and Yves Congar, OP." *U.S. Catholic Historian* 24 (2006) 33–44.

Dulles, Avery Cardinal. Foreword to *The Meaning of Tradition*, by Yves Congar, vii–x. San Francisco: Ignatius, 2004.

Dunn, James. "Church, State, and Soul Competency." *Review & Expositor* 96 (1999) 61–71.

Dupré, Louis K. *Passage to Modernity: An Essay in the Hermeneutics of Nature and Culture*. New Haven: Yale University Press, 1993.

Durso, Keith E. *Thy Will Be Done: A Biography of George W. Truett*. Macon, GA: Mercer University Press, 2009.

Ellis, Christopher J. *Gathering: A Spirituality and Theology of Worship in the Free Church Tradition*. London: SCM, 2004.

Ellis, William E. *A Man of Books and a Man of the People: E. Y. Mullins and the Crisis of Moderate Southern Baptist Leadership*. Macon, GA: Mercer University Press, 2003.

Erasmus, Desiderius. *On the Freedom of the Will: A Diatribe or Discourse*. Translated by E. Gordon Rupp. Philadelphia: Westminster, 1969.

Essick, John Inscore, and Mark S. Medley. "Local Catholicity: The Bodies and Places Where Jesus Is (Found)." *Review & Expositor* 112 (2015) 47–59.

Evans, Rachel Held. *A Year of Biblical Womanhood: How a Liberated Woman Found Herself Sitting on a Roof, Covering Her Head, and Calling Her Husband "Master."* Nashville: Thomas Nelson, 2012.

Fagerberg, David W. *Theologia Prima: What Is Liturgical Theology?* 2nd ed. Mundelein, IL: Hillenbrand, 2004.

Finney, Charles Grandison. *Lectures on Revivals of Religion*. Edited by William G. McLoughlin. Cambridge, MA: Harvard University Press, 1960.

Fitzgerald, Allan D., ed. *Augustine Through the Centuries: An Encyclopedia*. Grand Rapids: Eerdmans, 2009.

Forbis, Wesley L., ed. *The Baptist Hymnal*. Nashville: Convention, 1991.

Freeman, Curtis W. *Contesting Catholicity: Theology for Other Baptists*. Waco, TX: Baylor University Press, 2014.

---. "E. Y. Mullins and the Siren Songs of Modernity." *Review & Expositor* 96 (1999) 23–42.

Freeman, Curtis W., James Wm. McClendon Jr., and C. Rosalee Velloso Ewell, eds. *Baptist Roots: A Reader in the Theology of a Christian People*. Valley Forge, PA: Judson, 1999.

Furman, Richard. "Exposition of the Views of the Baptists Relative to the Coloured Population of the United States." In *A Sourcebook for Baptist Heritage*, edited by H. Leon McBeth, 252–55. Nashville: Broadman, 1990.

Gambrell, J. B. "A Historic Address." *Baptist Standard* 32, no. 23 (June 3, 1920) 1.

———. "Rome in World Politics." *Baptist Standard* 33, no. 19 (May 5, 1921) 1.

Garrett, James Leo. *Baptist Theology: A Four-Century Study*. Macon, GA: Mercer University Press, 2009.

George, Timothy. "James Petrigru Boyce." In *Theologians of the Baptist Tradition*, edited by Timothy George and David S. Dockery, 73–89. Rev. ed. Nashville: Broadman & Holman, 2001.

Gleason, Philip. "American Catholics and Liberalism, 1789–1960." In *Catholicism and Liberalism: Contributions to American Public Philosophy*, edited by R. Bruce Douglass and David Hollenbach, 45–75. Cambridge: Cambridge University Press, 1994.

Goen, C. C. "Baptists and Church-State Issues in the Twentieth Century." *American Baptist Quarterly* 6 (1987) 238–43.

Goodwin, Everett C., ed. *Baptists in the Balance: The Tension between Freedom and Responsibility*. Valley Forge, PA: Judson, 1997.

Gourley, Bruce T. "E. Y. Mullins: Public Spokesperson for Baptists in America." *Baptist History & Heritage* 43 (2008) 6–7.

Green, Joel B. *Practicing Theological Interpretation: Engaging Biblical Texts for Faith and Formation*. Grand Rapids: Baker Academic, 2011.

Greer, E. Eugene, ed. *Baptists: History, Distinctives, Relationships*. Dallas: Baptist General Convention of Texas, 1996.

Groppe, Elizabeth Teresa. *Yves Congar's Theology of the Holy Spirit*. New York: Oxford University Press, 2004.

Hankins, Barry. *Uneasy in Babylon: Southern Baptist Conservatives and American Culture*. Tuscaloosa: University of Alabama Press, 2002.

Hansen, Collin. "Young, Restless, Reformed." *Christianity Today* 50, no. 9 (September 2006) 32–38.

———. *Young, Restless, Reformed: A Journalist's Journey with the New Calvinists*. Wheaton, IL: Crossway, 2008.

Harmon, Steven R. *Baptist Identity and the Ecumenical Future: Story, Tradition, and the Recovery of Community*. Waco, TX: Baylor University Press, 2016.

———. *Towards Baptist Catholicity: Essays on Tradition and the Baptist Vision*. Waynesboro, GA: Paternoster, 2006.

Harrison, Richard L. "Alexander Campbell on Luther and the Reformation." *Lexington Theological Quarterly* 19 (1984) 123–52.

Hart, D. G. *Deconstructing Evangelicalism: Conservative Protestantism in the Age of Billy Graham*. Grand Rapids: Baker Academic, 2005.

Harvey, Barry. *Can These Bones Live? A Catholic Baptist Engagement with Ecclesiology, Hermeneutics, and Social Theory*. Grand Rapids: Brazos, 2008.

Hatch, Derek C. "George W. Truett and *Dignitatis Humanae*: Searching for a Theological Account of Religious Freedom." *Pacific Journal of Baptist Research* 11, no. 1 (May 2016) 59–71.

Hatch, Nathan O. *The Democratization of American Christianity*. New Haven: Yale University Press, 1989.

Hauerwas, Stanley. *A Better Hope: Resources for a Church Confronting Capitalism, Democracy, and Postmodernity*. Grand Rapids: Brazos, 2000.

———. *Hannah's Child: A Theologian's Memoir*. Grand Rapids: Eerdmans, 2012.

Healy, Nicholas J. "Henri de Lubac on Nature and Grace: A Note on Some Recent Contributions to the Debate." *Communio* 35 (2008) 535–64.

Helm, Paul. *John Calvin's Ideas*. New York: Oxford University Press, 2004.

Helwys, Thomas. *A Short Declaration of the Mystery of Iniquity*. Edited by Richard Groves. Macon, GA: Mercer University Press, 1998.

Herberg, Will. *Protestant, Catholic, Jew: An Essay in American Religious Sociology*. Garden City, NY: Doubleday, 1955.

Hill, W. J. "Báñez and Bañezianism." In *New Catholic Encyclopedia*. 19 vols. New York: McGraw-Hill, 1967.

Hinson, E. Glenn. "E. Y. Mullins as Interpreter of the Baptist Tradition." *Review and Expositor* 96 (1999) 109–22.

———. *Soul Liberty: The Doctrine of Religious Liberty*. Nashville: Convention, 1975.

Hobbs, Herschel H. *The Baptist Faith and Message*. Nashville: Convention, 1971.

Hobbs, Herschel H., and E. Y. Mullins. *The Axioms of Religion*. Rev. ed. Nashville: Broadman, 1978.

Hofstadter, Richard. *Anti-Intellectualism in American Life*. New York: Knopf, 1970.

Hoitenga, Dewey J., Jr. *John Calvin and the Will: A Critique and Corrective*. Grand Rapids: Baker, 1997.

Holcomb, J. David. "A Millstone Hanged about His Neck? George W. Truett, Anti-Catholicism, and Baptist Conceptions of Religious Liberty." *Baptist History & Heritage* 43 (2008) 68–81.

Hollon, Bryan C. *Everything Is Sacred: Spiritual Exegesis in the Political Theology of Henri de Lubac*. Eugene, OR: Cascade, 2009.

Horton, Michael. *For Calvinism*. Grand Rapids: Zondervan, 2011.

Hudson, Winthrop S. *Baptists in Transition: Individualism and Christian Responsibility*. Valley Forge, PA: Judson, 1979.

Hughson, Thomas. "From James Madison to William Lee Miller: John Courtney Murray and Baptist Theory of the First Amendment." *Journal of Church & State* 37, no.1 (Winter 1995) 15–37.

Hull, William E. "Mullins and Mohler: A Study in Strategy." *Perspectives in Religious Studies* 31 (2004) 311–24.

Humphreys, Fisher. "Edgar Young Mullins." In *Theologians of the Baptist Tradition*, edited by Timothy George and David S. Dockery, 181–201. Rev. ed. Nashville: B&H Academic, 2001.

Hunt, Dave, and James White. *Debating Calvinism: Five Points, Two Views*. Colorado Springs: Multnomah, 2004.

Ignatius of Antioch. *Smyrnaeans*. Translated by Alexander Roberts and James Donaldson. http://www.newadvent.org/fathers/0109.htm.

International Council on Biblical Inerrancy. "The Chicago Statement on Biblical Inerrancy." http://library.dts.edu/Pages/TL/Special/ICBI_1.pdf.

Irenaeus of Lyons. *Against Heresies*. In *Irenaeus of Lyons*, edited by Robert M. Grant, 55–187. New York: Routledge, 1997.

James, Powhatan W. *George W. Truett: A Biography*. Nashville: Broadman, 1939.

Bibliography

Johnson, William B. "Address to the Public." In *A Baptist Source Book, with Particular Reference to Southern Baptists*, edited by Robert A. Baker, 118–22. Nashville: Broadman, 1966.

Jorgenson, Cameron H. "Bapto-Catholicism: Recovering Tradition and Reconsidering the Baptist Identity." PhD diss., Baylor University, 2008.

Keathley, Kenneth. *Salvation and Sovereignty: A Molinist Approach*. Nashville: B&H Academic, 2010.

Kennedy, Rodney Wallace, and Derek C. Hatch. *Gathering Together: Baptists at Work in Worship*. Eugene, OR: Pickwick, 2013.

Kerr, Fergus. "French Theology: Yves Congar and Henri de Lubac." In *The Modern Theologians: An Introduction to Christian Theology in the Twentieth Century*, edited by David Ford, 105–17. 2nd ed. Malden, MA: Blackwell, 1997.

King, Larry. Interview with R. Albert Mohler Jr. *Larry King Live*. CNN, March 22, 2000.

Knox, Marv. "Baptist College Professors Discuss Influence of Calvinism on Campuses." *Baptist Standard* 115, no. 12 (March 24, 2003) 3.

Komonchak, Joseph A. "Murray, John Courtney (1904–67)." In *The Encyclopedia of American Catholic History*, edited by Michael Glazier and Thomas J. Shelley, 993–94. Collegeville, MN: Liturgical, 1997.

———. "Returning from Exile: Catholic Theology in the 1930s." In *The Twentieth Century: A Theological Overview*, edited by Gregory Baum, 35–48. Maryknoll, NY: Orbis, 1999.

———. "Theology and Culture at Mid-Century: The Example of Henri de Lubac." *Theological Studies* 51 (1990) 579–602.

———. "Vatican II and the Encounter between Catholicism and Liberalism." In *Catholicism and Liberalism: Contributions to American Public Philosophy*, edited by R. Bruce Douglass and David Hollenbach, 76–99. New York: Cambridge University Press, 1994.

La Soujeole, Benoît-Dominique de. "The Debate about the Supernatural and Contemporary Ecclesiology." In *Surnaturel: A Controversy at the Heart of Twentieth-Century Thomistic Thought*, edited by Serge-Thomas Bonino, translated by Robert Williams and Matthew Levering, 311–24. Ave Maria, FL: Sapientia, 2009.

Legaspi, Michael C. *The Death of Scripture and the Rise of Biblical Studies*. New York: Oxford University Press, 2010.

Leith, John H., ed. *Creeds of the Churches: A Reader in Christian Doctrine from the Bible to the Present*. 3rd ed. Louisville: Westminster John Knox, 1982.

Leithart, Peter J. "The End of Protestantism." *First Things*, online. November 8, 2013. http://www.firstthings.com/web-exclusives/2013/11/the-end-of-protestantism.

Leland, John. "Rights of Conscience Inalienable." In *A Sourcebook for Baptist Heritage*, edited by H. Leon McBeth, 178–81. Nashville: Broadman, 1990.

Lemke, Steve W. "The Inspiration and Truthfulness of Scripture." In *Biblical Hermeneutics: A Comprehensive Introduction to Interpreting Scripture*, edited by Bruce Corley, Steve Lemke, and Grant Lovejoy, 147–64. Nashville: Broadman & Holman, 1996.

Leo XIII, Pope. *Longinqua Oceani*. 1895. http://w2.vatican.va/content/leo-xiii/en/encyclicals/documents/hf_l-xiii_enc_06011895_longinqua.html.

———. *Rerum Novarum*. 1891. http://w2.vatican.va/content/leo-xiii/en/encyclicals/documents/hf_l-xiii_enc_15051891_rerum-novarum.html.

Leonard, Bill J. *Baptist Ways: A History.* Valley Forge, PA: Judson, 2003.
———. *Baptists in America.* New York: Columbia University Press, 2005.
———. *God's Last and Only Hope: The Fragmentation of the Southern Baptist Convention.* Grand Rapids: Eerdmans, 1990.
———. "Varieties of Freedom in the Baptist Experience." *Baptist History & Heritage* 25 (1990) 3–12.
———. "When the Denominational Center Doesn't Hold: The Southern Baptist Experience." *Christian Century* 110, no. 26 (September 22–29, 1993) 905–10.
Lincoln, Abraham. "Second Inaugural Address." http://avalon.law.yale.edu/19th_century/lincoln2.asp.
Locke, John. "A Letter Concerning Toleration." In *Two Treatises of Government; and, A Letter Concerning Toleration*, edited by Ian Shapiro, 215–56. New Haven: Yale University Press, 2003.
———. "On the Difference between Civil and Ecclesiastical Power, Indorsed Excommunication." In *The Life and Letters of John Locke*, edited by Lord Peter King, 300–307. London: Henry G. Bohn, 1858.
Lumpkin, William L., ed. *Baptist Confessions of Faith.* Rev. ed. Philadelphia: Judson, 1959.
Luther, Martin. *Disputation against Scholastic Theology.* In *Martin Luther's Basic Theological Writings*, edited by Timothy Lull, 13–20. Minneapolis: Augsburg Fortress, 1989.
MacCulloch, Diarmaid. *The Reformation: A History.* New York: Penguin, 2004.
Maddox, Timothy D. F. "E. Y. Mullins: Mr. Baptist for the 20th and 21st Century." *Review and Expositor* 96 (1999) 87–108.
Maring, Norman H., and Winthrop S. Hudson. *A Baptist Manual of Polity and Practice.* Rev. ed. Valley Forge, PA: Judson, 1991.
Marsden, George M. *Fundamentalism and American Culture.* New ed. New York: Oxford University Press, 2006.
Marsh, Charles. *God's Long Summer: Stories of Faith and Civil Rights.* Princeton: Princeton University Press, 1997.
Martin, James. *The Jesuit Guide to (Almost) Everything: A Spirituality for Real Life.* San Francisco: HarperOne, 2012.
McAfee, J. Thomas, ed. *Celebrating Grace Hymnal.* Macon, GA: Celebrating Grace, 2010.
McBeth, H. Leon. *The Baptist Heritage: Four Centuries of Baptist Witness.* Nashville: Broadman, 1987.
———. *A Sourcebook for Baptist Heritage.* Nashville: Broadman, 1990.
McCabe, Herbert. "The Trinity and Prayer." In *God Still Matters*, edited by Brian Davies, 54–63. New York: Continuum, 2002.
McClendon, James Wm., Jr. *Doctrine: Systematic Theology, Volume 2.* Nashville: Abingdon, 1994.
———. *Ethics: Systematic Theology, Volume 1.* Rev. ed. Nashville: Abingdon, 2002.
———. *Witness: Systematic Theology, Volume 3.* Nashville: Abingdon, 2000.
McCool, Gerald A. *The Neo-Thomists.* Milwaukee: Marquette University Press, 1994.
McGinn, Bernard, ed. *The Essential Writings of Christian Mysticism.* New York: Random House, 2006.
McGreevy, John T. *Catholicism and American Freedom: A History.* New York: Norton, 2003.

McLaren, Brian D. *A Generous Orthodoxy.* Grand Rapids: Zondervan, 2006.
McNutt, William Roy. *Polity and Practice in Baptist Churches.* Philadelphia: Judson, 1935.
Medley, Mark. "Catholics, Baptists, and the Normativity of Tradition: A Review Essay." *Perspectives in Religious Studies* 28 (2001) 119–29.
Metzger, Bruce M. *The Canon of the New Testament: Its Origin, Development, and Significance.* New York: Oxford University Press, 1987.
Michel, Dom Virgil. "The Liturgy the Basis for Social Regeneration." In *American Catholic Religious Thought,* edited by Patrick W. Carey, 424–32. 2nd ed. Milwaukee: Marquette University Press, 2004.
———. *The Liturgy of the Church, According to the Roman Rite.* New York: Macmillan, 1937.
———. "Mysticism and Normal Christianity." *Orate Fratres* 13 (1939) 545–48.
———. "Religious Experience: Liturgy Depersonalizes Piety?" *Orate Fratres* 13, no. 11 (October 1, 1939) 493–96.
Miller, John H., ed. *Vatican II: An Interfaith Appraisal.* Notre Dame: University of Notre Dame Press, 1966.
"Mohler Calls Catholicism 'False Church.'" *Baptist Standard* 112, no. 14 (April 3, 2000) 3.
Mohler, R. Albert, Jr. Introduction to *The Axioms of Religion*, by E. Y. Mullins, edited by R. Albert Mohler Jr., 1–32. Nashville: Broadman, 1997.
———. "Moralistic Therapeutic Deism—the New American Religion." *The Christian Post*, April 18, 2005. http://www.christianpost.com/news/moralistic-therapeutic-deism-the-new-american-religion-6266.
———. "When the Bible Speaks, God Speaks: The Classic Doctrine of Biblical Inerrancy." In *Five Views on Biblical Inerrancy*, edited by J. Merrick and Stephen M. Garrett, 29–58. Grand Rapids: Zondervan, 2013.
Morrow, Jeffrey L. "The Politics of Biblical Interpretation: A 'Criticism of Criticism.'" *New Blackfriars* 91 (2010) 528–45.
Mullins, E. Y. *The Axioms of Religion: A New Interpretation of the Baptist Faith.* Philadelphia: American Baptist Publication Society, 1908.
———. *The Axioms of Religion: A New Interpretation of the Baptist Faith* (2010). Edited by C. Douglas Weaver. Macon, GA: Mercer University Press, 2010.
———. *The Axioms of Religion.* Edited by R. Albert Mohler Jr. Nashville: Broadman, 1997.
———. *Baptist Beliefs.* Valley Forge, PA: Judson, 1925.
———. *The Christian Religion in Its Doctrinal Expression.* Valley Forge, PA: Judson, 1917.
———. *Freedom and Authority in Religion.* Philadelphia: Griffith and Rowland, 1913.
———. "A Message of the Baptist World Alliance to the Baptist Brotherhood, to Other Christian Brethren, and to the World." In *Baptist World Congress: Stockholm, July 21–27, 1923*, 223–33. London: Kingsgate, 1923.
———. *Soul Freedom Applied to Church Life and Organization.* Nashville: Baptist 75 Million Campaign, n.d., c. 1920.
———. "The Theological Trend." In *Proceedings of the Baptist World Congress*, 145–52. London: Baptist Union Publication Department, 1905.

Murray, John Courtney. "The Declaration on Religious Freedom." In *Bridging the Sacred and the Secular: Selected Writings of John Courtney Murray, SJ*, edited by J. Leon Hooper, 187–99. Washington, DC: Georgetown University Press, 1994.

———. "Leo XIII and Pius XII: Government and the Order of Religion." In *Religious Liberty: Catholic Struggles with Pluralism*, edited by J. Leon Hooper, 49–125. Louisville: Westminster John Knox, 1993.

———. "The Problem of Pluralism in America." *Thought* 29 (1954) 164–208.

———. "The Problem of Religious Freedom." In *Religious Liberty: Catholic Struggles with Pluralism*, edited by J. Leon Hooper, 127–97. Louisville: Westminster John Knox, 1993.

———. "Religious Freedom." In *The Documents of Vatican II*, edited by Walter M. Abbott, 672–74. New York: Herder & Herder, 1966.

———. *We Hold These Truths: Catholic Reflections on the American Proposition*. 1960. Reprint, Lanham, MD: Sheed & Ward, 2005.

Nettles, Thomas J. *By His Grace and For His Glory: A Historical, Theological, and Practical Study of the Doctrines of Grace in Baptist Life*. Grand Rapids: Baker, 1986.

Neufeld, Karl Heinz. "In the Service of the Council: Bishops and Theologians at the Second Vatican Council (for Cardinal Henri de Lubac on His Ninetieth Birthday)." In vol. 1 of *Vatican II: Assessment and Perspectives, Twenty-Five Years After (1962–1987)*, edited by René Latourelle, 74–105. New York: Paulist, 1988.

Nicholas of Cusa. *God as Not-Other: A Translation and Appraisal of De Li Non Aliud*. Translated by Jasper Hopkins. Minneapolis: University of Minnesota Press, 1979.

Noll, Mark A. *The Civil War as a Theological Crisis*. Chapel Hill: University of North Carolina Press, 2006.

———. *A History of Christianity in the United States and Canada*. Grand Rapids: Eerdmans, 1992.

O'Connor, Flannery. "Parker's Back." In *The Complete Stories*, 510–30. New York: Farrar, Straus and Giroux, 1971.

———. *Three by Flannery O'Connor: Wise Blood, The Violent Bear It Away, Everything That Rises Must Converge*. New York: New American Library, 1983.

Olson, Roger E. *Against Calvinism*. Grand Rapids: Zondervan, 2011.

———. *Arminian Theology: Myths and Realities*. Downers Grove, IL: IVP Academic, 2006.

Orchard, G. H. *A Concise History of Foreign Baptists*. Nashville: Graves & Marks, 1855.

Origen. *De Principiis*. In vol. 4 of *Ante-Nicene Fathers*, edited by Alexander Roberts and James Donaldson, translated by Frederick Crombie, 239–384. Peabody, MA: Hendrickson, 1994.

"Pastoral Letter of the Third Plenary Council of Baltimore." In *The Memorial Volume: A History of the Third Plenary Council of Baltimore, November 9–December 7, 1884*. Baltimore: Baltimore Publishing, 1885.

Payne, Ernest A. *The Fellowship of Believers: Baptist Thought and Practice Yesterday and Today*. London: Kingsgate, 1954.

Pecklers, Keith F. *The Unread Vision: The Liturgical Movement in the United States, 1926–1955*. Collegeville, MN: Liturgical, 1998.

Pelikan, Jaroslav. *Whose Bible Is It? A History of the Scriptures through the Ages*. New York: Viking, 2005.

Pelotte, Donald E. *John Courtney Murray: Theologian in Conflict*. New York: Paulist, 1975.

188 Bibliography

Percy, Walker. *Love in the Ruins: The Adventures of a Bad Catholic at a Time Near the End of the World*. New York: Farrar, Straus & Giroux, 1971.

Peterson, Robert A., and Michael D. Williams. *Why I Am Not an Arminian*. Downers Grove, IL: InterVarsity, 2004.

Pierce, John. "Truett's Famed Religious Liberty Sermon Celebrated by Baptists in Nation's Capital." *Baptists Today* 25, no. 8 (August 2007) 4–5.

Pinson, William M., Rosalie Beck, and Ebbie Smith. *Beliefs Important to Baptists*. Dallas: Baptistway, 2001.

Piper, John. *Desiring God: Meditations of a Christian Hedonist*. Expanded ed. Sisters, OR: Multnomah, 1996.

Pius IX, Pope. *Syllabus of Errors*. 1864. http://www.papalencyclicals.net/Pius09/p9syll.htm.

Placher, William C. *The Domestication of Transcendence: How Modern Thinking about God Went Wrong*. Louisville: Westminster John Knox, 1996.

Portier, William L. "Assembly Required: Christ's Presence in the Pews." *Commonweal* 140, no. 5 (March 8, 2013) 12–14.

———. "Theology of Manners as Theology of Containment: John Courtney Murray and *Dignitatis Humanae* Forty Years After." *U.S. Catholic Historian* 24, no. 1 (Winter 2006) 83–105.

Pseudo-Dionysius. "The Divine Names." In *Pseudo-Dionysius: The Complete Works*, translated by Colm Luibhéid and Paul Rorem, 47–131. New York: Paulist, 1987.

Ramm, Bernard. *Protestant Biblical Interpretation: A Textbook of Hermeneutics*. 3rd ed. Grand Rapids: Baker, 1970.

Ratzinger, Joseph Cardinal. Foreword to *Catholicism: Christ and the Common Destiny of Man*, by Henri de Lubac, 11–12. Translated by Lancelot C. Sheppard and Elizabeth Englund. San Francisco: Ignatius, 1988.

Rico, Hermínio. *John Paul II and the Legacy of "Dignitatis Humanae."* Washington, DC: Georgetown University Press, 2002.

Robinson, H. Wheeler. *The Life and Faith of the Baptists*. New York: George H. Doran Company, 1927.

Rogers, James A. *Richard Furman: Life and Legacy*. Macon, GA: Mercer University Press, 1985.

Ryan, T. "Congregatio de Auxiliis." In *New Catholic Encyclopedia*. 19 vols. New York: McGraw-Hill, 1967.

Schindler, David L. *Heart of the World, Center of the Church: Communio Ecclesiology, Liberalism, and Liberation*. Grand Rapids: Eerdmans, 1996.

Schlabach, Gerald W. *Unlearning Protestantism: Sustaining Christian Community in an Unstable Age*. Grand Rapids: Brazos, 2010.

Schloesser, Stephen. *Jazz Age Catholicism: Mystic Modernism in Postwar Paris, 1919–1933*. Toronto: University of Toronto Press, 2005.

Schmemann, Alexander. *Introduction to Liturgical Theology*. Crestwood, NY: St. Vladimir's Seminary Press, 1986.

Second Vatican Council. *Dei Verbum* (Dogmatic Constitution on Divine Revelation). 1965. http://www.vatican.va/archive/hist_councils/ii_vatican_council/documents/vat-ii_const_19651118_dei-verbum_en.html.

———. *Dignitatis Humanae* (Declaration on Religious Freedom). 1965. http://www.vatican.va/archive/hist_councils/ii_vatican_council/documents/vat-ii_decl_19651207_dignitatis-humanae_en.html.

———. *Gaudium et Spes* (Pastoral Constitution on the Church in the Modern World). 1965. http://www.vatican.va/archive/hist_councils/ii_vatican_council/documents/vat-ii_const_19651207_gaudium-et-spes_en.html.

———. *Sacrosanctum Concilium* (Constitution on the Sacred Liturgy). 1963. http://www.vatican.va/archive/hist_councils/ii_vatican_council/documents/vat-ii_const_19631204_sacrosanctum-concilium_en.html.

Shurden, Walter B. "The Baptist Identity and the Baptist *Manifesto*." *Perspectives in Religious Studies* 25 (1998) 321–40.

———. *The Baptist Identity: Four Fragile Freedoms*. Macon, GA: Smyth & Helwys, 1993.

———. *Not an Easy Journey: Some Transitions in Baptist Life*. Macon, GA: Mercer University Press, 2005.

———, ed. *Proclaiming the Baptist Vision: Religious Liberty*. Macon, GA: Smyth & Helwys, 1997.

Smith, Christian. *The Bible Made Impossible: Why Biblicism Is Not a Truly Evangelical Reading of Scripture*. Grand Rapids: Brazos, 2011.

Smith, Christian, and Melissa Lundquist Denton. *Soul Searching: The Religious and Spiritual Lives of American Teenagers*. New York: Oxford University Press, 2005.

Smith, James K. A. *Desiring the Kingdom: Worship, Worldview, and Cultural Formation*. Grand Rapids: Baker Academic, 2009.

———. *Introducing Radical Orthodoxy: Mapping a Post-secular Theology*. Grand Rapids: Baker Academic, 2004.

Smith, Ted A. *The New Measures: A Theological History of Democratic Practice*. New York: Cambridge University Press, 2007.

Southern Baptist Convention. *Annual of the Southern Baptist Convention*. Nashville: Southern Baptist Convention, 1963.

———. *The Baptist Faith and Message* (1925). http://www.johnstonsarchive.net/baptist/bf&m1925.html.

———. *The Baptist Faith and Message* (1963). http://www.baptiststart.com/print/1963_baptist_faith_message.html.

———. *The Baptist Faith and Message* (2000). http://www.sbc.net/bfm2000/bfm2000.asp.

Steinmetz, David C. "The Superiority of Pre-Critical Exegesis." *Theology Today* 37 (1980) 27–38.

Stephens, E. W. "At Washington with the Southern Baptists." *The Baptist* 1 (May 29, 1920) 8.

Strong, Augustus Hopkins. *Systematic Theology*. 3 vols. Philadelphia: Griffith and Rowland, 1907–9.

Talar, C. J. T. "Swearing Against Modernism: *Sacrorum Antistitum* (September 1, 1910)." *Theological Studies* 71 (2010) 545–66.

Taylor, Charles. *Sources of the Self: The Making of the Modern Identity*. Cambridge, MA: Harvard University Press, 1989.

Thompson, Philip E. "'As It Was in the Beginning'(?): The Myth of Changelessness in Baptist Life and Belief." In *Recycling the Past or Researching History? Studies in Baptist Historiography and Myths*, edited by Philip E. Thompson and Anthony R. Cross, 184–206. Waynesboro, GA: Paternoster, 2005.

———. "Dimensions of Memory: Challenges and Tasks in the Baptist Recovery of Tradition." In *Tradition and the Baptist Academy*, edited by Roger A. Ward and Philip E. Thompson, 46–66. Milton Keynes, UK: Paternoster, 2011.

Thuesen, Peter J. *Predestination: The American Career of a Contentious Doctrine*. New York: Oxford University Press, 2009.

Tilley, Terrence W. *Inventing Catholic Tradition*. Maryknoll, NY: Orbis, 2000.

Torbet, Robert G. *A History of the Baptists*. 3rd ed. Valley Forge, PA: Judson, 1963.

Truett, George W. "The Baptist Message and Mission for the World Today." *Southwestern Journal of Theology* 41 (1999) 107–29.

———. "Baptists and Religious Liberty." In *God's Call to America and Other Addresses Comprising Special Orations Delivered on Widely Varying Occasions*, 28–67. New York: George H. Doran, 1923.

———. "Baptists and Religious Liberty (1998)." *Baptist History & Heritage* 33 (1998) 66–85.

———. "The Prayer Jesus Refused to Pray." In *Follow Thou Me*, 34–50. Nashville: Sunday School Board of the Southern Baptist Convention, 1932.

Turner, Denys. *The Darkness of God: Negativity in Christian Mysticism*. New York: Cambridge University Press, 1995.

Underwood, William D. "The Future of Baptist Higher Education at Mercer University." In *The Baptist Summit at Mercer University: 19–20 January 2006, Three Addresses*, 47–77. Macon, GA: Mercer University Press, 2006.

Van Biema, David. "10 Ideas Changing the World Right Now: The New Calvinism." *Time* 173, no. 11 (March 23, 2009) 50.

Vincent of Lérins. *Commonitorium*. Translated by C. A. Heurtley. http://www.newadvent.org/fathers/3506.htm.

Voderholzer, Rudolf. *Meet Henri de Lubac: His Life and Work*. Translated by Michael J. Miller. San Francisco: Ignatius, 2008.

Walls, Jerry L., and Joseph R. Dongell. *Why I Am Not a Calvinist*. Downers Grove, IL: InterVarsity, 2004.

Warren, Rick. *The Purpose Driven Church*. Grand Rapids: Zondervan, 1995.

Wayland, Francis. *Notes on the Principles and Practices of Baptist Churches*. New York: Sheldon, Blakeman, 1857.

Weaver, Aaron Douglas. *James M. Dunn and Soul Freedom*. Macon, GA: Smyth & Helwys, 2011.

Weaver, C. Douglas. "The Baptist Ecclesiology of E. Y. Mullins: Individualism and the New Testament Church." *Baptist History & Heritage* 43 (2008) 18–34.

———. *In Search of the New Testament Church: The Baptist Story*. Macon, GA: Mercer University Press, 2008.

Weaver, C. Douglas, and Nathan A. Finn. "Youth for Calvin: Reformed Theology and Baptist Collegians." *Baptist History & Heritage* 39 (2004) 40–55.

Webber, Robert E. *Worship Old & New*. Rev. ed. Grand Rapids: Zondervan, 1994.

Whitsitt, William H. *A Question of Baptist History: Whether the Anabaptists in England Practiced Immersion before the Year 1641?* Louisville: C. T. Dearing, 1896.

Williams, D. H. *Evangelicals and Tradition: The Formative Influence of the Early Church*. Grand Rapids: Baker Academic, 2005.

———, ed. *Tradition, Scripture, and Interpretation: A Sourcebook of the Ancient Church*. Grand Rapids: Baker Academic, 2006.

Williams, Roger. *The Bloudy Tenant of Persecution*. Vol. 3 of *Complete Writings of Roger Williams*. New York: Russell & Russell, 1963.

———. *The Bloudy Tenant Yet More Bloudy*. Vol. 4 of *Complete Writings of Roger Williams*. New York: Russell & Russell, 1963.

Williams, Rowan. *Why Study the Past? The Quest for the Historical Church*. Grand Rapids: Eerdmans, 2005.

Wood, Susan K. "The Liturgy: Participatory Knowledge of God in the Liturgy." In *Knowing the Triune God: The Work of the Spirit in the Practices of the Church*, edited by James J. Buckley and David S. Yeago, 95–118. Grand Rapids: Eerdmans, 2001.

———. *Spiritual Exegesis and the Church in the Theology of Henri de Lubac*. Grand Rapids: Eerdmans, 1998.

Woodward, Kenneth L. "Sex, Sin and Salvation." *Newsweek* 132, no. 18 (November 2, 1998) 37.

World Council of Churches. *Called to Be the One Church*. February 23, 2006. http://www.oikoumene.org/en/resources/documents/assembly/2006-porto-alegre/1-statements-documents-adopted/christian-unity-and-message-to-the-churches/called-to-be-the-one-church-as-adopted.

York, Terry W. *America's Worship Wars*. Peabody, MA: Hendrickson, 2003.

Index

1 Corinthians, Letter, 75, 126, 127, 171, 172, 174
1 John, Letter, 68
2 Peter, Letter, 126, 170
2 Timothy, Letter, 66

Action française, 57, 157, 160
Akin, Daniel, 23n35
allegorical interpretation, allegorical sense, 73, 91–94. *See also* spiritual sense; multiple senses of scripture
Allen, Jason, 23n35
anagogical sense, 91–94. *See also* spiritual sense; multiple senses of scripture
Andrew of St. Victor, 94
antebellum biblical interpretation, 96–97, 74–76
anti-Catholicism, 44, 48–50, 140. *See also* Baptist attitudes toward Catholicism
Aristotle, 29, 53–54
Arminianism, 19–23, 34–35
Arminius, Jakob, 31, 35
Articles of Faith, Articles of Peace, 144, 146. *See also* John Courtney Murray
Athanasius of Alexandria, 126
Atlanta, Georgia, 141
Augsburg Confession, 28
Augusta, Georgia, 77
Augustine of Hippo, 21, 24–27, 30–31, 35, 40–42, 51, 54, 84n85, 90, 90–91n117

autocracy, 47, 49, 137, 140–41

Backus, Isaac, 117, 133
Bacon, Francis, 67
Baius, Michael, 40, 51
Balthasar, Hans Urs von, 43, 51, 95, 126, 126–27n126
Baltimore, Third Plenary Council of, 147
Bañez, Domingo, 40
"Baptifesto," "Baptist Manifesto," *see* "Re-envisioning Baptist Identity"
baptism, 35, 165, 170n29. *See also* sacraments
believers baptism, 2–7, 50, 100n3, 121–22, 132
immersion, 3n5, 4, 5, 100n3
children, 4, 5–7
rebaptism, 5, 6n16
Baptist attitudes toward Catholicism, 3n4, 44, 47–50, 82–83, 107, 109, 133, 140–42. *See also* anti-Catholicism
Baptist distinctives, 3, 7
Baptist Faith & Message (1925), 3n5, 22, 71n29, 80, 88–89n106, 100, 121–22
Baptist Faith & Message (1963), 3n5, 71n29, 80, 88, 88–89n106, 89, 112–13, 114, 121–22
Baptist Faith & Message (2000), 3n5, 80, 88, 88–89n106, 121–22
Baptist history, 7, 12, 21–22, 45, 105, 106

Index

Baptist Joint Committee on Religious Liberty, Baptist Joint Committee on Public Affairs, 48, 119, 134, 141
baptist vision, 81
Baptist World Alliance, 83n78, 100
Bapto-Catholic, 9n27
Barna, George, 166, 166–67
Barth, Karl, 5, 73n37, 99, 125, 125n122
Bell, Rob, 20
Bellarmine, Robert, 40, 53
Benedict XV, Pope, 49
Benedict XVI, Pope Emeritus, 43, 127
Bernard of Clairvaux, 91n118
Beza, Theodore, 31, 32
biblicism, 66–69, 78–79, 83, 87–89
Bill of Rights, 134
Billings, J. Todd, 29–31
Bismarck, Otto von, 142
Blanshard, Paul, 48, 153
Blondel, Maurice, 84–87, 95n140
Bloom, Harold, 118–19n88
body/soul dichotomy, 138, 152–53
Bonhoeffer, Dietrich, 56
Bowne, Borden Parker, 103
Boyce, James Petigru, 23n34, 68, 69
British Baptists, 128–29
Brownson, Orestes, 147n77

Cajetan, Thomas de Vio, 54–55
Calvin, John, 16, 17n11, 27, 28–31, 32, 78
Calvinism, 15–36, 40n10, 42, 44, 50, 51, 58
 doctrines of grace, 10, 17, 22
 resurgent Calvinism, 15–24, 32–36, 44, 50, 58, 175
 TULIP, 19–20, 22, 31–32
Campbell, Alexander, 66, 67, 68
Carson, D. A., 16
catholicity, 9, 123–30
Chan, Francis, 18
Chandler, Matt, 18, 20
Chenu, Marie-Dominique, 43, 145n67
Chesterton, G. K., 97–98
Chicago Statement on Biblical Inerrancy, 69

Christian tradition, 9, 10, 11, 23–24, 30–31, 35–36, 43, 44, 59, 61, 81, 84, 87–89, 91, 96, 101, 121, 155, 161, 162–63, 168, 172–73
Christian union, *see* ecumenism
Christians for Biblical Equality, 79n59
Christology, 11, 57, 59, 67, 87–88, 92, 98, 124–26. *See also* Jesus Christ
 as anthropology, 57, 59
church, 2, 10, 11, 44, 61, 80–81, 82, 85, 96, 97–98, 106, 108–110, 116–30, 136, 138–39, 149, 153–54, 158–61, 163, 169–71, 173, 175–76
 as catholic, 8, 12, 123–30
church growth, 166–68
Civil War, 74, 78
Clement VII, Pope, 40
Colossians, Letter to the, 75
commentatorial tradition, 42, 53–58. *See also* Thomas Aquinas, Thomism
Congar, Yves, 43, 80–82, 87, 95, 156–57, 160, 172
Congregatio de Auxiliis, 40–41
congregational polity, 3n5, 100n3, 107–108
Conner, Walter Thomas (W. T.), 3n4
conscience, 49, 114, 123n111, 132–33, 136–37, 139, 141, 151–52, 153, 158–59
Coste, René, 157
Council for Biblical Manhood and Womanhood, 79n59

Daniel, Book of, 75
Dawn, Marva, 167n14, 173
Dawson, James Martin (J. M.), 48, 134, 141–42, 144n63, 153
Day, Dorothy, 8, 172n34
de Lubac, Henri, 10–11, 38, 42–44, 50–58, 60–61, 92–95, 124, 125, 128, 149, 157, 158–59, 160, 163, 170n29, 172
Denton, Melissa Lundquist, 18–19
Descoqs, Pedro, 54–55, 57

discipleship, 6n14, 18, 93, 96, 124, 131–32, 155, 157, 159, 161, 165–66, 173
dissent, 44, 46, 118, 163
divine sovereignty, 7, 10, 15–24, 41
Dix, Dom Gregory, 173
Dockery, David, 21n28
Dostoevsky, Fyodor, 131
Driscoll, Mark, 18
dualism, 26, 27, 52, 55, 58, 118, 121, 123, 127, 129, 149, 151n94, 152–53, 158
Dunn, James, 119–20, 134
Dutch Remonstrants, 31

ecumenism, 80, 109n49
Emerson, Ralph Waldo, 147n77
Ephesians, Letter to the, 7, 127, 172
Erasmus, Desiderius, 39
Essick, John Inscore, 126
Eucharist, 99, 128, 168n17, 169–170, 173, 176. *See also* sacraments
evangelism, 17n7, 165, 168, 170, 171
"Evangelicals and Catholics Together," 47n34
Exodus, Book of, 75
extrinsicism, 52, 57, 58, 85, 87
Evans, Rachel Held, 96n144
Ezekiel, Book of, 126
Ezell, Kevin, 23n35

faith (virtue), 93, 96
Finney, Charles, 164–66, 168
Founders Ministries, 22
France, 142–43, 151n94, 160
   Third Republic, 57, 145, 157, 160
   Vichy France, 57–58, 157
free church, 9, 15–16, 32, 35, 37, 38, 44, 61, 66, 73, 78, 82, 95, 97, 144, 173, 174
freedom for, 152–54, 158
freedom from, 151–53, 156, 158
Freeman, Curtis, 5–7, 68n9, 89, 102, 112n62, 120n93, 129
Furman, Richard, 75–76

Galatians, Letter to the, 95, 151

Garrett, James Leo, 21n28
Garrigou-Lagrange, Reginald, 54–55, 57
Gelasius I, Pope, 143n58
General Baptists, 22, 127
Grudem, Wayne, 21n29
Guinness, Os, 21n27

Hansen, Collin, 15n3, 19
Harvey, Barry, 124, 126, 128
Hauerwas, Stanley, 155n107, 168n17
Hebrews, Book of, 95
Helwys, Thomas, 132–33
historical critical method, 72–73, 81, 92
historicism, 85–87
Hobbs, Herschel, 88, 112–14, 115n71, 116, 121
Hodge, Charles, 68–69
Hollon, Bryan, 58, 97
Holy Spirit, 71, 82, 90n114, 104, 113, 124, 127, 128–29, 162, 164, 169, 172
homo liturgicus, 174
hope (virtue), 93, 96
Hudgins, Douglas, 112, 114–116
Hudson, Winthrop S., 5, 117–118, 119
human free will, 7, 10, 15, 17, 20–21, 22–23, 24–25, 27–29, 31–32, 34–35, 38–42

Ignatius of Antioch, 88n102, 127
Incarnation, *see* Christology
individualism, 6, 19, 89, 108n43, 114, 117–18, 122, 125, 136, 140, 153, 168, 171
inerrancy, 69, 79–80, 95
inspiration, 66, 69, 79, 90
   verbal plenary theory, 69, 95
Irenaeus of Lyons, 31, 84

Jacobinism, 145, 146
James, William, 102–03
Jansenism, 10, 42, 50–52
Jansenius, Cornelius, 41–42, 51, 53
Jesuits, 38, 39–42, 44, 140, 142, 160, 163

Index

Jesus Christ, 3n4, 4, 22n32, 28, 39n5, 48n39, 61, 65, 71, 73-74, 75, 80, 84, 85, 86, 87-89, 98, 111, 113, 115, 120, 124, 126-27, 128, 131-32, 132n4, 153, 154, 155, 157, 158-59, 162-63, 164-65, 173, 175. *See also* Christology
Johannine Comma (1 John 5:7), 68n9
John, Gospel of, 61, 137n29, 161, 162, 175
John XXIII, Pope, 49
Johnson, William Bullein, 77
Joshua, Book of, 166

King, Martin Luther, Jr., 8
Kulturkampf, 142

lament, 167-68
la separation, 145
Leithart, Peter, 8
Leland, John, 117, 133-34, 168n17
Leo XIII, Pope, 111n54, 143n58
Leonard, Bill, 4, 6, 7, 22, 102, 118, 118n88
lex orandi, lex credendi, 12, 175
Lincoln, Abraham, 78
liturgy, worship, 12, 72n35, 80-81, 83n78, 121, 123, 162-76. *See also* worship songs
Locke, John, 15n2, 137-39, 152
London Confession of 1644, 3n5
love (virtue), 90, 93, 96
Luke, Gospel of, 75
Luther, Martin, 27-28, 32, 39, 54, 78
magisterium, 81-82

Maring, Norman H., 5
Marsh, Charles, 115-16
Matthew, Gospel of, 5, 95, 129, 137n29, 173
Maximus the Confessor, 92, 124
McBeth, H. Leon, 5, 16-17
McCabe, Herbert, 15, 34
McClendon, James Wm., Jr., 2, 9, 23-24, 32-33, 46n30, 80-81, 97, 122, 174-75
McLaren, Brian, 20n18, 21n27
Medley, Mark, 44, 46n30, 126

Melanchthon, Philip, 28
memory, 25, 45
metaphysical individualism, 122, 125
Michel, Virgil, 12, 169-172, 172-75
middle knowledge, 39
modern scientific hermeneutics, *see* historical critical method
Modernism, condemnation of, 49
modernity, 11, 55, 94, 129, 151, 159-60
Mohler, R. Albert, Jr., 22-23, 47, 69, 72n34, 123n109
Molina, Luis de, Molinism, 10, 39, 40n10, 41, 50-51, 52
monergism, *see* divine sovereignty
Moody, Dwight, 166
Moore, Russell, 23n35
Moralistic Therapeutic Deism, 18-20
Mother Teresa of Calcutta, 8
Mullins, Edgar Young (E. Y.), 47, 48, 70-72, 99-112, 112n62, 112-120, 121n101, 122, 123, 129, 136n24
multiple senses of scripture, 90-96. *See also* spiritual sense
Murray, John Courtney, 140-54, 155-57
mystery, 57, 60, 73, 93, 95, 97, 124, 157, 172, 174
mystical body of Christ, 12, 127, 168-75

natural desire to see God, 52, 53-55
nature and grace, 9, 24, 25-27, 28, 32, 43, 51-58, 59, 61, 132, 148-50, 151n94, 152-54, 155n107, 158, 160
  dualistic relationship between, 28, 52-58, 148-50, 151n94, 152-53, 155n107, 158, 160
Nazism, 57, 160
New Hampshire Confession of Faith, 22, 121
New Measures, 164-66, 168
Noll, Mark, 46, 74, 100n2
nominalism, 15n2, 29, 33, 51-52, 56, 59, 118
nuda scriptura, 66

O'Connor, Flannery, 35n84, 65, 74
Olson, Roger, 17, 20, 23n36
ordinance, 2–3, 3n4
Origen of Alexandria, 43–44, 89–90, 92
Orthodox Creed, 127
Oxford Movement, 121

Packer, J. I., 16, 18, 21n27, 21n29
participatory ontology, 27, 30n71, 34n82, 35–36, 58–59, 61
Passion Movement, 16
Patterson, Paige, 23, 69
Paul V, Pope, 40
Paul VI, Pope, 154
Pelagianism, 20, 29, 31, 39, 40–41
Pelikan, Jaroslav, 80n64
Percy, Walker, 44
personal experience, 71, 72, 79, 103, 110, 123n109
personal salvation, personal relationship with Jesus, 48n39, 89, 109n49, 115, 136, 153
Philadelphia Confession, 22
Pico della Mirandola, Giovanni, 43–44
Piper, John, 16, 18
Pius IX, Pope, 142
Pius XI, Pope, 57
plain reading/plain meaning of the Bible, 66, 72, 73, 78–79, 89n109, 97
Platt, David, 18, 23n35
political atomism, *see* individualism
postmodern denominationalism, 8–9
Poythress, Vern, 21n29
priesthood of believers, 3n5, 108, 113
private interpretation, 70, 79n62
Protestants and Other Americans United for the Separation of Church and State (POAU), 48
Proudhon, Pierre-Joseph, 43–44
Proverbs, Book of, 90n112
Providence, Rhode Island, 69, 133
Psalms, Book of, 17–18n11
Pseudo-Dionysius, 43, 58–59n80
pure nature hypothesis, 52–53, 58

racial discrimination, 115, 115–16n74, 116
Rainer, Thom, 23n35
Ratzinger, Joseph, *see* Benedict XVI, Pope Emeritus
"Re-envisioning Baptist Identity," 79n62, 97–98, 123n108
Reeve, James, 76n50
Reformational Catholicism, 8
Regent's Park College, 120
religious liberty, 3n5, 11, 12, 47, 48, 50, 119–20, 131–61, 173
re-membering the body, 128
ressourcement, 9–10, 11, 12, 38, 42–50, 58–61, 66, 81–89, 98, 101, 120–130, 132, 162–64, 169, 172–75
Robinson, H. Wheeler, 120–21, 122, 123
Romans, Letter to the, 21, 75

sacramental view of the world, sacramental ontology, 34n82, 35n84, 50, 95, 116
sacramentalism, 34, 59, 97, 140, 141
sacraments, 3n4, 35, 59, 109, 128nn131–32, 168, 171. *See also* baptism; Eucharist
Schaeffer, Francis, 21n27
Southern Baptist Convention (SBC), 3n5, 6–7, 22–23, 77, 77–78n55, 88, 100, 100–102, 108, 112–113, 114, 115n71, 134
spiritual but not religious (SBNR), 8
Scottish Common Sense Realism, 67, 68
scriptura pura, 78
Second Great Awakening, 74, 164
Second London Confession of Faith, 3n5, 22, 23n34
Second Vatican Council, 49–50, 57, 87–88, 142, 149, 154, 156, 157, 173
  Constitution on the Sacred Liturgy (*Sacrosanctum Concilium*), 173
  Declaration on Religious Freedom (*Dignitatis Humanae*), 49–50, 149, 154–59

Second Vatican Council *(continued)*
    Dogmatic Constitution on Divine Revelation *(Dei Verbum)*, 87–88, 92n123, 94n137
    Pastoral Constitution on the Church in the Modern World *(Gaudium et Spes)*, 57n75, 59–60n85, 157
sensus divinitatis, 29, 30n67, 31
separation of church and state, 48, 50, 57, 135, 137–39, 141–43, 144–54, 157, 158, 160
Shurden, Walter, 77–78n55, 118–119, 123n108, 135
slavery, 74–78, 96, 97
Smith, Christian, 18–19, 68n11, 78n58, 79, 80, 83
Smith, James K. A., 29–31, 174
Smyth, John, 132
social responsibility, 110–12, 114, 116
sola fide, 7, 38
sola gratia, 7, 20, 38
sola scriptura, 7, 11, 66, 72, 77, 78–81, 92, 98
Song of Songs, Book of, 91
soul competency, 3n5, 11–12, 101, 102, 105–08, 109, 110, 112–20, 129–30, 153
Southern Baptist Theological Seminary, 22–23, 23nn34–35, 47, 100, 103n13, 108n42
Southwestern Baptist Theological Seminary, 23, 135n17
spiritual interpretation, 93, 95
spiritual sense, 90n114, 91–97
Sproul, R. C., 16, 18, 21n27
Stone-Campbell Movement, 11n30
Suárez, Francisco, 53, 54, 148
subscribers, nonsubscribers, 68n9
Sunday, Billy, 166
supernatural beatitude, 54
Syllabus of Errors, 49, 142, 143n55, 154
synergism, *see* human free will
Synod of Dort, 19, 31–32, 32n75

Teilhard de Chardin, Pierre, 44
Tertullian, 83

theology in exile, 145n67, 151n94, 157, 160
theosis, divinization, 126, 170–71
Thomas Aquinas, Thomism, 21, 42–43, 52, 53–58, 57n77, 58n80, 91–92, 103n15, 143n56, 147n78, 148
Thompson, Philip, 45
Thuesen, Peter, 17, 34, 35n84, 59
tradition, 9, 10, 44–46, 50, 66–67, 70, 72, 78–84, 87–88, 92, 98
Trent, Council of, 38–39, 41, 92
Triennial Convention, 76–77
Trinity, 27, 57, 67, 83n78, 125, 126, 129, 166, 173, 175
tropological sense (moral), 91, 93. *See also* spiritual sense; multiple senses of scripture
Truett, George W., 47–48, 131–32, 134–37, 139, 140–42, 144, 152–54, 156, 157, 158, 159, 160–61

Underwood, William, 79n62
United States, 133, 134, 135, 137, 139, 143, 145–46, 147–48, 150, 151n94, 156, 157, 159, 160

Vincent of Lérins, 83–84, 125
Virginia Declaration of Rights, 134
Virginia Statute on Religious Freedom, 134
voluntarism, 29, 52, 118

Warfield, B. B., 68n11, 69
Washington, DC, 48, 134–35, 134n15
Wayland, Francis, 69–72, 117
Whitsitt Controversy, 100, 105–06
Williams, Roger, 100n3, 133, 144
Williams, Rowan, 45
World Council of Churches, 129n136
worship songs, 17, 72n35, 99, 123, 167–68, 176. *See also* liturgy, worship

Zacharias, Ravi, 21n27
zero-sum game, 33, 34, 59, 118